BOB HEPPLE

Race, Jobs and the Law in Britain

Allen Lane The Penguin Press London 1968

Allen Lane The Penguin Press
Vigo Street, London W1

Printed in Great Britain by
Latimer Trend & Co Ltd. Plymouth
Bound by Mansell, London N1

Contents

Contents

Contents

Acknowledgements

This study of voluntary and legal controls over racial discrimination in employment in Britain would not have been written but for the encouragement of Dr Paul O'Higgins, who inspired me with his own enthusiasm for the role lawyers can play in the solution of social problems, commented on drafts of the manuscript and directed me to many sources which otherwise might have been neglected. Most of the work was undertaken at Cambridge and it is with pleasure that I record my appreciation for many kindnesses to the Master and Fellows of Clare College, and especially to Mr Colin Turpin. Several colleagues at Nottingham University have given me the benefit of their counsel in the later stages of preparation: notably Mr David Harris, Miss Mary Robertson and Mr Dan Lawrence. Professors O. Kahn-Freund and K. W. Wedderburn, to whose writings on labour law I owe a great deal, made valuable criticisms of an early draft of the manuscript and for these I am most grateful.

My practical understanding of the issues involved is derived from interviews with many trade union officers, employers and officials of employers' organizations, community relations workers and leaders of immigrant bodies and officers of the Ministry of Labour and the Race Relations Board. I would ask them all to accept my deepest thanks for their courtesy and helpfulness. I was also fortunate to enjoy the cooperation of 103 trade union officers and twenty-one liaison officials who replied to my questionnaires and some of whom took the time and trouble to write me explanatory letters and to supply me with relevant documents. I was privileged to have discussions with experts in particular areas of interest: notably Mr H. S. Kirkaldy, Mr Paul Keating and Mr Anthony Lester. Correspondence with several parliamentarians has proved most helpful, in particular with Lord Brockway, Mrs Shirley Williams M.P., Mr Roy Hattersley M.P., Mr Maurice Orbach M.P. and Mr Harold Walker M.P. The contribution of my colleagues on the Nottingham Commonwealth Citizens' Consultative Committee, especially Mr Bill Taylor, has lain in their enabling me to participate in the day-to-day work of integration, so deepening my practical experience.

In collecting the scattered library sources I was fortunate to have the careful guidance of Mr A. Sivanandan and Miss M. Yhap at the Institute of Race Relations, whose library of newspaper cuttings enabled me to compile Appendix I. In that task I was also able to make use of the files of the National Council for Civil Liberties, to which I am grateful for permission to relate the facts of certain cases without identifying the parties involved. I had the advantage of some helpful advice on sources from Mr Nicholas Deakin, and it was my good fortune to be allowed to consult the manuscript of Mrs Sheila Patterson's important forthcoming book on immigrants in Croydon industry and Dr Peter Wright's thesis on the position of coloured workers with special reference to the North and Midlands.

Needless to say, none of those mentioned shares my responsibility for the contents of this book.

Finally, I wish to acknowledge with thanks the permission of the following to quote from their publications: Rediffusion Television Limited for excerpts from the post-production script of the *This Week* programme on coloured school-leavers, of 4 November 1965; the Institute of Race Relations for extracts from Dr R. B. Davison's three books *Commonwealth Immigrants*, *West Indian Migrants* and *Black British* and from various issues of the I.R.R. *News Letter*; Mrs Sheila Patterson for extracts from *Dark Strangers*; the Twentieth Century Fund for an extract from Michael L. Sovern's *Legal Restraints on Racial Discrimination in Employment*; the Columbia University Press for extracts from Paul H. Norgren and Samuel E. Hill's *Toward Fair Employment*; Bow Publications Limited for extracts from *Commonwealth Immigration*; the National Maritime Board for a quotation from the National Standard Rates of Pay and Conditions Applying only to Deck and Engine-Room Ratings, printed in their Year Book 1966; and the Engineering Employers' Federation for their agreement regarding racial discrimination in employment.

1 February 1968.

Introduction

The notice in the tailor's shop window read: 'Junior salesman required.' Colin, aged seventeen, applied and received the half-apologetic answer: 'Sorry, the job is already taken.' Shortly afterwards his schoolmate, William, applied for the same position and was offered an immediate interview.

Colin then went to a kitchen equipment company which had advertised staff vacancies and was told that they had all been filled. William went to the same firm and was informed that jobs were still available. Colin was refused sixteen jobs in this way. At the time both he and William were in the sixth form working for their Advanced Levels. They had similar results at Ordinary Level and both were school prefects. There was one visible difference between them: Colin is coloured, William is white.[1]

Britain is entering a new phase in race relations in which unequal treatment of the kind endured by Colin is to be contrary to the law. In the period ahead legal controls will supplement voluntary action against racial discrimination in employment.

The decision to legislate was preceded by the publication in April 1967 of a Report by Political and Economic Planning (P.E.P.) which revealed the existence of substantial discrimination, largely based on colour, against Britain's one million coloured people. Discrimination in employment was found to be 'the biggest single criticism in immigrants' spontaneous criticisms of life in Britain'.[2] Tests carried out provided hard evidence that their claims were well-founded.

Of 974 West Indian, Indian, Pakistani and Cypriot immigrants interviewed, 36 per cent claimed job discrimination and provided verbal evidence to this effect, the claimed incidence of discrimination being

1. This case was first reported on the Independent Television Programme *This Week* on 4 November 1965. The names used here are fictitious. Other illustrations of reported racial incidents in employment will be found in Appendix I, below, p. 201
2. P.E.P. *Report on Racial Discrimination*, p. 8. The investigation was sponsored by the Race Relations Board and the National Committee for Commonwealth Immigrants and the research was conducted by Research Services Ltd. It was financed by a grant from the Joseph Rowntree Memorial Trust

highest for West Indians (45 per cent) and lowest for Cypriots (6 per cent). In over one third of the cases the discrimination was obvious, the reasons for not employing them being stated in terms such as 'No black bastards wanted' and 'We don't want any more Indians'.

In other cases the evidence was more circumstantial but 'situation tests' conducted during the P.E.P. Survey established that the great majority of claims made by immigrants were valid. Forty firms against which allegations had been made were selected. An Englishman, a Hungarian and a person of the appropriate coloured group, all with a work-history of comparable experience and qualifications, applied for the same type of job as had the original claimant. The results were as follows:

Number of cases where no job available   10
Number of cases where employment possible   30
Discrimination against English tester   —
Discrimination against Hungarian tester   13
Discrimination against coloured tester   27

The experience of the Hungarian tester in comparison with that of the coloured tester, together with the relatively low percentage of Cypriots who claimed personal experience of job discrimination, indicates that the discrimination against coloured work-seekers is primarily on grounds of colour. There is, in fact, reason to believe that the level of discrimination reported by immigrants is lower than that which actually exists, in particular (1) the situation in which discrimination occurs often makes it impossible for the immigrant to know that it has taken place (e.g. he is told the vacancy has been filled); (2) many immigrants, particularly Indians and Pakistanis, control their exposure to situations in which they might experience discrimination (e.g. working in one type of job or industry through contacts within their own community); and (3) the overwhelming majority of informants in the P.E.P. Survey were seeking unskilled and semi-skilled jobs in manufacturing industry and here they were least likely to be discriminated against. Indeed, it is significant that those immigrants who had English trade qualifications made the highest claims of discrimination, and that employment bureaux interviewed by the P.E.P. researchers stated that ninety per cent of their clients would not accept coloured office staff.

These findings had to a considerable extent been anticipated by several earlier local studies. But the publication of the P.E.P. Report, backed by its impressive research in six areas which had not previously been intensively surveyed, at a time when there was mounting pressure on the Government to act, provided a political justification for legal intervention. In addition, the Government was able to point to the recommendations of the National Committee for Commonwealth Immigrants (N.C.C.I.) and the Race Relations Board that the Race Relations Act 1965 should be extended to cover job discrimination. The N.C.C.I., set up by the Government 'to promote and coordinate the integration of Commonwealth immigrants into the community', had declared in its Report for 1966 that 'many firms operate and parade a colour bar without apology'. The Race Relations Board was established under the Race Relations Act which came into operation on 8 December 1965, to deal with complaints of discrimination in places of public resort. In its Report for 1966–7, published shortly after the P.E.P. Report, it stated that up to 31 March 1967 it had received 327 complaints. Of these no less than 238 fell outside its jurisdiction, 101 complaints relating to employment discrimination, most of the others to housing (37), publications (24), shops (7), financial facilities (12) and the police (14).[1] The fact that so many persons bothered to complain to the Board about matters with which it could not deal was due, in part at least, to the activities of bodies such as the Campaign Against Racial Discrimination (C.A.R.D.), a group set up to unite the efforts of all immigrant-based organizations, whose summer project in 1966 had revealed many instances of discrimination against coloured youngsters.

Adding to the pressure for legislation was a spate of pamphlets, debates and reports from Labour, Liberal and Conservative groups. A Conference on Racial Equality in Employment held in London at the end of February 1967 under the auspices of the N.C.C.I. showed that despite reservations there was influential support for the view that voluntary action against discrimination did not preclude legislation from playing a useful role. In Parliament on 16 December 1966, Mr Maurice Orbach (Labour) with the support of M.P.s of all parties moved the second reading of a Bill to amend the Race Relations Act to extend its scope to employment, housing and the provision of insurance and credit services. This was withdrawn only after a Government assurance that it was giving serious consideration to the need for strengthening the existing law and administrative machinery.[2] A similar Bill introduced by Lord Brockway was defeated by sixty votes to twenty-three in favour at its second reading in the House of Lords on 19 December 1966.[3]

1. Between 18 March and 30 November 1967 there was a sharp upswing in the number of complaints received by the Board. Of 519 complaints, 386 fell outside the Board's jurisdiction. Of the latter, 190 related to employment
2. 738 House of Commons Debate, col. 940
3. 278 House of Lords Debate, cols. 1838–1912

Despite the protests of individual Conservatives that special privileges were being created for coloured persons[1] and that 'the process of trying to change psychological prejudice by Act of Parliament is . . . a violation of the liberty of the individual',[2] the tide was beginning to flow towards legislation. This was emphasized by an opinion poll among a representative quota sample of 1,000 electors conducted by Opinion Research Centre in May 1967 for the *Sunday Times*, which showed that 58 per cent of those asked were in favour of laws ensuring equal treatment for everyone in housing and jobs regardless of race or colour; 31 per cent were against and 10 per cent were 'don't knows'. When the question was put in the form: 'Do you think it should be illegal to refuse a job to someone because of his race or colour?' there was still a small majority in favour of legislation. Upper middle-class and Conservative voters were significantly more opposed to legislation than were the lower occupational classes and Labour and Liberal voters. A small majority of the trade unionists asked favoured legislation. [3]

The most concerted opposition to legal action came from the Trades Union Congress (T.U.C.) and the Confederation of British Industry (C.B.I.) both of which, while expressing strong disapproval of racial discrimination, preferred a strictly voluntary approach, seeing in legislation a threat from without to the delicate balance of conflicting interests maintained by understanding, tact and compromise, which characterizes the British system of industrial relations and marks its maturity. In a joint statement reported to have been presented by these organizations at a meeting of the National Joint Advisory Council of the Ministry of Labour in January 1967 (but never published by themselves) they said:

. . . We point to the existence of negotiated agreements establishing procedures for the settlement of grievances and disputes, and expect all those associated together in the operation of industries and services to utilize to the full the methods of voluntary settlement which have been successfully developed over many years. We ask our members on both sides of industry to ensure that joint agreements relating to wages and conditions of employment are enforced for all employees irrespective of their colour, race, or national or ethnic origins.

Accordingly, the T.U.C. and the C.B.I. ask their members to examine and

1. 738 House of Commons Debate, col. 918 (Mr H. Gurden)
2. 278 House of Lords Debate, col. 1879 (Lord Milverton)
3. *Sunday Times*, 7 May 1967

subsequently keep under continuous review the employment policies, practices and procedures in their industries and services which bear on the full achievement of integration and to eliminate any which militate against it.[1]

Subsequently, various schemes were mooted between the C.B.I. and the T.U.C. as an alternative to legislation and moves were made in some industries to set up special machinery to deal with questions of racial discrimination in cases where the ordinary procedures for avoiding disputes were inapplicable. One such scheme was agreed between the Engineering Employers' Federation and the Confederation of Shipbuilding and Engineering Unions in July 1967 to embrace 4,764 federated establishments employing some 2,150,000 people. The parties declared:

Discriminatory practices, either by employer or employed, can more suitably be considered and dealt with through voluntarily established machinery than through statutory measures.[2]

In the country's largest union, the Transport and General Workers' Union (T. & G.W.U.) and elsewhere in the unions and among some prominent industrialists, however, there was support for the principle of legislation.

It was in this atmosphere of controversy that the Home Secretary (Mr Roy Jenkins) announced the Government's intention to legislate against discrimination in housing, employment, and credit and insurance facilities on 26 July 1967. Only two years before, his predecessor in office, Sir Frank Soskice (as he then was), had vigorously resisted pressure from his own Labour backbenchers and the immigrant lobby to illegalize job discrimination and had predicted when moving the third reading of the Race Relations Bill: 'It would be an ugly day in this country if we had to come back to Parliament to extend the scope of this legislation.'[3]

With dramatic speed in these two years Britain was transformed from a country in which the law had no part in improving race relations to one in which it came to be believed that legislation was capable of acting as an instrument of change and that it was desirable to use legal sanctions in the area of employment in which, by tradition, social conflicts have been institutionalized by norms and sanctions which

1. *Sunday Times*, 29 January 1967
2. The full text of the Agreement will be found in Appendix III below, p. 226 and the scheme is discussed below, p. 169
3. 716 House of Commons Debate, col. 1056 (16 July 1965)

exist *outside* the law and in which the law intervenes, if at all, only marginally.

At once we can dismiss the suggestion that the decision to legislate was simply a panic reaction to the unprecedented racial violence in Detroit and other Negro ghettoes in the United States in the summer of 1967. Some considerations of this kind, prompted by the fear of similar civil strife erupting in the ghettoes developing in Britain's cities, may have played their part. But this ought not to obscure the fact that, in addition to the P.E.P. Report and other studies, there had been detailed consideration of the workings of legislation in other countries and on the type of legislation which Parliament might consider suitable by a committee consisting of Professor Harry Street (as chairman), Mr Geoffrey Howe, Q.C. and Mr Geoffrey Bindman (legal adviser to the Race Relations Board) and sponsored by the Race Relations Board and the N.C.C.I.

At the same time, the very speed with which the Labour Government had made its turnabout intensified immigrant suspicions that the extension of legislation was yet another example of hypocritical 'tokenism', of 'too little, too late'. They could point to the White Paper on *Immigration from the Commonwealth* (Cmnd 2739) published in August 1965 which, under the heading 'Integration', dismissed the employment situation in less than 250 words with a note of the 'considerable progress' made by employment exchanges, the youth employment service and the trade unions in solving what was perceived as an 'immigrant problem'. While apparently rejecting such complacency in 1967 the Government retained the strict control on immigration, unrelated to economic need, announced in that White Paper.

Legislation, then, has intruded into a social situation aptly described by *The Times* Midland correspondent as one of 'worry, ignorance, superstition, fear and dislike'.[1] As the country prepares to operate novel voluntary and legal controls over discrimination, the time seems appropriate for a study of the dichotomy between, on the one hand, what people *believe* the law can achieve in the improvement of race relations, and, on the other hand, what the *reality* of social inequality and the nature of the law renders possible. Nowhere is this contradiction between utopianism and social and legal reality more in need of examination than at the matrix of class conflict and social compromise. It is in the area of industrial relations that most of the questions about the aims and limits of the law have been raised in the sharpest and most controversial way.

1. *The Times*, 27 July 1967

The main areas of debate are: (1) the nature and extent of racial discrimination in employment; (2) the character and efficacy of (a) voluntary conciliation procedures, and (b) the existing law, to deal with the problem; (3) the capacity of law to affect the situation; and (4) the desirability of using the law in an area in which social conflicts are normally controlled by extra-legal codes and sanctions.

These are underlying themes of this book.

Part One

RACIAL DISCRIMINATION IN EMPLOYMENT

1. Strangers and Sub-citizens

One million coloured people live in Britain; by 1975 their number is likely to be one and three-quarter million and by 1985 three and a half million. Most of them have arrived from the West Indies since the early 1950s and from India and Pakistan since the late 1950s. The problems they face in earning a living spring from the facts that they are (1) immigrants (2) dark-skinned and (3) in general, low-paid manual workers.

Often these problems are looked at in a one-sided and static way. Those who are preoccupied with an 'immigrant problem' usually concentrate on the adjustment of immigrants to the values, customs and beliefs of the host society; consciously or unconsciously the assumption tends to be made that the British way of life is superior to that of the immigrants and that the latter must conform to it. Those who see a 'colour problem' tend to over-emphasize the importance of prejudice in shaping the situation and make facile comparisons with the United States and South Africa. There are those, too, who are unwilling to see either of these aspects and treat attempts to isolate and deal with the special difficulties of the immigrants and their children as manifestations of misguided liberalism creating special 'privileges' for one section of the working-class. Rarely, if ever, is the interaction between immigration, colour and social inequality seen as part of a dynamic social process. This leads to a failure to comprehend the very real differences between the problems of the first generation of coloured immigrants and those being encountered by the second generation. It results in misunderstandings about the significance of racial discrimination.

The first generation's difficulties are more complicated, particularly because of the colour factor, than were those of earlier waves of immigrants to Britain such as the Irish and the Eastern European Jews and of the half million aliens, most of them Poles and East Europeans, resident in this country.

The major determinants of their work situation are (1) their educational attainments, employment experience and language ability; (2) trends in immigration; (3) the housing situation; and (4) discrimination on grounds of race or colour.

There are significant variations in the skills and educational levels possessed by members of the different immigrant groups and sub-groups. No information is available about the educational background of Barbadians and Trinidadians coming here, but in the case of Jamaicans a survey conducted under the auspices of the University College of the West Indies among persons collecting their passports during a seven-week period in 1961 in Kingston[1] showed the following levels attained on leaving full-time school among the *men*: 4 per cent had no education; 16 per cent had grades 1–3; 78 per cent had grades 4–6; 2 per cent had secondary education; 5 per cent had further education. Among the *women* standards were slightly higher. Language can also be a problem for West Indians, especially those from rural areas, who speak a Creole differing from standard English in vocabulary, idiom and grammar. As a rule, language and cultural differences are a far greater barrier for those coming from India and Pakistan, most of whom neither speak nor write English on their arrival in this country and many of whom are illiterate in their own tongues. The consequences are manifold: for example, jobs involving dealings with members of the public are automatically beyond their reach; they tend to become self-segregating; and employers find it convenient to set up ethnic work units under English-speaking Asian 'go-betweens'.[2]

No overall statistical information is available about the employment experience of immigrants. Several field studies indicate that a large number of the West Indians were working on their own account before migrating, either in agriculture, or, to a lesser extent, in clothing and other trades. Those who were working for wages were mostly employed in agriculture, the building trade or light manufacturing. A considerable number were unemployed. Widely divergent estimates of their skills have been made. These fall into three main categories: (a) those based on the migrant's own statement of his skills; (b) those based on work being done in Britain by the migrants; and (c) those based on British assessment of their abilities. In the first category are the figures given by the Department of Labour in Dominica regarding those emigrating from Dominica to Britain between 1955 and 1960.[3] Of those in employment 42 per cent claimed that they were unskilled

1. R. B. Davison, *West Indian Migrants* (London 1962), p. 19
2. The consequences are discussed in Chapter 5, below, p. 77
3. R. B. Davison, op. cit., p. 20

and 34 per cent that they were skilled. The remainder were domestic servants (15 per cent) or in clerical or professional work.

Another study, that by Mrs Ruth Glass,[1] indicated that Jamaica, Barbados and the small Caribbean territories send comparatively fewer black-coated workers to Britain than Trinidad and Guyana. The majority of men from Barbados had previously been skilled manual workers, while a relatively large proportion of those coming from Jamaica had been engaged in agriculture. Taking all these territories together, she found that 24 per cent had been professional and other black-coated workers, 46 per cent had been skilled manual workers, 5 per cent semi-skilled and 13 per cent unskilled manual workers. 12 per cent had been agricultural workers.

In the third category (British assessment) is a memorandum by the Ministry of Labour Staff Association which estimated that roughly 13 per cent of West Indian work-seekers were skilled; 22 per cent semi-skilled and 65 per cent unskilled. These percentages were apparently arrived at by drawing on the experience of members of the Association working at local employment exchanges in 1954. The divergences between the various estimates do little more than emphasize the conflict which exists between the migrants' job expectations and British assessment of what their abilities are.

Most of the Indian immigrants have an agricultural background to which their families were attached by tradition. The rest are craftsmen. Relatively few have been in industrial employment before coming to Britain and status in India may affect job preferences here. Moreover different standards of training in India result in their crafts not being recognized in Britain. The majority of Pakistanis working in the North and Midlands appear to come from a landless and impoverished agricultural background. No useful information is available about their skills but the impression is that they are relatively lower than those found among the Indian immigrants.

Trends in immigration also affect the status of the coloured working population. Prior to 1961 the rise and fall in immigration was closely related to the number of available jobs in Britain. This has been convincingly demonstrated in relation to West Indian immigration by Dr Ceri Peach, an Oxford geographer, who found that the economic regulator was the main determinant of the size of West Indian migration.[2] Paradoxically, the introduction of the Commonwealth Immigrants Bill

1. *Newcomers: The West Indians in London* (London 1960), p. 24
2. 'West Indian migration to Britain: The Economic Factors' (1965) VII *Race*, p. 31; see too, Kenneth Leech, 'Migration and the British population 1955–62' (1966) VII *Race*, p. 401

in 1961 resulted in an element of political uncertainty and caused an exceptional influx of 230,000 immigrants between January 1961 and July 1962, a period of economic decline. There is reason to believe (although no global information is available to test this assertion) that the majority of arrivals in this period immediately before the Act came into operation were of low socio-economic status. Moreover it seems likely that the restrictions on immigration caused more immigrants to settle here permanently and to bring their wives and children over, while at the same time allowing in fewer workers.

On the other hand, the effect of the system of employment vouchers introduced by the Act has been to reduce the overall proportion of unskilled and semi-skilled persons allowed into Britain from the 'coloured' Commonwealth countries. Commonwealth immigrants coming to work are required to be in possession of current Ministry of Labour employment vouchers. These are in three categories: category A is for applications by employers who have a specific job (whether skilled or unskilled) to offer the immigrant, category B is for those without a specific job to come to but with certain special qualifications, and category C is for all others. Since 2 August 1965, category C has been discontinued and, in fact, no vouchers in this category were issued in 1965. Since the same date the list of special qualifications eligible under category B has been reduced and is now limited to doctors, dentists, trained nurses, qualified teachers, graduates in science and technology with a minimum of two years' experience since graduation and certain professionally qualified non-graduates with similar experience. This has meant the exclusion of shorthand-typists, arts graduates and building trades craftsmen who previously qualified under category B. The total number of vouchers for the Commonwealth, apart from Malta which has an allocation of 1,000, is not to exceed 7,500 a year.[1]

In 1962, 75 per cent and in 1963, 63 per cent of all the vouchers in respect of the principal 'coloured' Commonwealth countries were issued in category C. In 1964, however, this proportion dropped to a mere 9 per cent and the effect of the discontinuance of this category since 1965, coupled with the reduction in category A, has been to reduce the overall proportion of unskilled and semi-skilled persons coming into Britain from these countries. In category A, waiters, kitchen and domestic staff and unskilled factory workers still predominate, but of the B vouchers (skills) the overwhelming proportion goes to teachers, doctors and nurses. Taking the A and B categories together it is

1. *Immigration from the Commonwealth*, Cmnd 2739, 1965

apparent that most of those now entering from the 'coloured' Common-wealth possess skills.

This presents yet another paradox. So far from lessening the danger of future conflict (as the protagonists of immigration control have maintained) the limitation of entry to the professional *élites* of their own countries has made more immediate the possibility of wide-scale dis-crimination. The P.E.P. Report showed that it is precisely those coloured immigrants with the highest qualifications who are likely to experience the most discrimination. In the process downward job mo-bility among the coloured population will be accentuated.

The housing situation is closely linked to the job opportunities of both first and second generations. Coloured immigrants and their families are not spread evenly over the whole country but are concen-trated in a few areas. It was estimated in 1965 by the Survey of Race Relations in Britain that there were 350,000 in Greater London (com-prising 4·2 per cent of the total population of the area), 70,000 in Birmingham (4 per cent), 10,000 in Manchester (1·5 per cent), 10,000 in Liverpool (1·3 per cent), 12,500 in Bradford (4·1 per cent) and 12,500 in Nottingham (4 per cent).[1] Moreover they are concentrated in par-ticular neighbourhoods – for instance most of Birmingham's coloured immigrants are to be found in three or four of the city's eighty-one square miles. The reasons for the growth of a segregated ghetto in Sparkbrook have been subjected to close scrutiny by Rex and Moore who conclude that:

a tendency towards segregation of coloured immigrants in cities will con-tinue . . . and the inhabitants of these areas will more and more become the targets of punitive policies and racial hostility.[2]

The indirect effects must include increased racial hostility in other relationships (such as work) and a growing number of socially handi-capped coloured children unable to compete for jobs on a basis of equality with children from the white suburbs. They will tend to stay at the bottom of the occupational scale and hence in the worst housing. So the vicious circle may continue.

The link between the generations is provided by those young people who arrived from the 'coloured' Commonwealth while in their teens in time to complete their schooling in Britain. Of those coloured immi-

1. More up-to-date and precise information about the distribution of the main immigrant groups in Britain will be found in Table 5, below p. 233, which is based on the 1966 sample 3 census figures (published in December 1967)
2. *Race, Community and Conflict: a study of Sparkbrook* (London 1967), p. 271

grants eligible to leave school at the end of the summer term in 1966, half had been less than two years at school in this country. It is fair to assume that many of them came on to the employment market poorly educated, and to some extent creating unfavourable stereotypes of young coloured people, thus adversely affecting the chances of the true second generation born or wholly educated in Britain. Some 200,000 children of Commonwealth citizens may have been born in Britain since immigration began on a large scale. In January 1966, there were 130,000 immigrant schoolchildren (i.e. those born abroad or born in this country of parents who emigrated to the U.K. after 1956). Allowing for the fact that the latter figure is based on returns from schools with ten or more immigrant pupils and excludes children of 'mixed' parentage, and for further immigration, the Hunt Committee in its Report on *Immigrants and the Youth Service* (1967) estimated that the percentage of immigrants in the age range 14–20 may be as much as two and a half to three within a few years. In Birmingham it may go up four times in the next ten years.

The most striking differences between the generations are the educational attainments and qualifications of the young and their far greater expectations. These may to a limited extent be frustrated by the 'old country' values of their parents and their lives within a closed community. Far more important, however, is their reception at the hands of their white fellow-citizens. For them, the extent of racial discrimination is likely to be the key determinant of employment opportunities.

Racial discrimination, then, cuts across the generations but is of primary importance only in the second. The P.E.P. Report emphasized how extensive discrimination is, and that managements justify the non-employment of coloured immigrants on the grounds (a) that existing staff will not like it; (b) that customers will not like it; and (c) that immigrants are under-skilled, indolent or unlikely to stay with the company. Each of these reasons is capable of concealing management prejudices and it is worth noting, in regard to the third, that almost half the immigrants interviewed in the P.E.P. Survey had been in their jobs for three years and the higher the qualifications of the immigrant the more frequently was discrimination claimed. But this must not allow it to be assumed that personal colour prejudice is the sole or even the major cause of discrimination.

Personal prejudice, in the sense of an emotional and rigidly hostile disposition towards members of a given group arising from the individual's own inadequacies and resulting in displaced aggression, must be distinguished from mere antipathy which results from factors such as ignorance, conflicts of interest and other objective factors. Both these types of unfavourable disposition may be found together with discrimination. Theoretically they are distinct. Prejudiced people do not always discriminate: thus, white employees may object to the employment of a coloured worker but withdraw their complaint when threatened by management or union action. Similarly, discrimination is not always the result of prejudice: thus an employer may refuse to employ coloured salesmen, although he himself is well-disposed towards coloured people, because he fears a loss of custom. In other words, social factors regulate discrimination.

This is borne out by studies of the position of immigrants in industry. Mrs Sheila Patterson, in a survey in Croydon, found that English workers' reactions to immigrants were compounded of economic fears and preoccupations with status in addition to a mild antipathy to foreigners and second-hand derogatory notions.[1] Dr Peter Wright found in the North and Midlands that British workers were generally prepared to accept coloured immigrants in work relationships, although many would have preferred to work where only white people were employed; the level of social acceptance of each group by the other was relatively low due to the difference in cultural backgrounds, the beliefs of white workers about social status, the fears of rejection on the part of West Indians, and the choice of Asians to remain in their own social groups.[2] Mrs Patterson found that most managers approached the employment of immigrants from a pragmatic industrial viewpoint. Dr Wright, as well, found that coloured labour was taken on 'as necessary' in the light of labour shortages and subject to factors like the attitude of white workers. In those factories which did not employ coloured labour, management prejudice played some part, but so did adverse assessment of the standards of coloured workers, fears of racial friction and the objections of white workers.

How is the antipathy to coloured workers to be explained? In the case of the newcomers an attractive hypothesis is that formulated by Dr Michael Banton as a result of his survey of six areas, four of which had a settlement of recent coloured immigrants.[3] The attitudes of white towards coloured people, he explains, must be traced back to the late eighteenth century when apologists for the slave trade attributed

1. *Immigrants in Industry* (London 1968)
2. *The Coloured Worker in British Industry with special reference to the Midlands and North of England* (Unpublished Ph.D thesis, Edinburgh University 1966)
3. *White and Coloured: the behaviour of British people towards coloured immigrants* (London 1959) esp. pp. 177–84

inferiority to the Negro. Nineteenth-century imperialism fostered the belief that Britons were socially and morally superior to the colonial peoples, and the missionaries were thought of as taking benefits to the black heathen. Anthropological and biological doctrines were concocted to 'prove' European superiority.

In the modern post-colonial era, Banton points out, British people have had to realize that the old forms of relationship are untenable, largely because coloured people have rejected them. At the same time, Britons are not sure about the proper course of conduct to adopt towards coloured people. For one thing, coloured people are believed to be unfamiliar with the ordinary norms of British life and the coloured man seems to be 'the farthest removed of strangers – the archetypal stranger'. Secondly, colour may affect social prestige. The result, Banton concludes, is that Britons are apt to avoid entering certain types of relation with coloured people, especially those in which the norms are implicit and the sanctions against deviant behaviour weak: for example, while British workers may not invite coloured workmates home they are likely to find them more acceptable in a work relationship where the sanctions for failure to conform (e.g. loss of job) are far clearer. Discrimination, according to this view, is a form of avoidance of strangers, and it is likely to be relatively unimportant in the workshop.

This explanation is of considerable value in relation to the first generation and helps to explain why opposition to discrimination in public places has always been more forthcoming than that against discrimination in the private relations of life. It is inadequate, however, in relation to the second generation who are no longer strangers. In this context one is drawn to the view put forward by Dr Kenneth Little as a result of his study in Cardiff's Bute Town where coloured people are socially and geographically segregated, have poor housing, low standards of living and restricted educational and job opportunities.[1] He suggests that British people tend to identify those who are coloured with the lowest social class. This theory has the merit of showing the connexion between colour and class prejudice, although as Dr Little himself points out, social contact is avoided not so much because of personal prejudice but rather as a result of social pressures. This does not entirely account for the non-acceptance of coloured people by the white British working class since the former cannot be 'beneath' the latter in terms of class, but only in terms of status. For this reason

1. *Negroes in Britain: a study of racial relations in English society* (London 1947); and *The Race Question in Modern Science* (Paris, Unesco 1956), p. 165 and p. 175

Dr Wright suggests in his study that Little's thesis is really a 'colour status consciousness' theory of social distance.

The attitudes which treat coloured people as belonging to an inferior status group result in their relegation to low-paid work. In this capacity they belong to Britain's 'new poor', whom a recent study has estimated[1] number between seven and eight million (or 14 per cent of the total population) living around subsistence rates. The Report of the Central Advisory Council for Education (England) [the Plowden Report] *Children and their Primary Schools* (1966) showed a disproportionate number of immigrant children in deprived areas. In this social inequality the coloured immigrants share problems common to the poor generally: such as inadequate social security benefits, wage-related unemployment and sickness schemes which do least for those with lowest wages, and the worst effects of a 'squeeze' on incomes. Racial discrimination and the wider inequality of class act upon one another. The former helps to swell the ranks of the poor and keeps immigrants fitted only for unskilled and semi-skilled labour and this, in turn, diverts economic pressure for technological change and political pressure for social change.[2] At the same time, the continuing association, in the minds of white people, of poverty with a dark skin colour ensures racial stereotyping of all coloured people as belonging to an inferior group. The process has gone full circle.

It is in the light of this that the solutions offered by Government, employers and trade unions, must be considered.

THE POLICY OF INTEGRATION

'Integration' is the universally accepted answer. Mr Roy Jenkins defined this aim as follows:

In my view integration is rather a loose word, because I do not regard it . . . as meaning the loss by immigrants of their national characteristics and culture. I do not think that we need or want, in this country, a sort of melting pot which will turn everybody out in a common mould as one of a series of carbon copies of someone's misplaced idea of the stereotyped Englishman. It would be bad enough if this were to happen to the few people in this country who happen to have pure or almost pure Anglo-Saxon blood in their veins. If it were to happen to the rest of us, to the Welsh like myself, to the Scots, to the Irish, to the Jews, to the mid-Europeans, and to the still more recent arrivals, it would be little short of a national disaster. It would deprive us of the most positive advantages of immigration . . . which I think can be great.

1. B. Abel-Smith and P. Townsend, *The Poor and the Poorest* (London 1965)
2. See below, Chapter 3, p. 60

I would therefore define integration not as a flattening process of assimilation, but as equal opportunity accompanied by cultural diversity in an atmosphere of mutual tolerance.[1]

In theory, this definition is excellent. It surmounts the mistakes in regard to immigrants which in the United States were symbolized by the 'melting pot' thesis that European immigrants would fuse with American society as a homogeneous culture in the natural course of events (the Negro, however, would remain outside the mainstream because of his visibility!). American sociologists later modified this one-sided view of assimilation with the notion of a 'fusion' of cultural heritages, a process which was neither inevitable nor rapid and which involved reciprocity and conscious and unconscious changes on both sides. From this grew the notion of 'cultural democracy', a situation in which, on the one hand, different groups retained their cultural distinctiveness and, on the other hand, there was an interaction and a body of shared values among groups.

S. N. Eisenstadt, in his comprehensive theory of absorption, used this term to describe all stages in the adaptation and acceptance of migrant groups, a lengthy process in which the immigrant changes his status image and values and the host society makes the necessary changes in its institutional structure. The index of absorption is the extent to which the structure of the immigrant group is *balanced* in relation to the total social structure; such a balance is only possible if its internal status structure is not completely opposed to that of the absorbing society, the hosts are prepared to accept the additional status premises of the ethnic group, and the immigrants accept the status positions allotted to them. For all practical purposes, 'integration' is the level of absorption regarded as legitimate in contemporary Britain.

The concept of absorption has proved a useful one in some studies of the position of immigrants in British industry. In particular, Mrs Patterson has demonstrated the development of attitudes on the index of absorption from that of initial contact (where managements will not employ immigrants and local labour will not work alongside them) through the stage of accommodation (in which managements try various modes of selection and local labour agrees to accept them subject to quotas etc.) to the level of assimilation (in which managements are willing to start promoting them and local labour will accept them in supervisory posts). On the part of immigrants there are corresponding levels in which, at first, they keep together in groups and later start

1. 735 House of Commons Debate cols. 1233-4 (8 November 1966); italics added

to mingle and become capable of supervisory work. In an intermediate stage of 'pluralistic integration' managements use ethnic work gangs and individual immigrants emerge as leaders of these gangs.

When used as a statement of *political* objective, however, 'integration' is as elusive a term as 'democracy' or 'equality', meaning different things according to the interests and outlook of the user. The Government's White Paper in August 1965 on *Immigration from the Commonwealth* discussed integration explicitly as an 'immigrant problem'. This is an approach dominated by the assumptions of social work which place their emphasis on the maladjusted individual rather than on low wages, inadequate housing and other environmental factors. In Dipak Nandy's words:

There is a persistent tendency to shy away from problems of *discrimination*, to forget that the 'problem' is not a person, whatever his personal qualities may be, but the denial of equal rights to a person, and to a whole group.[1]

The emphasis on cultural diversity may, moreover, not accord with the trade union view of integration. An example of this is the attitude taken by some union branches to cultural distinguishing marks, such as the wearing of turbans and beards by Sikhs which, they argue, emphasize differences between workers. The development of the factory system has universally been accompanied by the blurring of tribal, religious and cultural distinctions between workers; in this sense, it is odd to talk of 'cultural diversity'. Some trade unionists look with a measure of suspicion on national organizations, such as the Indian Workers' Association, because these are seen as potentially divisive. Actual experience, however, suggests that such organizations have helped to strengthen trade union organization in industries where it is weak.

Again, it is relevant to ask: what are the limits of cultural diversity? An ethnic work-unit based on language differences seems, at first sight, to be compatible with the classic definition of integration. In practice it may lead to permanent segregation. Moreover, the comparison between the Welshman who belongs to a Welsh-speaking society and the coloured immigrant is an over-simplification. The former lives and works in an integrated society and chooses to keep up his own language and culture as a means of retaining his identity. By contrast, the coloured immigrant, in the words of the Hunt Committee, 'is obliged to feel and confirm his national identity because the door to integration has been, or appears to him to have been, closed in his face'.[2]

1. *Policies for Racial Equality* (eds. Lester and Deakin) Fabian Research Series 262 (1967) p. 38
2. *Immigrants and the Youth Service* (H.M.S.O. 1967), para. 52

The other aspect of the definition of integration is equal opportunity. But British society *is* highly stratified and even if every vestige of racial discrimination was eliminated today, the wider social inequalities would remain. Obviously, integration can mean no more than a *Times* leader suggested: 'It must be possible for individual coloured people to find *their own level* in British society.'[1]

It is precisely because racial discrimination aggravates inequalities of opportunity and wealth and makes it infinitely more difficult to resolve them, that its elimination is a matter of grave urgency.

1. *The Times*, 5 August 1967; italics added

2. The Concept of
Racial Discrimination

In everyday speech all actions which involve choice or selection are acts of discrimination. Without them, any kind of group social life would clearly be impossible. In the language of sociologists, the word is used in a pejorative sense to mean 'the unequal treatment of equals, either by the bestowal of favours or the imposition of burdens'.[1] There is also said to be discrimination when the competitors are unequal but the burdens are disproportionate to the inequalities between them.

To say that all people are entitled to equal opportunities is not to say that they are, by nature, equal. On the contrary, it is to assert that the only valid criterion for judging an individual is an assessment of his aptitudes and abilities in the light of what the job requires. Other distinctions based on race, colour, ethnic or national origin, religion, social origin, sex or political opinion, are irrelevant to the performance of work and ought to be disregarded.

The particular pretext for discrimination ought to be of little importance in any attempt to remove the underlying causes of discriminatory behaviour. Personal prejudice or antipathy may lead to discrimination against an individual because he is coloured; the underlying reason might have been the same had he been singled out because he is a Moslem. To attack some pretexts and not others is to encourage the manifestation of the causes in other ways. As a long-term objective, therefore, it is proper to seek the eradication of all forms of employment discrimination. The I.L.O. Convention Concerning Discrimination in Respect of Employment and Occupation 1958 (No. 111) (not yet ratified by the U.K. Government[2]) specifically defines discrimination as:

any distinction, exclusion or preference made on the basis of race, colour,

1. Hankins, 'Social Discrimination', *Encyclopaedia of the Social Sciences* (ed. Seligman; New York 1934)
2. See below. Chapter 11, p. 190

sex, religion, political opinion, national extraction or social origin, which has the effect of nullifying or impairing equality of opportunity or treatment in employment or occupation.

The I.L.O.'s Committee of Experts has insisted that members ratifying the Convention must take measures against *all* these forms of discrimination.

In Canada, the Fair Employment Practices Act 1953[1] prohibits religious as well as racial discrimination and this is also the case with provincial anti-discrimination legislation. (Nova Scotia cautiously includes 'religious creed and religion'.) In the United States, Title VII of the Civil Rights Act 1964 applies to religious and sex discrimination in addition to racial discrimination in employment, and the thirty-nine states with enforceable laws against discrimination all include discrimination on grounds of 'creed' (i.e. religious belief). Several states outlaw discrimination on grounds of age or sex, and in the Canadian province of Quebec discrimination on grounds of 'social origin' is unlawful. In Britain, by contrast, the Race Relations Act illegalizes only such discrimination as is on the grounds of 'colour, race, or ethnic or national origins'.

The author has argued elsewhere[2] that the omission of religion from this definition may provide a loophole for the seasoned discriminator who could claim that his unequal treatment of a Jew or Moslem was on grounds of religion and not race. This was a point made by several M.P.s during the committee stage of the Race Relations Bill 1965 and in its Report for 1966–7 the Race Relations Board recommended that the position of groups such as the Jews, Sikhs and Gypsies should be clarified. The Solicitor-General (Sir Dingle Foot, Q.C.) took the view during the debates on the 1965 Bill that Jews were to be regarded, for its purposes, as a 'race' or 'ethnic group'.[3] Further reflection leads the author to the view that the problem is not really one of definition but of proof and that it is erroneous to lay down, in the abstract, whether discrimination against Jews or Sikhs is on racial grounds rather than for religious reasons. In each case, it is now suggested, the actual relationship of the parties must be examined to determine whether the discriminator believed his victim to be a member of some distinct race and for that reason discriminated against him. In most instances there will be little difficulty because the refusal to employ, say, a Sikh is unlikely to be on the grounds of his beliefs.

1. Statutes of Canada, 1 & 2 Eliz. 2, c. 19, s. 2
2. (1966) 29 M.L.R. 306
3. 711 H.C. Deb. col. 1043; H.C. Standing Committee B, 27 May 1965, cols. 65–9

Similar considerations apply to the question whether discrimination against Gypsies can be unlawful. In 1965 the Lord Chancellor opined that the Race Relations Act would probably cover Gypsies as an 'ethnic group'.[1] Indeed, the Oxford English Dictionary definition of a Gypsy is 'a member of a wandering race (by themselves called Romany) of Hindu origin'. But the 'true' Gypsy descendants of certain wandering Indian tribes have to be distinguished from other nomads who travel around the English countryside in search of agricultural work and other means of making a living. (Recent research in England and Wales[2] found that of 15,000 Gypsies, or 3,400 families, more than half the men were dealers, mainly in scrap metal, other occupations being road work, building work and general labouring; the vast majority were illiterate and unwilling to work for others.) As a group Gypsies have been subjected to repressive legislation since a statute of 1530 which treated them as felons. Local authorities today use the Highways Act 1959, and the Caravan Sites and Control of Development Act 1960, and various private Acts to discourage Gypsies in their area. In the context of the Highways Act 1959, a Divisional Court had recently to decide whether the word 'Gypsy' used in section 127, which makes it an offence for a Gypsy to encamp on a highway, was to be understood in its dictionary sense. The Court decided that it was not, and applied the popular meaning of nomad. Their Lordships pointed out the difficulty in ascertaining whether a man is 'of the Romany race' ('How pure-blooded a Romany must one be?') and were not prepared to believe that Parliament had intended to penalize a man merely because of his race.[3] This decision does not mean, however, that discrimination against a Gypsy can never be on grounds of race, simply that Parliament could not have intended in the Highways Act to use the word in that way. As a matter of practice, the Race Relations Board has been prepared to consider complaints in regard to discrimination in places of public resort against Gypsies.

The apparent ambiguity of the position of groups such as the Jews and Sikhs is not in itself a strong enough argument for extending the Race Relations Act to religious discrimination. But a case for doing so could be made out on independent grounds in the light of evidence of widespread religious discrimination in Northern Ireland. This would

1. 268 H.L. Deb. col. 1067 (26 July 1965)
2. Report of the Sociological Research Section of the Ministry of Housing and Local Government, *Gypsies and other Travellers* (H.M.S.O., 1967) esp. p. 34; see, too, *Children and their Primary Schools* (H.M.S.O. 1966) App. 12. Note by Mrs B. Adams and Mr D. M. Smith
3. *Mills* v. *Cooper* [1967] 2 Q.B. 459, criticized by the editor of *Antiquity*, 46 (1967) p. 258, on the ground that Gypsies are an ethnic group although not a race

involve, as well, extending the Act to the whole of the United Kingdom since at present it applies only in England, Wales and Scotland, where religious discrimination in employment does not appear to be a significant problem.

A case could also be made for illegalizing discrimination on grounds of political opinion. The anti-Communist views of some Polish refugees after the war resulted in some discrimination against them. In certain industries, particularly those with Government defence contracts, suspected Communists have been refused employment without any legal right to contest the decision that they are 'security risks'.[1] This is contrary to the standards laid down in the I.L.O. Convention Concerning Discrimination in Respect of Employment and Occupation 1958 (No. 111) which provides:

Any measures affecting an individual who is justifiably suspected of, or engaged in, activities prejudicial to the security of the state shall not be deemed to be discrimination, *provided that the individual concerned shall have a right to appeal to a competent body established in accordance with national practice* [article 4]

Sex discrimination, too, falls outside the ambit of the law. Ministry of Labour statistics for October 1966 showed that the average hourly earnings of male workers in manufacturing industries was 9s 2·8d. and for female workers 5s. 3·6d. Although the Government has announced its acceptance of the principle of equal pay for equal work, it has not yet ratified the I.L.O. Convention on Equal Remuneration for Men and Women Workers for Work of Equal Value 1951 (No. 100) on the ground that 'the present position in the U.K. is not fully in accordance with the detailed requirements of the instrument'.[2] Legislation may not be the best way to deal with any of these forms of discrimination, but there can hardly be an excuse for failing to pursue an active policy to eradicate them.

---

1. For a full discussion see H. Street, *Freedom, The Individual and the Law* (Harmondsworth: Penguin Books 1967), p. 237; and David Williams, *Not in the Public Interest* (London 1965), p. 177. The position in the civil service is discussed below, p. 178

2. 725 H.C. Deb., cols 178–9. A Government-T.U.C.-C.B.I. working party was set up in 1966 to study the technical problems involved. The C.B.I. prefer the more limited provisions of the Treaty of Rome which require equal pay for the same work, to those in the I.L.O. Convention which insist on equal pay for work of equal value. The Government view is that equal pay 'is not possible in present economic circumstances' (*The Times*, 8 December 1967). A point which recurs in feminist literature is the striking parallel between individual male attitudes to women and those towards so-called 'inferior' races: see e.g. Simone de Beauvoir's *The Second Sex*, and Olive Schreiner's earlier classic, *Woman and Labour* (London 1911)

THE DEFINITION OF DISCRIMINATION

Apart from limiting the grounds of unlawful discrimination to racial ones, the Race Relations Act sets out a definition of 'discrimination'. In relation to discrimination in places of public resort section 1 (3) of the 1965 Act states:

. . . a person discriminates against any other person if he refuses or neglects to afford him access to the place in question, or any facilities or services available there, in the like manner and on the like terms in and on which such access, facilities or services are available to other members of the public resorting thereto.

The Race Relations (Amendment) Bill introduced by Mr M. Orbach in 1966[1] to cover employment discrimination defined the term as a refusal or neglect '. . . to afford . . . like treatment in the like manner and on the like terms to that afforded to any other person'. The Committee, under the chairmanship of Professor Street, which examined in detail the shape that Britain's extended Race Relations Act ought to take,[2] made no proposals about the definition of 'discrimination'. Basically, the alternative drafting techniques which could be adopted are either to set out a definition of discrimination, such as that in the Orbach Bill accompanied by a list of complicated exceptions, or to follow American precedent.

The attempt to attach a definite legal meaning to discrimination in Britain is in contrast to the position in the U.S.A. and Canada where this term is nowhere defined (except so as to include segregation). Subtle and complex questions have arisen as to whether particular conduct is 'discriminatory'. For example, if a Negro is refused a job as a counterhand because of the fear of customer reaction but is offered another position with higher pay and better prospects in the same establishment, is this 'discrimination'? From the subjective standpoint the applicant has been refused the job of his choice; objectively speaking, he is better off because of his race. As a matter of statutory interpretation there may have been discrimination in respect of a particular occupation, but not in respect of 'employment'.

Difficulties such as these are not necessarily avoided by the British definitions. Indeed, the legal definition of 'discrimination' may introduce unnecessary rigidity. This could present a problem in relation to (1) quota arrangements; (2) 'positive discrimination' in deprived areas.

1. See above, p. 3
2. See above, p. 6

Inasmuch as a quota of, say, 10 per cent coloured labour results in the exclusion of suitably qualified coloured workers it is obviously discriminatory within the meaning of the definitions. The administering agency may, however, consider it desirable to allow, or even encourage, quotas as a temporary measure (a) where an employer has previously refused to employ coloured workers and now agrees to 'try a few'; and (b) to prevent the growth of all-coloured departments or factories and aid dispersal as part of a planned policy of integration. The difficulty has been recognized in the United States. The Californian Attorney-General in an opinion in 1964[1] said that a requirement by the sponsor or producer of a television series that a specific number of workers in each work crew was to be of a specified race would be a violation of the state's Fair Employment Practices Law because setting a racial quota 'constitutes a limitation of the civil rights of all citizens to seek and hold employment without discrimination'. But he added that efforts to obtain a 'reasonable balance' in the work force would not be unlawful. A definition that requires 'like treatment of like people' would not allow for the concept of 'reasonable balance' as a temporary social measure. In other words, lawyer-like precision might defeat the very purposes of the law, or otherwise lead to the provisions of the law being disregarded in practice.

'Positive discrimination' is a concept which has gained acceptance since the publication of the Plowden Report which recommended that every local authority should be more generous to schools in areas where the 'social need' was greatest, and this was to be ascertained by reference to factors like occupations, family size, cash supplements, over-crowding, poor school attendance, proportion of handicapped children, incomplete families and the number of children unable to speak English.[2] The Hunt Committee also recognized that 'special provisions' of a temporary nature, and depending on their motivations, might be required to meet some of the needs of young immigrants, although it emphasized that 'an over-emphasis on distinctiveness rather than on shared values and attitudes can widen rather than narrow the gap.'[3] In the field of employment a case exists for preferential treatment for immigrants to overcome the disparities in education, language and skills between them and the host population. Similar arguments could apply to long-resident coloured families whom past discrimination has condemned to poor education and deprivation.

1. No. 63/48 30 April 1964, reported in (1964) 9 *Race Relations Law Reporter*, p. 1051
2. *Children and their Primary Schools* (H.M.S.O. 1967) paras. 148–53
3. *Immigrants and the Youth Service* (H.M.S.O. 1967) para. 58; see too, paras. 151–2, 201–4

The United Nations' Convention on the Elimination of All Forms of Racial Discrimination (not yet ratified by the U.K.[1]) recognizes that:

special measures taken for the sole purpose of securing adequate advancement of certain racial or ethnic groups or individuals requiring such protection as may be necessary in order to ensure such groups or individuals equal enjoyment or exercise of human rights and fundamental freedoms [including the right to work] shall not be deemed racial discrimination, provided, however, that such measures do not as a consequence lead to the maintenance of separate rights for different racial groups, and that they should not be continued after the objectives for which they were taken have been achieved.

The I.L.O.'s Committee of Experts has pointed out that such measures can be evaluated only in the light of the actual situation in the country concerned. It has accepted as legitimate such policies as the 'Africanization' of the public service in Tanzania and special measures in favour of the 'scheduled castes' in India.[2]

In Britain, measures of 'positive discrimination' might include (a) preference for those without British qualifications in industrial training schemes; (b) intensive language teaching courses for immigrants; (c) recruitment drives among coloured people who have not applied for jobs because of past experiences of discrimination; and (d) ability tests that make allowances for the cultural background of the person. This does not mean preferring coloured applicants over white applicants with similar qualifications (although in the U.S.A. demands of this kind are increasingly made) but simply assessing each man on his merits and making allowance for past deprivation. Unfortunately, a rigid interpretation of 'discrimination' could make measures such as these unlawful. The Street Report proposed, in effect, that the law should not compel this kind of 'positive discrimination'. But voluntary plans by employers to reduce racial imbalance would be permitted provided they received the prior approval of the authority administering the law.

The problems relating to quotas and 'positive discrimination' emphasize the social nature of a problem which cannot be reduced to the precise formula desired by the lawyer. The P.E.P. Survey used the term 'discrimination' in the sense of:

a practice or policy which affects members of minority groups differently because of colour or country of origin, in ways that are either of significance to them personally or of significance socially.

1. See below, Chapter 11, p. 192
2. Report of the Committee of Experts on the Application of Conventions and Recommendations, Report III (Part IV) International Labour Conference, 47th Session, 1963 (Geneva I.L.O. 1963) Part Three, para. 39

This is a wide and flexible concept. British legislation might do well to follow the American lead by declining to attach any exact meaning to 'discrimination' (except so as to include segregation and hence ethnic work units) and to leave it to the good sense of those enforcing the law to determine the social significance of the particular conduct in question.

The final limitation on the legal definition of racial discrimination is that the act in question must be of one of the types specified. In the U.S.A. and Canada the activities specified include discrimination by employers in the hiring, discharge, compensation, terms, conditions or privileges of employment, discrimination by labour organizations in admission to and expulsion from those organizations, discrimination by employment agencies in job referrals, and discriminatory job advertisements. The Street Report recommended that the Race Relations Act should cover a similar list of activities in the field of employment.

Certain forms of racial discrimination are excepted from the statutory prohibition in the U.S.A. and Canada. One of these is where the colour, race, creed or national origin of a person is a bona fide occupational qualification.[1] The exemption tends to be strictly interpreted by the supervising agencies. While it is generally considered to be legitimate for a Chinese restaurant to refuse to employ non-Chinese waiters in order to maintain the appropriate atmosphere for its commercial activities, it is not a ground for exemption that customers or existing staff object to the employment of a Negro, even though a loss of business may result from these objections. Another possible exemption is in respect of so-called 'intimate personal relationships'. The Street Report suggested that 'some relationships may well be so personal and intimate that legal intervention is either likely to be ineffective or is politically or socially unacceptable'. Examples are domestic servants and a personal hairdresser employed by a film star. This does not seem a very satisfactory basis for exemption. If, as the Street Report proposed, it should be unlawful for a hairdresser to discriminate in the choice of his customers despite the personal nature of the services rendered, there seems no logical reason to permit the film star to discriminate on racial grounds in the choice of her personal hairdresser. A more compelling, and separate, ground for granting an exemption exists in the case of small employment units. In the early stages of legislation the supervising agency cannot reasonably be expected to assume responsibility for these units. For this reason Title VII of the federal Civil Rights Act 1964

---

1. The Federal Civil Rights Act 1964 and a model anti-discrimination statute drawn up by the Uniform Law Commissioners in 1966 do not allow this exemption where the discrimination is on grounds of race or colour

originally exempted employers with less than 100 employees, and provided for this figure to be reduced annually until it reached twenty-five. The Street Report suggested that it might be unnecessary to write any exemption of this kind into the law; instead, the matter could be left entirely to administrative practice. Alternatively, the Act might originally apply to establishments with more than fifty employees and provide for subsequent reduction by order of the supervising agency. Such a provision would enable the authorities to concentrate their attention in places where they are likely to make the greatest impact in changing employment patterns. It would also render unnecessary any separate exemption in respect of domestic employees because it is highly unlikely that any one household would include as many as fifty domestic servants.

In summary, it can be said that the sociological concept of discrimination deals with all kinds of differential treatment of persons ascribed to particular social categories. The sociologist's factual descriptions of relations between groups enable him to evaluate the extent of discrimination and to generalize about social distance. He is concerned with discrimination as part of a continuing relationship; isolated group conflict is not his real concern, nor is it his task to pass moral judgements about discrimination exercised against, or in favour of, particular groups (e.g. 'benign quotas'). On the other hand, the legal definition of discrimination is the result of ethical and political judgements, and deals with single (or a few) conflicts between particular individuals belonging to different social groups. If the proposals in the Street Report are adopted, the lawyer will confine his attention to discrimination 'on grounds of colour, race or ethnic or national origins'. The law will permit racial imbalance schemes (although these are, strictly speaking, discriminatory) provided they have received the prior approval of the administering authority. And, while covering all the main areas of employment, it will exempt certain employment relationships where the use of the law is likely to be politically or socially unacceptable. The reader should keep the differences between the sociological and legal concepts of discrimination clearly in mind throughout this book.

DISCRIMINATION AGAINST FOREIGN NATIONALS

Discrimination is at the very heart of the distinction between aliens and nationals, yet this is not, in the generally accepted sense, racial discrimination. In Britain 'national origin' and not 'nationality' is a ground of unlawful discrimination, and it is therefore necessary to distinguish the two concepts.

'National origin' is not defined in the Race Relations Act. In some American states it is defined as 'including ancestry'; in others 'ancestry' is mentioned as a separate ground of unlawful discrimination. It seems clear that the British terminology includes ancestry or extraction (the term used in the I.L.O Convention is 'national extraction') and foreign birth.

'Nationality' on the other hand, means the status of an individual as the subject or citizen of a particular sovereign or state. The basic distinction is between British subjects and aliens. Broadly speaking, the former are persons born within the Queen's dominions, or a person whose father was a British subject at the time of that person's birth. Aliens are all persons who are not British subjects.[1] Since 1948 there has been a further distinction between those British subjects who are citizens of the U.K. and colonies and those who are Commonwealth citizens.[2] The latter may register as U.K. citizens, generally after a period of five years' ordinary residence in the United Kingdom. In 1965, for example, 2,265 Indians, 852 Jamaicans and 628 Pakistanis were among those acquiring U.K. citizenship.[3]

There is an overlap between these concepts. Discrimination against a U.K. citizen who has acquired his citizenship in a particular way, e.g. by naturalization, or by birth in England of alien parents, is discrimination on grounds of 'national origin'. Moreover, the mere fact that a person is a foreign national does not mean that he is excluded from the scope of the Race Relations Act if the discrimination arises not on grounds of his foreign nationality but on one of the grounds specified, e.g. ethnic or national origins.

Discrimination between aliens and British subjects in employment is an accepted principle of legislation and industrial practice. Aliens who are permitted to enter the United Kingdom generally do so subject to the condition that they may not enter into employment without the permission of the Ministry of Labour. In practice, the Ministry needs to be satisfied that the employment is reasonable and necessary, that there is no suitable British or long-resident foreign labour available and that there will be no undercutting of wage standards. Where there is strong trade union organization, the Ministry consults the unions and opposition from that quarter may result in the exclusion of the alien. Each year between 2,000 and 3,000 applications to employ foreign

---

1. Status of Aliens Act 1914, 4 & 5 Geo. 5, c. 17, s. 1
2. British Nationality Act 1948, 11 & 12 Geo. 6, c. 56 as amended
3. Statistics of Persons Acquiring Citizenship of the U.K. and Colonies 1965, Cmnd 3091

nationals are turned down.[1] An example of the cooperation between the Ministry and an industry employing foreign labour is to be found in the Conditions for the Importation of Foreign Striptease Performers as approved by the Variety & Allied Entertainments Council of Great Britain (dated 15 May 1961). These provide that the foreign performer's contract of engagement must be submitted to the V.A.E.C. and that engagements for more than twenty-six weeks in any total of fifty-two weeks will not, as a rule, be allowed. It is laid down that applications for work permits must be made to the Ministry of Labour and *copies* of the application must be *made simultaneously* [*sic*] to the joint secretaries of the V.A.E.C. 'Although the Ministry of Labour will normally be prepared to issue permits on the basis of this agreement', it is said, 'they must retain discretion to refuse permits in particular cases.' This neatly sums up the role of the Ministry. (The agreement also requires foreign striptease performers to 'carry their permits with them for production to the competent authority *at any time*'. Facetiously, one might ask whether the permit has supplanted the fig leaf!)

By statute, certain occupations are closed to aliens. An alien is not permitted to hold a pilotage certificate, nor to act as master, chief officer or chief engineer of a British merchant ship, nor as skipper or second-hand of a fishing boat registered in the U.K.[2] Aliens may not be employed in the Civil Service without certificate,[3] are barred from public office[4] and are subject to restrictions in regard to military service.[5] An alien promoting industrial unrest in an industry in which he has not been bona fide engaged for at least two years is liable on conviction to up to three months' imprisonment.[6]

A number of collective agreements between employers and unions discriminate against aliens. A summary of the principal ones will be

---

1. During 1966, 69,104 applications were made of which 66,054 were allowed, nearly half of them for domestic, catering and nursing work (Ministry of Labour *Gazette*, LXXV, 3, p. 223) In earlier years the figures were:

	1964	1965
Applications made	60,762	68,723
Applications allowed	58,338	66,126

The condition of entry is imposed under Aliens Order, S.I. 1953/1671, art. 22 (subject to S.I. 1960/828 and S.I. 1954/394). When an alien has been in approved employment in the U.K. for four years the condition is normally cancelled

2. Aliens Restriction (Amendment) Act 1919, 9 & 10 Geo. 5, c. 92, ss. 4 & 5. For certain racial provisions in s. 5 (2) of this Act, see below, p. 44

3. Aliens Employment Act 1955, 4 & 5 Eliz. 2, c. 18, s. 1. The Civil Service Nationality Rule is discussed in Chapter 10, below, p. 178

4. Act of Settlement 1700, 12 & 13 Will. 3, c. 2

5. Army Act 1955, 3 & 4 Eliz. 2, c. 18, s. 21; Air Force Act, 3 & 4 Eliz. 2, c. 19, s. 21 (both as amended by S.I. 1964/488)

6. Aliens Restriction (Amendment) Act 1919, s. 3

found in Appendix II[1] and their origins and effect in producing a norm in regard to other 'outsiders' is considered in the next chapter.[2] Some of these agreements use precise language so as to indicate that they are to apply only to 'foreign nationals' (i.e. aliens) and that the restrictions they impose are to cease when the alien is naturalized. An example is the agreement dated 20 May 1959, between the National Union of Railwaymen and the Railway Management, which provides that if foreign nationals are recruited for starting grade positions or positions above starting grade, they are to be employed on a temporary basis only. However, on becoming a naturalized British subject, a foreign national will be transferred from the temporary to the permanent staff if there are permanent staff vacancies in the grade in which he is employed at the time of naturalization. Since July 1960, the temporary service of foreign nationals who become British subjects and are transferred to the permanent staff, counts for seniority for future promotion.

Most of the agreements, however, lack this admirable precision. While a few refer to specific groups (e.g. Spanish females or Italians) the majority relate to 'foreign' workers, a vague term which could be interpreted to include those of foreign origin or ancestry. For instance, it was alleged in 1962 that miners at a colliery near Barnsley had asked the management to refuse to sign on any worker who was not 'British by birth'. What this really meant was that Poles and Hungarians at the pit, some of whom were British by naturalization, were unwelcome.

Union rule books sometimes restrict membership to British subjects (e.g. the British Airline Pilots' Association). The Association of Cinematograph and Television and Allied Technicians limits membership to British subjects and protected persons, Irish citizens and aliens of long residence, but allows those not otherwise qualifying to be admitted as temporary members with the same privileges as members. The Musicians' Union requires twelve months' residence in the U.K. as a condition of membership. The Professional Footballers' Association requires two years' residence.

Are laws and practices of this kind justifiable? Judged by the standards of international law they would appear to be so. According to the 'practice of civilized states' a host country is entitled to place restrictions on the employment of aliens within its territory. It is generally said that aliens must be afforded civilized treatment but there

1. Below, p. 218
2. Below, p. 49

is no agreement as to how to decide what is 'civilized'.[1] Attempts have been made to formulate certain fundamental 'human rights' which aliens and nationals are entitled to share equally. In regard to migrant workers a series of international labour conventions expressly prohibit certain forms of discrimination between aliens and nationals. The Migration for Employment Convention (Revised) 1949 (No. 97), which has been ratified by the U.K., imposes an obligation to treat migrant workers not less favourably than nationals in respect of matters such as remuneration, conditions of work, membership of trade unions and enjoyment of the benefits of collective bargaining, accommodation and social security. The Migration for Employment Recommendation (Revised) 1949 (No. 86) provides that as far as possible migrants for employment should be admitted to employment on the same terms as nationals, and that where restrictions are imposed these should cease to apply to those immigrants who have resided in the country for a certain period which should not, as a rule, exceed five years. The Social Security (Minimum Standards) Convention 1952 (No. 152) (ratified by the U.K.), the Workers Housing Recommendation 1961 (No. 115) and the Equality of Treatment (Social Security) Convention 1962 (No. 118) also prohibit discrimination on grounds of *nationality*. Standards are bound to vary according to national conditions, but it is interesting to observe that the Canadian Fair Employment Practices Act 1953, and the anti-discrimination laws of Ontario, New Brunswick and British Columbia outlaw discrimination on grounds of nationality in the same way as racial discrimination.

If Britain enters the European Economic Community, an influx of European workers into Britain may be expected, particularly if Britain is able to maintain its relatively high wage rates for skilled workers. Article 48 of the Treaty of Rome provides that the free movement of labour shall be secured within the Community not later than 1 January 1970, and that 'such freedom of movement shall entail the abolition of any *discrimination based on nationality* between workers of the member States as regards employment, remuneration or other labour conditions'.

Article 49 lays down the procedure by which this objective is to be reached. When and if Britain becomes subject to these provisions it is possible that the other member states will have abolished all restrictions which might hinder a worker from one member state taking up paid private employment in another member state in the same way as if he were a national of that other member state. At present certain transi-

1. See I. Brownlie, *Principles of Public International Law* (Oxford 1966), p. 427, for a clear account of the opposing views.

tional regulations are in force which indicate the progress made towards the achievement of free movement of workers and non-discrimination. These provide, among other matters, that after one year no obstacle may under any circumstances be placed in the way of employment in the same occupation; the right to take up employment becomes absolute after two years' regular employment in the particular country; and migrants must be eligible for election to representative workers' bodies after three years' employment in the same undertaking in the country concerned. Other equal rights include those of obtaining accommodation, and of assistance from employment officers (even if the worker is not yet resident in the country). Member states are under a positive duty to ensure equality of opportunity.[1] This shows that, should Britain become tied to the E.E.C., there is bound to be insistence that laws, agreements and union rules regarding foreign labour be revised.

A simultaneous development is likely to be an increase of discrimination on grounds of nationality against Commonwealth citizens. The precise effect of British entry into the E.E.C. on the position of migrant workers from the Commonwealth will be a subject of political and economic controversy. The analogy used may be that of the Netherlands which does not have the equivalent of the Commonwealth Immigrants Act and allows citizens of Surinam (Dutch Guiana) and other overseas Dutch territories unrestricted entry into Dutch territory in Europe and free choice of employment there. But they have no similar rights in other member states.

Even if Britain stays out of the E.E.C. the tendency to restrict the rights of British subjects who are not also citizens of the U.K. and Colonies is likely to continue. This is shown not only by the contraction of the number of employment vouchers issued under the Commonwealth Immigrants Act, but also by the growing practice of placing restrictions on the employment of Commonwealth visitors and students coming to Britain. In 1962, the *Instructions to Immigration Officers*[2] authorized officers to impose a prohibition on the taking up of employment by a Commonwealth visitor whom he had reason to suppose was contemplating getting a job. The 1966 *Instructions*,[3] replacing the earlier ones, repeated this and added that where an immigration officer thinks it is desirable for the Home Office to confirm that a person is a bona fide intending student he should restrict that person's initial period of stay and prohibit the taking up of employment in the meantime. It is

1. Arts. 8–16 of Reg. 38/64/E.E.C. of the Council of Ministers of 25 March 1964
2. Cmnd 1716
3. Cmnd 3064

not inconceivable that demands to check the alleged 'evasion' of the Commonwealth Immigrants Act might lead in time to conditions being imposed on all visitors and students in regard to employment. From this it would be a relatively short jump to impose conditions on holders of employment vouchers requiring Ministry of Labour permission to subsequent changes of employment.

Within industry, employers and employees who are prevented from discriminating on racial grounds against coloured immigrants, may be tempted to resort to distinctions of nationality (where these immigrants are still nationals of their own countries) to uphold local privileges. So whilst citizenship may lose its significance as between citizens of the U.K. and Colonies and foreign E.E.C. nationals, it may tend increasingly to be the criterion of discrimination between the workers of the advanced and under-developed countries. In this sense, ending racial discrimination does not inevitably result in greater internationalism.

3. The Development of Attitudes and Institutions

Hewers of wood and drawers of water has long been the white man's stereotype of the 'black sons of Ham'. To some extent the legend has been based on the actual position in society occupied by coloured men and women. What effect has myth and reality had in the shaping of institutions? What effect have they, in turn, had upon the situation?

The first confrontation between the organs of government in England and Negroes as a distinct body of labour occurred in 1596. As an aftermath of the Spanish wars there was a small influx of 'blackamoores', some of them slaves, the others destitute mercenaries. Elizabeth I's Privy Council ordered their removal on grounds which have been repeated through the centuries:

[These blackamoores] may well be spared in this realme so populous and nombres of hable persons the subjectes of the land and Christian people that perish for want of service, whereby through their labour they might be mayntained.[1]

The reasons, it is to be noted, were primarily economic but were buttressed by a religious distinction. At this stage, as with the expulsion of the Jews from England in 1290, the racial justification was not advanced. In the case of the Jews traditional religious superstitions continued to be put forward in the seventeenth century against their readmission to England. While London merchants expressed their alarm that this would deliver a fatal blow to English commerce, William Prynne 'as a Christian and English Freeman' put out a spate of anti-semitic propaganda. 'As I kept on my way . . . in Lincolns-Inne Fields passing by seven or eight maimed Soldiers on Stilts who begged me', he wrote, 'I heard them say aloud one to another, *We must now all turn Jews, and there will be nothing left for the poor.*'[2] The financial and

1. Acts of the Privy Council, 18 July 1596
2. Preface to his pamphlet, *A short Demurrer to the Jews' long discontinued Remitter into England.* 2nd ed. (London 1656), as quoted in L. Poliakov, *The History of Anti-Semitism*, Vol. I (London 1965), p. 207

political services which the Jews were able to render Cromwell, however, proved to be more significant than the hostile public opinion
aroused by Prynne and others. The Jews, without being officially
admitted, were tolerated and their community flourished. They continued until the nineteenth century to labour under severe legal disabilities. Yet the basis of this discrimination was a religious one, felt
particularly in the form of oath which they were required to take before
carrying on a number of trades and professions.[1]

NEGRO SLAVERY

In the case of Negroes in Britain, however, the religious excuse for
inequality and discrimination was not viable. When they reappeared in
England, also in the late seventeenth century, it was in the status of
slavery. At first imported as serving-boys and manservants to satisfy a
fashion, the use of Negro slaves in domestic service became extensive and
by 1770 there were thought to be some 14,000 to 20,000 in London alone.

The presence of this body of unfree servants confronted the common
lawyers with a cruel dilemma. On the one hand, as Granville Sharp, a
lawyer and leading emancipator argued,[2] slavery as a status could be
justified only by enforcing the ancient laws of villeinage but this could
not be done because it would lay the foundation for a 'most dangerous
vassalage' in which the poorer English classes might be involved. On
the other hand, in the colonies and plantations slavery was not only
permitted but the Imperial Government applied legal and financial
pressures to meet an insatiable demand for Negro slaves.

At first the religious justification was attempted. In 1677 a court
declared that slavery was legal in England because Negroes were
infidels and therefore beyond the rights enjoyed by Christian men.[3]
This would have meant that baptism set free a slave and so it was soon
repudiated. A century of vacillation followed in which the judges
delivered conflicting opinions about the legality of slavery in England.
Not least among the forensic arguments was the economic consequences
of emancipation. Lord Mansfield declared in 1771: 'I do not know
what the consequences may be if the masters were to lose their property

---

1. Doubt persists even to-day whether a Jew may hold the office of Lord High Chancellor. The better view is that he can: H. S. Q. Henriques, *The Jews and English Law* (London
1908). The position of Roman Catholics in relation to this office is a little more dubious:
Lord Simon in 127 H.L. Deb. col 463 and correspondence in the *Sunday Times*, 6 & 13
February 1966
2. *A representation of the injustice and dangerous tendency of tolerating slavery in England*
(London 1769) and *Appendix* (London 1772) esp. pp. 77-8, 108-9
3. *Butts* v. *Penny* (1677) Levinz 201

by bringing slaves to England. I hope it will never be finally discussed. . . .'[1]

The following year he estimated that if some 14,000 to 15,000 slaves were freed the owners would be involved in a loss of £700,000. Granville Sharp countered this with the argument that a master could, at the time, obtain the services of an apprentice for six or seven years or more without any wages at all, so why the need for slavery?

At the end of 1771, when an escaped Negro slave, James Somersett, was recaptured and placed on board a ship which was to have returned him to Jamaica, Lord Mansfield was unable to avoid a decision. He twice adjourned the case, twice suggested that the owner might settle the matter by selling the slave and he advised the merchants to apply to Parliament for a remedy.[2]

When all this failed he was led to say:

The state of slavery is of such a nature that it is incapable of being introduced on any reasons, moral or political, but only by positive law . . . It is so odious that nothing can be suffered to support it, but positive law. Whatever inconveniences, therefore, may follow from the decision I cannot say this case is allowed or approved by the law of England; and therefore the black must be discharged.[3]

This decision is sometimes treated as a declaration that there was from that time a complete prohibition on slavery in England. However, it has been shown by a learned writer that 'the legal position [Lord Mansfield] established was not that a slave on setting foot in England became free but that he could not be forcibly removed to the rigours of American slavery'.[4] After the decision, Negro slaves continued to be bought and sold in England and Lord Mansfield himself held that a slave who continued to work for his master after being brought to England was not a 'hired' servant and, it would follow, had no claim to wages.[5]

1. *Minutes of the trial of Thos. Lewis at the Court of King's Bench,* 20 February 1771
2. When this suggestion was taken up in 1773, the attempt to promote legislation to tolerate slavery in England failed: K. Little, *Negroes in Britain* (London 1948), p. 182
3. *The Case of James Somersett* (1772) 20 St. Tr. 1 at 82
4. E. Fiddes, 'Lord Mansfield and the *Somersett* case' (1934) 50 L.Q.R. 499. The Scottish courts, on the other hand, went much further: in *Knight* v. *Wedderburn* (1778) 33 Mor. 14545, the Court of Session approved the view that 'the state of slavery is not recognized by the laws of this kingdom, and is inconsistent with the principles thereof.' It needs to be added that at this time those who entered employment as colliers and salters in Scotland were bound in perpetuity
5. *The Inhabitants of Thames Ditton* (1785) 4 Dougl. 299. Most of the mythologizing about Somersett's case arose in the nineteenth century. Lord Campbell in his *Lives of the Chief Justices,* 3rd ed. (London 1874) iii, p. 293, made the fanciful claim that Lord Mansfield had said 'the air of England has long been too pure for a slave, and every man is free who breathes it'.

In 1827, Lord Stowell held that temporary residence in England suspended but did not extinguish the status of slavery, which revived when the slave voluntarily returned to America.[1] Indirectly as well, the courts continued far into the nineteenth century to countenance slavery. While Parliament was endeavouring to stamp out the slave trade, a court held in 1820 that a foreigner could recover damages in England in respect of the wrongful seizure by a British subject of a cargo of slaves on board a ship being used by him in the African slave trade.[2]

As late as 1860 four eminent judges could find nothing in the anti-slave trade statutes to invalidate a contract by a British subject for the sale of slaves held by him in Brazil where the possession of slaves was lawful. Nor did they think it necessary to consider the question whether to recognize slavery in this way was contrary to the public policy of the English courts.[3] One must conclude, therefore, that the majority of the judges were slow and reluctant emancipators. It appears, moreover, that Somersett's case had little immediate impact on the social status of Negroes. After 1772, Negroes brought to England as slaves usually remained with their masters in the same occupations and with the same lowly status as before that year. Some, indeed, tried to live as free men but were unable to find work. Distressed ex-slaves and Negro ex-soldiers who had served in America, stood out among the London poor as the 'St Giles Blackbirds'.[4] Among the attempts to solve the problem was a Government scheme under which 411 Negroes with sixty white prostitutes were shipped to Sierra Leone. Others went to the West Indies. But in 1814 it was still possible for a Select Committee to draw the attention of the Commons to the distressed condition of many Negroes in London.

Gradually, however, coloured people ceased to form a visibly distinct section of the population. There are records of Negro workmen and beggars in the first half of the nineteenth century but by 1870 they had become almost completely assimilated in white English society. Apart from visiting colonial students, they did not reappear until the 1914–18 war when several thousand coloured labourers were brought to England to fill the jobs of Englishmen on active service. When the war industries closed, many were repatriated. The remainder sought

---

1. *The Slave, Grace* (1827) 2 St. Tr. (N.S.) 273
2. *Madrazo* v. *Willes* (1820) 3 B. & A. 353
3. *Santos* v. *Illidge* (1859) 6 C. B. (N. S.) 841; (1860) 8 C. B. (N. S.) 861. To-day, of course, laws concerning slavery and the like are regarded as contrary to English public policy: *Reggazoni* v. *Sethia* [1956] 2 Q. B. 490 at 524 per Parker L. J.
4. M. D. George, *London Life in the Eighteenth Century* (London 1925), p. 137

what Dr Kenneth Little describes as the 'only employment open to them', namely seafaring around places such as Cardiff.

THE SHIPPING INDUSTRY

The shipping industry has, in fact, been a traditional source of occupation for coloured men. Although jobs have been more readily available at sea than on land, coloured seamen have always fallen between two stools. When they have secured employment in their native countries on British ships they have been paid less and had worse conditions of service than British seamen. When they have come to England to seek work they have had to face resentment and discrimination.

Present law and policy in this regard remain deeply rooted in laws passed to regulate the East India Company. In 1814 the Company was compelled to provide food, clothing and necessary accommodation for Asiatic sailors in England until they could be conveyed back to India. This measure[1] was enacted without debate because of the large number of Lascars (i.e. sailors who were natives of India) and other Asiatic seamen who had been discharged on the arrival of their ships in England and left destitute.

An amending Act of 1823 (4 Geo. 4, c. 80) introduced a racial division between British subjects. It provided that Lascars and other Asiatic sailors 'although born in territories . . . under the Government of His Majesty' were not to be regarded as British sailors. At the same time, Negro seamen born in the West Indian colonies were said to be 'as much British seamen as a white man would be'.[2] This distinction had two consequences. The first was that Lascars received less in cash and kind than British (including Negro West Indian) seamen. A shipowner testifying before a Parliamentary Select Committee in 1847 estimated that the cost of victualling a ship was one shilling a day per European seaman and sixpence a day per Lascar. It was suggested, however, that more men were required in a ship manned by Lascars and consequently the overall cost to the shipowners of hiring Lascars was greater than that of hiring Europeans.[3] The second result was that Lascars could not be discharged in England, while other British subjects who were sailors could be. The reason advanced for this was the

1. 54 Geo. 3, c. 134, ss. 2 and 3; *Hansard's Parliamentary Debates*, vol. 27, cols. 214, 225–8 (29 November 1813). A Committee on Lascars and other Asiatic Seamen, 1814–15, subsequently advised the setting up of a regular establishment, with legal powers to provide for the care and treatment and 'the preservation of an efficient police' among the Lascars

2. First Report from the Select Committee on the Policy and Operation of the Navigation Laws, 1847–8, Minutes of Evidence, p. 10, para. 67

3. Ibid. Second Report, pp. 420–1, para. 4666

same as with the 1814 Act, namely to prevent Lascars becoming a charge on charity in England.

The normal rule which applied whenever a ship was manned by non-British sailors was that at least three fourths of the seamen had to be British.[1] But this was not applied in respect of Lascars, who were technically 'British'. Instead, where part of the crew of a ship with a British master was Lascar, only four seamen for every one hundred tons of the ship's load had to be 'British' (here meaning European) and the rest could be Lascars. This lends weight to the view that these discriminatory measures were not enacted to protect British seamen from direct Lascar competition. A Board of Trade Committee report in 1903 confirms this by saying that while preference was shown to British seamen over foreigners 'for patriotic and sentimental reasons' this did not apply in regard to preference over Lascars.[2]

What then were the reasons for the differential treatment of Lascars? Among the pretexts put forward in evidence to the Board of Trade Committee in 1903 were that the Atlantic climate was 'unfitted to their constitutions', that 'they were decidedly inferior to European men in physique', that 'they were not always sober' and that they were prepared to accept 'lower conditions and standards of comfort than British seamen'. The Committee itself, after hearing the evidence of Lascars, commented that 'there is no reason to think that many of them do, in any appreciable degree, suffer in the colder climates' and the Committee was impressed by 'their manly character'. It suggested that the Lascars had some claim to employment because British vessels had displaced native trading ships.

Behind the declarations made by the shipowners of their 'humanity and consideration' one suspects that the roots of the discrimination lay in the relative cheapness per head of Lascars and their suitability for work in the tropics. This was of especial importance at a time when, as the 1903 Committee reported, British seamen could not be recruited in sufficient numbers. A further reason was the need to prevent the presence of a mass of unemployed Lascars on English soil.

The 1823 Act was not removed from the statute book until 1963.[3] But the result of its repeal was not to put Indian sailors in the same position as other British subjects. This is because the Merchant Shipping Act 1894, which is still in force, continues to differentiate between seamen on a racial basis.

1. Report to Board of Trade on the supply of British seamen, by Thomas Gray (Assistant Secretary), 1886, pp. 3, 16
2. Report of Committee appointed by the Board of Trade to inquire into certain provisions affecting the mercantile marine, 1903, Cd. 1607, Minutes of Evidence, I, 3542
3. Statute Law Revision Act 1963, 11 & 12 Eliz. 2, c. 30

The relevant sections of the Act are too long to be quoted here in full. In summary, they provide that: (1) a master or owner is liable to a fine 'if any person being a native of any country in Asia or Africa, or any Island in the South Sea or the Pacific Ocean or of any other country not having a consular office in the U.K.' is brought as a seaman and left in the U.K. and within six months of being so left is awarded social security benefits. There is an exception in the case of a master or owner who can show that the person quitted the ship without consent or was afforded due means of returning to his native country.[1] (2) The Secretary of State is bound 'to take charge and send home or otherwise provide for all Lascars and other seamen who are natives of India' who are found destitute in the U.K.[2] (3) A master or owner may enter into an agreement with a Lascar or any native of India binding him to proceed either as a seaman or as a passenger to any part of the U.K. and there enter into a *further* agreement to serve as a seaman on any ship which may happen to be there and to be bound to any port in India. If an appointed officer then certifies that the further agreement is a 'proper' one relating to a 'proper' ship, the Lascar is 'deemed to be engaged under the further agreement and to be for all purposes one of the crew of the ship to which it relates'.[3] The last of these provisions means, in effect, that a native of India becomes bound to work his passage home, although he may not wish to do so, and must work on terms and conditions in which he has had no say and to which he may positively object. This unusual provision, imposed on a racial basis, becomes all the more remarkable when one remembers that for a breach of his 'contract' the seaman concerned will be subject to the criminal sanctions laid down by the Merchant Shipping Act for desertion or indiscipline.

Racial differentiation is also at the heart of another subsisting statutory provision. Section 5 (2) of the Aliens Restriction (Amendment) Act 1919 provides that no alien may be employed on board a British ship at a rate of pay less than the current standard rate of pay on British ships for his rating. However, where aliens of '*any particular race* are habitually employed afloat in any capacity or in any climate for which they are specially fitted, nothing in this section shall prejudice the right of aliens *of such race* to be employed upon British ships at rates of pay which are not below those for the time being fixed as standard rates for British subjects *of that race*.' This is striking legislative confirmation that British subjects employed at sea are paid differently

1. 57 & 58 Vict. c. 60, s. 184 (1) as amended by Ministry of Social Security Act 1966, Sch. 6
2. Ibid. s. 185
3. Ibid. s. 125

according to their race. It means, for example, that a British sailor from Hong Kong will be paid the same as a Chinese sailor from Shanghai working on a British ship but he may earn considerably less than a French sailor on a British ship. The French sailor is entitled to be paid at the same rate as European British subjects.

These provisions crystallize and reinforce the custom of the shipping industry. This custom is evidenced, as well, in the current agreement on manning entered into between the Shipping Federation (the owners) and the National Union of Seamen, with effect from 1 March 1965, which limits the employment of 'Non-Europeans' on British ships. The term 'Lascar' is no longer used to describe Indian seamen, having been replaced by 'Non-European' which, according to the National Union of Seamen,[1] is used to describe any crew members on British vessels who are not working on national maritime rates. This too, confirms that on British ships there are two classes of sailor: Europeans and Non-Europeans.

Between the wars the agonies of economic depression led to a rein-forcement of traditional discrimination in the shipping industry. While shipowners were anxious to sign on Non-European sailors abroad because they could be employed below national rates of pay, European sailors looked on all coloured sailors (whether signed on here or abroad) as an alien group responsible for keeping white sailors out of work. This led to union pressure behind the slogan 'British seamen only'. The experience of those years helps in some measure to explain the current manning agreement.

During the acute conflicts of the inter-war years the white seamen's demands were met by two legislative measures. The Special Restrictions (Coloured Alien Seamen) Order 1925,[2] obliged *coloured* seamen, many of whom were in fact British colonial subjects, to register as aliens unless they could produce documentary proof of their nationality. Once registered they were liable to deportation at any time. Secondly, it was made a term of payment of subsidies by the Government to British tramp owners under the British Shipping (Assistance) Act 1935 that first preference in employment must be given to seamen of British nationality. In the popular mind 'coloured' and 'alien' were strongly identified. Moreover, many coloured British seamen were unable to prove their British nationality and consequently held alien

1. The terms and application of the current agreement are discussed in Chapter 5 below, p. 65
2. S. R. & O. 1925/290 (made under the Aliens Order 1920, S. R. & O. 1920/448). The effect of this is discussed by Little, op. cit., p. 64 et seq., and in *The Race Question in Modern Science* (Paris 1956) at p. 198

registration certificates. In effect this meant that they could not serve on subsidized vessels and, according to one estimate,[1] several hundred lost their livelihood in this way. After the Second World War both these measures were repealed.

THE SECOND WORLD WAR AND AFTER

During the war itself coloured workers experienced far less discrimination than in earlier generations. The shortage of skilled and unskilled labour in factories led to a number of West Indians being brought to England.[2] The Ministry of Labour employed Learie Constantine, a well-known West Indian cricketer, to assist in the adjustment of some of these workers. He has recounted how, by telling cricketing stories, he managed to reduce tension when it arose and to persuade white workers not to discriminate.[3] At the end of hostilities many West Indians were repatriated when they became redundant. For those that remained in areas such as Liverpool there was a substantially higher rate of unemployment than among white workers.

The immigration from the Caribbean, India and Pakistan, which has been going on since the early 1950s, has been primarily motivated by the labour needs of the British economy.[4] This easily identifiable group of workers, many of them of low socio-economic status, unskilled and poorly educated, became the target of wild allegations and a ready ploy for unscrupulous politicians. The charges that they were ousting English workers from their jobs, working for lower rates of pay and longer hours than local workmen became loud and frequent in the areas of greatest immigrant concentration.[5]

These charges bore a striking resemblance to those levelled against the poorer classes of Jews who fled from Eastern Europe to Britain between 1880 and 1905. A Select Committee of the House of Commons in 1888 reported that these 'aliens' generally 'worked for longer hours and for less wages than English workmen' and that they were 'dirty

1. Little, op. cit., p. 74; of 690 unemployed firemen on the Cardiff Docks Register on 11 March 1936, 599 were coloured men. Caradog Jones, *The Economic Status of Coloured Families in the Port of Liverpool* (Liverpool U. P. 1940) states that in 1938, seventy-five per cent of the males in coloured families in Liverpool were out of work, a very much higher figure than that among whites in similar jobs
2. The problems of one group of 345 West Indians who came between 1941–3 are discussed by A. H. Richmond, *Colour Prejudice in Britain: A Study of West Indian Workers in Liverpool, 1941–1951* (London 1954)
3. *Colour Bar* (London 1954), p. 147
4. See Chapter 1 above, p. 13, and Chapter 4 below, p. 58
5. There is an excellent account of the development of immigration as a political issue in Paul Foot, *Immigration and Race in British Politics* (Harmondsworth: Penguin 1965)

and uncleanly in their habits'. The solution proposed by the Committee was legislation to halt the flow of immigration. Attempts were made by the Marquis of Salisbury and the Earl of Hardwicke to introduce restrictive measures and ultimately a Royal Commission was appointed which reported in 1903. The Commission rejected the complaint of several trade union witnesses that alien Jews were displacing native labour but added that 'leaving the skilled labour market out of the question we think it proved that the industrial conditions under which a large number of aliens work in London fall below the standard which ought . . . to be maintained'.[1]

Above all, the evils of 'sweated' labour became associated, by popular misconception, with the worst-off section of sweated labour, the alien Jews. The 'sweater' was graphically described in evidence to the Commission by Mr Herbert Evans, an assistant Factories Inspector in East London:

He is usually found in a basement or garret, concealed from the outside world altogether. His workshop reeks with foul smells; the atmosphere is loaded with human vitiation; the combustion from burning refuse and the emission of sickly fumes by cheap oil lamps and other implements of work and from processes of manufacture, together with an absence of natural light, make this particular class of workplace a danger to the community. Here the alien is imprisoned day and night and kept at work in a semi-nude state for starvation allowance. . . . Not a little of the ill-feeling and strife evinced towards the foreigner in East London is attachable to this wretched [sweater]. He is neither amicable to law or reason. . .[2]

In spite of evidence like this, the Commission made no recommendations to improve the conditions of labour (although some proposals were made about overcrowding). Instead, it suggested that the immigration of certain classes of aliens be subjected to state control and legislation. The result was the Aliens Act 1905, which did precisely this.

The restrictions on immigration failed to rid East London of its sweated garrets. The reform of industrial conditions for Jewish labour came through other avenues. Before 1901, as one writer has expressed it, 'the inadequacy of inspecting staff, the limitations of the law, the absence of even a list of workshops, the ruses to evade the Inspector's visits and queries, all combined practically to nullify English factory

1. Report of the Royal Commission on Alien Immigration, Cd. 1741, 1903, p. 20, para. 133, and see p. 19, paras. 127–30
2. Ibid, p. 393, paras 11685, 11690

legislation in Jewish workshops.'[1] The Factory and Workshop Act of 1901, however, ushered in a new era of effective factory legislation. Coupled with the growth of Jewish trade unions, which jumped in number from thirteen in 1896 to thirty-two in 1902, it was this which rid the country of sweated Jewish labour.

In 1962, however, the lessons of 1905 were lost and faith was again placed in the panacea of immigration control. The Commonwealth Immigrants Act, like the Aliens Act of 1905, said nothing about the real problem, namely the disparities in socio-economic position between the immigrant and host populations. In fact, as we have seen, one of the ironic consequences of the agitation for immigration control was that for the first time there was a large influx of coloured immigrants unrelated to the labour needs of the British economy.

Before turning to a consideration of the occupations and socio-economic status of coloured workers, it is necessary to refer to two other groups of immigrant workers in Britain whose presence has helped to mould the present patterns of employment in relation to coloured workers.

FEARS OF DILUTION: THE IRISH

Irish immigrants have been subjected to various forms of control and discrimination, probably since the reign of Henry IV, if not earlier.[2] Yet Irish labour was indispensible to the success of the industrial revolution. This was not simply because it was cheaper than any other labour in Western Europe (which it was) but particularly because the destitute Irish peasantry was ready and willing to fill a large variety of manual occupations, at the base of the industrial pyramid, which English workers considered too menial. To this extent they were tolerated. However, in the 1830s and 1840s they brought with them a squalor which threatened to debase the conditions of the English workers themselves and in some trades, such as the building industry and on the docks, they occasionally came into direct competition with the English poor. In those trades in which unionism was weakest Irish labourers were not infrequently brought in to 'dilute' the standards of local labour and to act as strikebreakers, which in turn resulted in anti-Irish rioting.

In times of depression in this century, such as the 1930s, Irish

---

1. L. P. Gartner, *The Jewish Immigrant in England, 1870–1914* (London 1960), p. 67
2. Paul O'Higgins, 'English Law and the Irish Question' (1966) 1 *Irish Jurist* (New Series), p. 59; and E. P. Thompson, *The Making of the English Working Class* (London 1963), pp. 429–440

workers have continued to be looked at with suspicion. Yet, in general, since the Second World War they have become more widely distributed in the occupational structure (although, as we shall see later, labouring remains the typical employment for Irishmen) and Irish workers and their descendants participate in trade unions far beyond the proportion of their numbers in industry. In recent times, Irish workers have not, as a rule, complained of hostility or discrimination by their fellow employees. From the employers' standpoint Irish workers, especially as labourers in the building industry, have been welcomed as an essential reservoir of casual and highly mobile labour.

Thus, while social inequality remains, the Irish workers in Britain are rarely thought of with hostility as an alien group. The legacy of suspicion and the fears of 'dilution' have been transferred to the newest section of workers: the coloured immigrants.

INSTITUTIONALIZED DISCRIMINATION: THE E.V.W.S

The second relevant group is that known collectively as the European Volunteer Workers (E.V.W.s), allowed to work in Britain after 1947 in order to meet critical labour shortages. The E.V.W.s consisted of three groups: 100,000 members of the Polish armed forces and their dependants who elected to stay in the United Kingdom at the end of the war, 85,000 displaced persons of many nationalities brought to Britain under various schemes, and men and women brought from the Continent temporarily to work in undermanned industries. Nearly all the latter have now gone home and those in the first two groups have been integrated into the British working population.

The restrictions on these workers were of two kinds: those imposed by the Home Office as 'conditions of entry' and which the recruit was required to sign, and those laid down in collective agreements between unions and employers. The gist of the conditions of entry was that the E.V.W.s could not change the employment selected for them by the Ministry of Labour without consent and they had to be of good behaviour. This led to a complaint at the Fourth Session of the United Nations General Assembly in November 1949 that displaced persons in Britain were the 'victims of an official policy of discrimination' because in other countries where they were accepted for permanent resettlement no such restrictions were imposed. After an assurance to trade unions that industrial agreements would not be affected, the Government lifted these restrictions on E.V.W.s from 1 January 1951.[1]

1. J. A. Tannahill, *European Volunteer Workers in Britain* (Manchester 1958), p. 54

A similar restriction, however, remains today in regard to aliens.[1]

Collective agreements regarding these workers were concluded around 1947 in nearly forty industries.[2] Among the usual provisions were: (1) the placing of E.V.W.s was 'subject to no suitable British labour being available'; (2) in the event of redundancy they were the first to be dismissed or they were to go 'as soon as the position can be met by British labour'; (3) wages and conditions of the foreign workers were to be 'in accordance with existing agreements regarding British workers'; (4) in some instances they were not to be engaged unless they joined the appropriate union, in others union membership was to be 'encouraged'; (5) in some industries or occupations a quota of foreign labour was imposed (for example, 15 per cent of the total number of operatives in specified groups in the weaving industry); (6) at least two agreements restricted the upgrading and promotion of foreign workers. In coal-mining and the cotton industry there were informal limits on promotion.

These collectively-imposed restrictions had their origin in trade union fears about the standards of their 'own' workers and the fear of employers that if their industries had a large influx of foreign workers, there might be a corresponding exodus of long-established labour. The E.V.W.s themselves complained frequently that they were forced to do unskilled manual work, although they possessed technical skills. Part of the machinery set up by the Ministry of Labour to deal with the E.V.W.s were *ad hoc* committees at employment exchanges to handle trade union complaints that foreign workers were being employed in agriculture while British workers remained unemployed. In other industries the agreements were enforced by the ordinary non-legal collective sanctions.

These agreements have influenced the position of coloured workers in two ways. The vague and flexible definitions of the affected workers have occasionally led to interpretations that extend the restrictions to Commonwealth immigrants.[3] Secondly, the agreements have provided a pattern of conduct towards immigrant workers, in which restriction is looked upon as normal and proper.

1. See above, Chapter 2, p. 32
2. A summary of some of the principal agreements will be found in Appendix II below, p. 218
3. See, for example, John Goodall, Supplement to I.R.R. *News Letter* October 1966, regarding a post-war restriction on Poles and E.V.W.s now alleged to operate against Commonwealth immigrants. See above, Chapter 2, p. 34 regarding the terminology in some agreements

4. Employment Patterns

There are no statistics about the colour of Britain's working population. There are obvious disadvantages in introducing a racial classification into official information, yet the statistical vacuum means that all discussion of the position of coloured workers in employment has to rest on what is, at best, intelligent guesswork. The three main sources upon which reliance has to be placed are (a) census information about Commonwealth immigrants, classified according to place of birth; (b) the statistics presented to Parliament under the Commonwealth Immigrants Act 1962, for the period since 1 July 1962; and (c) various sample surveys conducted in certain areas of immigrant settlement and among particular immigrant groups.

The major limitations of the Census and Commonwealth Immigrants Act figures are that they include an unspecified number of white persons born in those countries and that they take no account of coloured persons born in Britain. The first of these limitations is particularly significant in the case of the 198,998 persons enumerated in the 1961 Census as having been born in India and Pakistan. It seems probable that a large number of these were white British-educated children of officers, civil servants and professional and managerial classes. They would themselves be disproportionately concentrated in the Census enumeration in professional, managerial and white-collar occupations. Another reservation about the 1961 figures is that there appears to have been an under-enumeration in areas which are known to have a large number of new arrivals of low socio-economic status. During the Census the full range of questions was answered by 10 per cent of the population and a shorter list by the other 90 per cent. Most of the information about immigrants comes from the 10 per cent sample. In regard to the latter it has been shown that there was at least a 20 per cent under-enumeration of West Indians[1] and the 10 per cent sample of Jamaicans has been described as 'more like an 8 per cent sample'.[2]

1. G. C. K. Peach, 'Under-enumeration of West Indians in the 1961 Census' (1966) 14 *Sociological Review* (New Series), p. 73
2. P. J. Jenner and B. G. Cohen, I. R. R. *News Letter*, November/December 1966, p. 28 at 30

Until more accurate statistical evidence becomes available, however, some use has to be made of the 1961 figures. Where possible, they ought to be compared with information obtained from external sources.

HOW MANY ARE THERE?

About 1·7 million people who are economically active[1] were enumerated in 1961 as having been born outside England and Wales. This means that eight out of every 100 workers are 'immigrants'.

One of the most useful ways to find out how many coloured workers there are in Britain is to look at the number of persons arriving from overseas applying for national insurance cards. The Ministry of Pensions and National Insurance supplied such figures for the period 1956–63 to Dr R. B. Davison, who has recently published them.[2] These reveal that during this period 1,380,785 persons from overseas joined the labour force. Of these 43 per cent came from the Commonwealth, 29 per cent from the Irish Republic and 28 per cent were aliens. Of those from the Commonwealth 163,464 were from Asia, 233,084 from the Caribbean and 58,006 from Africa. If one adds to this an estimated figure of 30,000 workers from 'coloured' Commonwealth countries who joined the work force between 1964 and 1966 (exact figures are not available) it might be said that more than half a million coloured workers from overseas have taken up jobs in Britain in the past decade. There are no figures as to how many of these left the national insurance scheme in this period. One might conclude that two or three out of every 100 workers in Britain are coloured, but this would be misleading because they are concentrated in particular industries and regions.

The xenophobic assertion that 'they came here to live off us' is belied by the fact that in 1961 two thirds of all immigrants from the 'coloured' Commonwealth were in the labour force, as compared with less than one in two of the total population. Dr Davison's analysis of the 10 per cent Census information in regard to twenty-eight London boroughs[3] reveals that while 66 per cent of the English-born males in the sample were economically active, the percentages for immigrants were 88 per cent of the men born in Jamaica, 75 per cent of those born in India and 76 per cent of those born in Pakistan. Among the women 39 per cent of the English-born were economically active, but 62 per cent of the

1. Those not 'economically active' include all children under the age of fifteen, retired persons, housewives, students and similar groups

2. *Black British* (London 1966), p. 66

3. Op. cit., p. 68. For convincing proof that immigrants do not constitute a drain on the social services, see: K. Jones, 'Immigrants and the Social Services', N.I.E.S.R. *Economic Review*, no. 41, August 1967, p. 28

Jamaican-born, 48 per cent of the Indian-born and 31 per cent of the Pakistan-born.

The reasons for the higher proportion of persons who are economically active among those born abroad appear to be that (a) a higher proportion of the immigrants are aged between 18 and 34; (b) more English-born males are receiving education after the age of 15; (c) there is a greater proportion of retired persons among the English-born; and (d) more English women seem to stay at home as housewives than do Jamaican and other West Indian women.

WHAT JOBS DO THEY DO?

West Indians are mostly concentrated in London and the Midlands in a wide range of light industries such as food, drink and tobacco, clothing and footwear, vehicles, light engineering and chemicals, in public transport and communications, on building sites, and in laundries and the nursing profession. Asians are most often found in the North and Midlands in steel works, textile factories and the production of some engineering, electrical and chemical goods, as well as services like hotels, laundries and catering. Only a bare handful of coloured workers are found in agriculture, mining and quarrying, shipbuilding, insurance, banking and finance. Coloured women immigrants from the Commonwealth appear to be mainly concentrated in clothing and footwear, professional and scientific services, and in particular, nursing. There are smaller concentrations of women in transport, the distributive trades, engineering and the manufacture of food, drink and tobacco.

It has been asserted that the general work pattern among immigrants from the 'coloured' Commonwealth 'closely resembles that for the country as a whole'.[1] However, the occupation tables of the 1961 Census, which are analysed in Table 1,[2] reveal several striking differences between the occupations of all economically active persons in England and Wales and those of immigrants. The most significant of these is that Pakistani men and Caribbean-born men and women are over-concentrated in labouring jobs. But it is to be observed that (white) men born in Ireland are in much the same position. Another feature is that persons from the Caribbean seem to be virtually excluded from sales work (involving contact with the public) and they are grossly

1. Ruth Glass, 'The New Minorities', *The Times*, 30 June and 1 July 1965
2. Below, p. 228. The figures in respect of immigrants are limited in these tables to those who, at the Census date, were Commonwealth and Irish citizens, so excluding an unspecified number with U.K. citizenship. The reader must guard against converting the 'nationality' figures into 'colour' ones; the Census questions on nationality are often misunderstood by those who have to answer them

under-represented as clerical workers. Here, too, the explanation cannot rest simply on colour because more Pakistani men and women are sales and clerical workers than is the case with the Irish-born. On the other hand, the heavy concentration of Caribbean-born women in the professional bracket is not surprising in view of the large number that have gone into nursing. The statistics confirm familiar patterns: immigrants are virtually unknown in farming and forestry jobs; Irishmen tend to be building navvies; Pakistanis to work in textile mills and West Indians in transport services. The most baffling figures are those in respect of persons born in India, which show higher proportions of Indian males as clerical workers, administrators and managers and professional workers and fewer as labourers than is the case with the population as a whole. This distribution must be due to the shortcomings of the 10 per cent sample and the misleading consequences of classifying persons by nationality for Census purposes. Little reliance ought to be placed on the statistics in relation to Indians.

WHAT IS THEIR STATUS IN INDUSTRY?

These figures tell us something about the spread of immigrants in different kinds of occupations. It is now necessary to consider their status, that is, what position they occupy in terms of social class and prestige.

Census figures are available in regard to the industrial and socio-economic status of persons born in Jamaica, the rest of the British Caribbean, India, Pakistan, Africa (other than South Africa), Cyprus and Malta, resident in the six major conurbations.[1] These are analysed and compared with the industrial and socio-economic status of the population of England and Wales as a whole, in Tables 2 and 3.[2]

From these tables it will be observed that a smaller percentage of immigrants is classified as employers, managers, foremen and supervisors than is the case with the population as a whole. Yet the surprising aspect of these figures is that the differences are so small that they could be explained in terms of regional peculiarities and the fact that many immigrants have not been here long enough to qualify for supervisory and managerial work or to accumulate sufficient capital to become employers. Even more remarkable is the fact that a greater proportion of the male immigrants are employed as professional workers and semi-skilled manual workers than is the case with the population as a whole. Moreover, there are statistically insignificant differences between the

1. Tyneside, West Yorkshire, S.E. Lancashire, Merseyside, West Midlands, Greater London
2. Below, pp. 230 and 231

percentage of male immigrants who are intermediate and junior non-manual workers and skilled manual workers, and the percentages of those classified in these groups in the population as a whole. In fact, the only major differences that emerge are that 17·7 per cent of the female immigrants are intermediate non-manual workers, compared with 9·3 per cent in the whole population, and 18·3 per cent of the male immigrants are unskilled manual workers, compared with 8·5 per cent in the whole population.

A more accurate comparison would require the breakdown of the various immigrant groups and a comparison of these percentages with those for English-born workers in each conurbation. This has been done in respect of twenty-eight London metropolitan boroughs by Dr Davison,[1] based on the answers given in the Census by the individuals in the 10 per cent sample of the population who were asked to give their occupation. For each separate birthplace the economically active males (aged fifteen years and over) were classified into six broad occupational categories. This revealed that proportionately more males born in Jamaica (34 per cent), the rest of the Caribbean (30 per cent), Pakistan (21 per cent), Ireland (31 per cent) and Cyprus (18 per cent) than those born in England (14 per cent) were engaged in unskilled manual occupations, the armed forces and various inadequately described occupations. Similarly, proportionately more males born in Jamaica (22 per cent), the rest of the Caribbean (24 per cent), Pakistan (24 per cent), Poland (18 per cent), Ireland (20 per cent) and Cyprus (30 per cent) than those born in England (15 per cent) were engaged in personal services (such as barmen, maids, cooks and hairdressers) and semi-skilled manual and agricultural occupations. At the top end of the occupational scale fewer males born in Jamaica (below 0·5 per cent), the rest of the Caribbean (1 per cent), Ireland (2 per cent) and Cyprus (1 per cent) than those born in England (3 per cent) were engaged in the professions and fewer were employers and managers.[2] The percentage of males born in these countries who were foremen, skilled manual workers and persons working on their own account closely resembles the percentage of those born in England engaged in these occupations.[3]

The figures which appear in Dr Davison's analysis in respect of males

1. Op. cit., p. 70
2. The figures in respect of employers and managers, given by birthplace are: England—9 per cent; Jamaica—1 per cent; Caribbean—1 per cent; Ireland—3 per cent; Cyprus—10 per cent
3. The figures given by birthplace are: England—36 per cent; Jamaica—39 per cent; Caribbean—33 per cent; Poland—34 per cent; Ireland—30 per cent

born in India are, as he points out, rather surprising. They suggest that of the Indians 76 per cent (as compared with 71 per cent of the English) are in the top four occupational categories. The Pakistan-born males had 55 per cent in the top four categories, which is also higher than that of Jamaicans and other Caribbeans and the Irish.

The figures given by Dr Davison in respect of Pakistanis are probably to be explained on the basis that very few Pakistanis were included in the sample, as a high proportion have settled in the north of England. The figures relating to Indians are probably unreliable for the reasons given earlier. These reasons might also provide some explanation for the surprising general figures about immigrants resident in the six conurbations. A further reason might be a deliberate upgrading of their status by those answering the Census questions. It is impossible, however, to give a full explanation of these figures until further field work has been done, particularly in relation to Indian and Pakistani workers.

A number of local studies have been made about the occupational status of coloured workers. No summary can do justice to them but they all appear to confirm that coloured workers are concentrated in unskilled and semi-skilled manual labour and that this tendency is more pronounced among Pakistanis and Indians than among West Indians. For example, in Halifax Pakistanis are mainly to be found in unskilled and semi-skilled jobs in textile factories, and the same applies in Huddersfield. In Smethwick, Punjabi Sikhs are concentrated in unskilled jobs in foundries. A study of West Indians at work in Nottingham[1] revealed that 47·1 per cent of those interviewed were doing unskilled, 32·8 per cent semi-skilled and 16·1 per cent skilled work.

A second conclusion from these local studies is that it is relatively rare for West Indians to be engaged in white-collar work and even rarer in the case of Pakistanis and Indians. Finally, it must be remembered that there are important regional variations. For example, in Sheffield Pakistanis are concentrated as labourers in steel works and heavy engineering. In Halifax, on the other hand, although engineering is the second largest industry, very few Pakistanis are employed in it, most of them being labourers and machine minders in textiles.

UNEMPLOYMENT

There is a general belief that economic recession in Britain is likely to be felt more severely by immigrants than by the local population. A rise in

1. F. J. Bayliss and J. B. Coates, 'West Indians at Work in Nottingham', *Race* VII, 2 (1965), p. 157. Similar results in respect of Jamaicans (all over England) are to be found in R. B. Davison, *Black British*, p. 74

unemployment, it is said, is generally accompanied by a far greater rise in joblessness on the part of coloured workers. This in turn leads to the dilemma that either the immigrants become a public liability in times of recession or, if they are kept at work while native workers are on the dole, there is bound to be an increase in racial conflict. To what extent are these fears warranted by the available evidence? Table 4[1] indicates that at the time of the 1961 Census 5·6 per cent of economically active males and 5·2 per cent of active females born in Jamaica, the rest of the Caribbean, India, Pakistan, Africa (other than South Africa), Cyprus and Malta residing in the major conurbations[2] were unemployed. This can be compared with the 2·8 per cent of all economically active males and 2·4 per cent of all active females resident in England and Wales who were unemployed at that date. Dr Davison[3] has made a detailed analysis of the Census figures in respect of unemployment among persons born in selected birthplaces, resident in twenty-eight metropolitan boroughs. These reveal that the unemployment rate was lowest among men born in England (3·2 per cent) and highest (7·4 per cent) among males born in Jamaica. Six per cent of men born in the rest of the Caribbean were unemployed. These figures can be compared with those from the 'white' countries: 5·8 per cent of the Cypriots (who have a language problem) and 4·8 per cent of the Irish were unemployed. Unemployment amongst Jamaican and Caribbean-born women was higher than that amongst those born in Ireland, Cyprus and England.

A continuing record of unemployed persons registered on the books of local employment exchanges is kept by the Ministry of Labour. Prior to July 1962 a tally was kept of coloured unemployed workers and this is a reliable guide to the extent of unemployment because registration is a condition precedent for the payment of unemployment benefits. The figures[4] reveal a marked increase in coloured unemployment after November 1961 which may have been due to the large influx of immigrants at that time to beat the ban threatened by the Commonwealth Immigrants Bill. This suggests that the relatively high rate of coloured unemployment in this period related to political rather than economic or racial factors. Unfortunately it is not possible to know the rate of unemployment amongst coloured workers because, as indicated earlier, there are no reliable figures about the number of coloured people at work. From local studies it seems that there was a

1. Below, p. 232
2. See above, note 1 p. 54
3. Op. cit., pp. 88–9
4. Published in Davison, op. cit., p. 83

concentration of coloured unemployed in the 1961-2 period in particular areas. In Huddersfield, for example, coloured men and women
made up 45·2 per cent of the total unemployed in May 1962.[1] In
Nottingham West Indian females made up 39 per cent of the total
female unemployed during 1962.[2]

After the Commonwealth Immigrants Act came into operation the
Ministry of Labour changed the way in which it counted unemployed
from the Commonwealth. The 'coloured' tag has been dropped and
instead, immigrants are recorded according to their country of origin.
Consequently the figures from August 1962 are not exactly comparable
with those before that date. In the period between August 1962 and
August 1965 the national unemployment rate remained fairly steady
around less than 2·5 per cent apart from the high rate of 3·9 per cent in
the extreme winter of February 1963. The figures[3] in respect of unemployed persons from the West Indies, India and Pakistan as a percentage
of the total number of unemployed persons in this period reveal a
downward trend in the proportion of those among the unemployed
who are immigrants, roughly corresponding with the downward trend
in the national rate of unemployment. The rapid decline may be due,
in part, to the high level of mobility amongst single coloured immigrants.

It is difficult to make any firm deductions from these figures. On the
whole, apart from the period immediately preceding the passing of the
Commonwealth Immigrants Act, coloured Commonwealth unemployment seems to have stayed well within the bounds set by unemployment
nationally. It is, however, true to say that coloured immigrants appear
to constitute a disproportionate number of the total unemployed. This
may be due to several causes, for example, the kind of jobs they do,
redundancy policies in which coloured workers are the first to go, and
the difficulties they experience in finding work.

DO IMMIGRANTS PROVIDE CHEAP LABOUR?

The association of immigrants with 'sweating' and 'dilution', as we
have seen, has been one of the factors retarding their industrial integration in the past. To what extent are trade union fears justified that
coloured immigrants provide a source of cheap labour which is a threat
to the standards of British workers?

1. John Goodall, Supplement to I. R. R. *News Letter* October 1966
2. Daniel Lawrence, Supplement to I. R. R. *News Letter* June 1966
3. Published in Davison, op. cit., p. 87. The figures for the period of Britain's economic
squeeze in 1966-8 were not available at the time of writing. These may indicate with
greater accuracy the effect of national unemployment on Commonwealth immigrants

Information about the earnings of coloured immigrants is notoriously unreliable. But the little there is suggests that the hourly wage rates of coloured immigrants are not dissimilar from those of indigenous workers doing the same jobs. There does, however, seem to be a difference in the average weekly take-home pay of British workers and those of immigrants whose wages have been investigated. A study in Nottingham[1] revealed that while two thirds of British men took home over £12 a week, only half of the West Indian men interviewed did so. This was explained on the basis that British men tend to work longer hours (up to eight hours a week overtime) than West Indians. In October 1962 the average weekly earnings for male manual workers in Britain were £15 17s. 3d. and for women £8 0s. 10d. The Jamaican immigrants included in Dr Davison's survey[2] at that time averaged £10 15s. 0d. a week (30 per cent less than average) in the case of men and £6 13s. 0d. (20 per cent less than average) in the case of women. These figures are quite understandable in the light of the fact that Jamaicans tend to work in lower-paid jobs and lower-paid industries than British workers. Moreover, the figures quoted were those earned at the end of the immigrants' first year in Britain; in the case of the men their average weekly earnings went up by 6 per cent by the end of their second year in the country. Because more members of the average Jamaican household are at work than is the case with British families, it has been estimated that the annual gross income of a Jamaican family is £1,200 or 10 per cent larger than that of the average British household. On the scanty evidence available therefore, the superficial judgement must be that job-for-job West Indian immigrants are not underpaid in comparison with British workers. There is no useful information on this regarding Asian workers.

The more fundamental question is whether in relation to their role in the British economy immigrants are a source of cheap labour. This problem has long been the subject of vague speculation and, until recently, no serious academic study of it had been attempted.

For twenty years or more it has been asserted that acute labour shortages exist in Britain and that this in turn is a cause of the persistent problem of inflation. The shortages have had a regional character and in those areas in which there has been a growing demand for labour at a time of full employment, employers wishing to expand production have had to choose between: (a) increasing investment of a labour-substitution nature, i.e. automating the production process; (b) attracting

1. Bayliss and Coates, above, note 1 p. 56
2 *Black British*, pp. 93-4

internal migrants from other parts of Britain by the lure of higher wages; or (c) employing immigrant labour, particularly from the 'coloured' Commonwealth.

The first of these alternatives offers an ideal solution but for several reasons, such as the imperfections of the money market, failure to make correct technical innovations, and bottlenecks in the production of investment goods and services, it has not happened fast enough to solve the problem. The second alternative has proved to be less attractive than that of employing immigrant labour because wages in the development areas have not been high enough to attract internal migrants nor, prior to 1966–7, was there unemployment on a scale likely to induce workers to look elsewhere for jobs.

Immigrants have moved to those areas in which they have had the best chances of getting work. This has meant going to areas of full or over-full employment where, in turn, there has been the least resistance from local labour to their recruitment. Theoretically the effect of the influx of immigrant labour might have been to keep down the pressure emanating from local labour for higher wages. In practice there is no evidence that this has happened. The wages of British workers have continued to rise during the period of immigration and the curbs on this trend have been Government-imposed rather than due to any dilution of the bargaining strength of local labour.

Without the immigrants a great many jobs, especially in hospital and transport services and of a labouring kind, would have had to be done by indigenous labour but then, undoubtedly, it would have cost employers more because, in the absence of labour-substitution investment, internal migrants would have had to be induced to take up these jobs at relatively high rates of pay. It is in this sense and this alone that immigrants have been a source of 'cheap' labour.[1]

FUTURE TRENDS

Chapter Three began with the oft-repeated assertion that coloured workers are relegated to the status of hewers of wood and drawers of water. This belief, we have seen, has been impressed upon the established institutions of our society through slavery, the shipping laws,

1. This discussion leaves out of consideration the controversial question whether immigrant labour results in excess demand and a worsening of the balance of payments situation. For the view that it does, see: E. J. Mishan and L. Needleman, 'Immigration: some economic effects' (1966) *Lloyds Bank Review*, p. 129, and for a more technical treatment by the same writers 'Immigration: Excess Aggregate Demand and the Balance of Payments' (1966) 46 *Economica*, p. 129. For the contrary view: P. J. Jenner and B. G. Cohen in I. R. R. *News Letter*, November/December 1966, with a reply by Needleman, I. R. R. *News Letter*, February 1967

and written and unwritten codes of industrial relations. Fears of economic insecurity have been kindled to divert attention from real problems of exploitation and poverty on to the largely imaginary question of immigration control. This has left unresolved the vital issue: will coloured workers be integrated on the basis of equal opportunity into Britain's economic life?

The statistical evidence provides tantalizing clues as to the position occupied in industry by coloured workers, yet in many respects it is baffling and contradictory. Doubtless, coloured workers are frequently engaged in labouring and dirty work and in unskilled and semi-skilled occupations. It is rarer for them to penetrate into white-collar and sales jobs. But it is equally clear that colour does not in itself provide the reason for what appears to be their inferior position. White Irish workers in Britain also tend to do labouring work far out of proportion to their numbers, yet in their case allegations of racial discrimination are rarely heard. In fact a number of them choose labouring work because it offers higher wages than many white-collar jobs. Economically, Irish labour has served an essential function as a cheap, mobile and efficient labouring force. The coloured immigrants of the fifties and sixties seem to have served a similar function.

What the Irish share in common with the newer immigrants is an economically depressed background. In other words, the explanation for the relatively low status of both groups of immigrants must be found in poor education, low standards of living, lack of industrial experience and training.[1] In the case of immigrants from India and Pakistan and to a lesser extent those from the West Indies, language barriers complicate the problems of inequality. This is a difficulty faced, as well, by certain other immigrant groups such as the Cypriots and Poles.

Although unskilled labour is the 'typical' employment for Irishmen, it is equally true to say that since the Second World War they have become widely distributed in the occupational structure. This development has been even more marked in the case of Poles. In the case of the Jews there has been, during the past few decades, a diversification of jobs, with the emphasis on self-employment, professional and white-collar work. These minority groups have gradually been accepted into the labour market.

Will coloured workers be satisfactorily integrated in the same way? On the one hand there is evidence that in the South-east and Midlands individual coloured immigrants are moving up the occupational scale,

1. Described in Chapter I above, p. 12

getting jobs which were formerly beyond their reach. On the other hand it is precisely at this point when coloured workers cease to do the jobs that white workers do not want and become qualified for skilled jobs and more senior positions that white workers object most strongly to them. They are seen as direct competitors for the same jobs. Potentially, the greatest danger of conflict arises in times of general unemployment. But even in times of full employment the employees' interest in keeping up the pressure for higher wages tends to be translated into a policy of limiting the available supply of labour. The precise way in which this limitation is achieved varies according to historical, political and local circumstances. When it takes the menacing shape of racial discrimination, visible differences between workers are seized upon as the justification for excluding members of minority groups from the labour market. In this respect the present coloured immigrants have to jump a hurdle which did not confront earlier immigrant groups. The second and later generations of Jews, Irish and Poles have lost the 'alien' features of their fathers and have won acceptance in industry. For coloured persons their outward physical differences remain. The disturbing reports that second generation coloured school-leavers are finding it difficult to obtain jobs is a grave harbinger. In particular, their exclusion from white-collar work may lead to a rapid growth in inequality. This point needs little underlining when one remembers that the white-collar labour force in Britain increased by 147 per cent between 1911 and 1961, while the number of manual workers increased in that period by only 2 per cent, having actually decreased in numbers since 1931.[1] The white-collar section of the labour force increased from 18·7 per cent to 35·9 per cent of the total, while the manual share decreased from 74·6 per cent to 59·3 per cent, between 1911 and 1961. This trend is likely to continue until, by the 1980s, the labour force as a whole is dominated by white-collar workers. The danger is that coloured workers will find themselves relegated, by reason of discrimination, to the declining activity of manual labour.

This troubled situation becomes even more complex when one considers the employers' angle. In several industries immigrants have provided cheap labour. The decision to relieve labour shortages in this way places the employer under conflicting pressures. On the one hand, the habit of utilizing immigrant labour may make him reluctant to introduce technical innovations and automation. On the other hand, the longer he employs immigrant labour the more pressure mounts from the immigrants themselves to move up into senior positions and skilled

1. Guy Routh, *Occupation and Pay in Great Britain* (Cambridge 1965), pp. 4–5, Table 1

jobs. This leads to resistance from British workers who feel their positions threatened and this in turn induces the employer to resolve the conflict by dispensing with cheap labour and introducing automation. This could result in a growing pool of unemployed unskilled and semi-skilled coloured labour. Such a reservoir of redundant coloured workers would inevitably be a threat to the living standards and jobs of other workers.

From the workers' angle, therefore, the only feasible solution is to reject the apparent short-term advantages to be gained from resisting the advancement of coloured workers and, instead, to insist that they be rapidly trained and promoted on merit. If patterns of inferiority are allowed to develop so that second and third generation coloured people become a constant source of casual, cheap, unskilled labour there will be a permanent threat to the wages and jobs of the lowest categories of white workers. On the other hand, if coloured workers are successfully integrated they will cease to perform their function of cheap labour and, in economic terms, they will be indistinguishable from all other workers.

These, then, are the seeds of future conflict. How are institutions reacting to the growing confrontation between the policy of integration and the facts of discrimination? We have seen that political and legal developments up to 1965 did little to improve the prospects for integration. On the contrary, it was the agitation for restrictions on immigration which exacerbated racial feeling and at the same time led to a relatively large influx of immigrants, probably of low socio-economic status, on the eve of the Commonwealth Immigrants Act. It may be that if the voucher system under the Act continues on its present basis the intake of skilled and professional migrants will increase. But they, too, may face the resentment of local employees and, in any event, the majority of immigrants and their offspring arrived here before July 1962.

In this analysis the key points of conflict are those at which coloured school-leavers seek jobs and immigrants try to move up the occupational scale and into white-collar employment. On their success or failure in overcoming discrimination at these points will depend the future patterns of employment of coloured workers.

5. The Main Types of Discrimination

Recruitment policies of managements resulting in the exclusion of suitably qualified coloured workers are the most commonly reported instances of discrimination. Some exclude coloured workers altogether, while others maintain a racial quota restricting the proportion of coloured workers to white workers in the establishment or in certain occupations.

The origins of quotas in formal collective agreements in the immediate post-war period were discussed in Chapter 3.[1] Occasionally a quota of coloured workers might result from the application to them of one of these formal agreements originally intended to apply to European workers. More frequently, quotas are the result of informal shop floor understandings between workers and management or of unilateral management decisions induced by the belief that working techniques can be more rapidly communicated to newcomers in industry if they are spread over the labour force, that dispersion minimizes the risk of conflict between different groups and that the 'character' of the enterprise ought not to be changed by the sudden influx of a large number of outsiders – the latter is important to the employer who does not want to risk losing the bulk of his long-established labour force. Of course, quotas originally applied for these reasons might ossify into permanent employment practices.

It is difficult to gauge the precise extent of quota systems. Only two informants admitted to the P.E.P. researchers that they operated a quota (one of 50 per cent, the other 20 per cent).[2] Against this, there were a number of allegations in the press during the five-year period 1961–5 of white workers taking or threatening strike action where an

1. Above, p. 50
2. P.E.P. *Report on Racial Discrimination*, p. 49

employer was alleged to have broken his promise about how many coloured workers he would employ.[1]

Apart from quota arrangements an employer's discretion may be limited by an agreement to 'consult' local workers or their union before engaging certain classes of worker. This practice seems to be limited. Of 151 companies seen during the P.E.P. Survey, only 51 had any contact with trade unions (49 of these were manufacturers) and in 45 of these cases it was claimed that the employment of immigrants had never been discussed with union representatives. In the other six cases, shop stewards were said to have exerted pressure against the employment of coloured immigrants.[2] Several formal agreements relating to European workers negotiated immediately after the war required 'consultation' but were silent as to how the 'consent' of local workers was to be obtained, and whether or not it had to be unanimous. Disputes which arose were normally dealt with according to customary local and national procedures in the particular industry. Some agreements made it a condition for the employment of foreign labour that 'no suitable British labour' was available. To determine whether or not this condition had been fulfilled some agreements required a consensus between employers' and workers' associations in consultation with the manager of the local employment exchange. In the agricultural industry the procedure was for *ad hoc* committees to be set up consisting of a non-official chairman, two representatives of the National Farmers' Union and two of the appropriate trade union together with a Ministry of Labour official and a member of the County Agricultural Executive Committee. The *ad hoc* committees sat at employment exchanges where they considered complaints by trade unions that foreign workers were being employed in agriculture whilst British workers had no work.

Most of these agreements are now dead letters and formalized procedures do not appear to have been evolved in relation to the employment of coloured workers. One agreement which stands on its own needs, however, to be mentioned. This is the current manning agreement between the Shipping Federation Ltd. and the National Union of Seamen, operative from 1 March 1965. This provides that no existing ship registered in the U.K. may change over to 'non-European' labour without the approval of the National Maritime Board (on which employers and union are represented) and an owner who wants to employ 'non-Europeans' on a newly built or newly acquired ship must

1. See Appendix I below, p. 203. The quota system in relation to the definition of discrimination is discussed above, p. 27
2. P.E.P., op. cit., pp. 47–8

submit his case to the National Maritime Board. In making its decision the Board is bound to take into account traditional trades in which 'non-Europeans' are employed, the intended pattern of trading of the vessel concerned, the availability of suitable manpower and any other relevant factors.[1] Before this Agreement came into force, shipowners could change over to 'non-European' crews whenever they chose to do so for economic reasons. From the standpoint of the N.U.S., therefore, the Agreement represents a safeguard for sailors on European articles. However, the Agreement does nothing to ensure satisfactory conditions for those signed on outside the continent of Europe; in fact it confirms their relegation to certain ships and lower-paid occupations.

It must be emphasized that this Agreement only applies to 'non-Europeans' who are domiciled outside the U.K., but allegations have been made that it reinforces traditional discrimination against coloured seamen recruited in the U.K. Of the 142,000 employees in the Merchant Navy Establishment, an estimated 2,500 are coloured seamen recruited in the U.K.[2] This belies any suggestion of outright exclusion; in fact, the discrimination which occurs is the outcome of the policy of segregating ratings of different races on board the same ship. This is customary except on some larger ships where the ratings in one department may be of a different race to those in another. A consequence of the fact that a large number of ships carry white engine-room crews is that there is a greater demand for white trainees than for recruits of a different colour. This means, in effect, that white U.K. citizens have a better chance of being accepted for training than coloured citizens with similar qualifications.[3] The Minister of Labour (Mr R. J. Gunter) has explained the segregation on the ground that the merchant shipping industry presents features peculiar to a sea-going life, such as living in close quarters for prolonged periods, in which dangers of racial conflict must be avoided. Official policy has been to regard this as an 'industrial' matter in which the Government ought not to intervene.

Apart from arrangements with long-established local labour, employers advance the supposed objections of white customers as a reason for not employing coloured workers. This is particularly the case in work which involves contact with the public. Yet in practice there is little evidence to support these fears. The racial prejudice of customers, as the magazine *Hotel and Restaurant Management* told

1. See above, Chapter 3, p. 45, regarding the meaning of 'non-European' and the general position in the shipping industry
2. Figures (as at July 1965) kindly furnished by the Merchant Navy and Airline Officers Association. 43,000 of all the employees are Commonwealth citizens
3. See Appendix I below, p. 202

caterers in 1965, is largely a myth. Significantly, objections are not often heard from white patients about being treated by coloured hospital staff!

Such excuses indicate that personal prejudices do play a part in management discrimination, although the blame is usually shifted elsewhere. Moreover, those who turn coloured work-seekers away, as the P.E.P. Report showed,[1] are frequently relatively low down the management scale – such as receptionists, secretaries and gatekeepers who operate their own 'screening' system.

ENGAGEMENT OF COLOURED SCHOOL-LEAVERS

The general view, reflected in a Report of the Inner London Education Authority in 1966, is that it takes longer and is often more difficult to place coloured boys and girls in employment than white schoolleavers. Banking, insurance and retail sales work are said to be virtually closed to them, although this is denied by the banks and insurance companies who are able to point to a fair number of coloured staff behind-scenes (although exceptionally few as tellers or insurance salesmen). In some industries, it is said that employers tend to demand a higher standard from coloured youngsters than from their white counterparts. This often results, it is claimed, in their accepting jobs which make relatively low demands on their abilities.

A Youth Employment Officer summed up the position as follows:

I think it has been equated with the problem that we have in placing handicapped youngsters. . . . It takes longer to place them. Sometimes they have to accept a job that doesn't require quite such high qualifications as they've got, but it's more difficult to place a well-qualified coloured youngster than an equally qualified white youngster. Indeed sometimes I think they are rather in the same position as women used to be and still are to some extent. Certain firms within an industry are not prepared to accept youngsters. . . . We . . . find variations in acceptability. . . . There are some employers who will take West Indians and not West Africans, or Indians and Pakistanis, or Indians and perhaps not Pakistanis. . . . We also find, too, that some employers will say, we'll take them if they're not too dark. I think it depends very often on the depth of colour of the skin.[2]

When it is remembered that one third of all girls leaving school go into office work, the difficulties which coloured girls experience in getting this kind of work are particularly disturbing. The preference of employers in terms of depth of skin colour indicates the significance of colour discrimination in this context.

1. P.E.P., op. cit., pp. 9, 41
2. *This Week*, Independent Television programme, 4 November 1965

The other side of the picture is the effort being made by Youth Employment Officers and others. A spot check by the Ministry of Labour in June 1965 at four youth employment offices in areas with high proportions of coloured immigrants showed that of nineteen immigrant boys and twenty-one immigrant girls known to have left school that Easter, only four boys and three girls were still without work at the beginning of June. All but three of those placed were in jobs which were said to have prospects for training and advancement.[1] The general approach which Youth Employment Officers are expected to follow was stated as follows in a Ministry of Labour circular towards the end of 1966:

Discrimination against persons solely on grounds of race, colour, creed or sex is contrary to the general policy of the Government and should not be practised or condoned by Y.E.O.s in selecting or putting forward young persons for submission to employment. In submitting young people for employment the Y.E.O.s should not normally raise the question of an individual's race, colour or creed with a prospective employer, unless the young person concerned has specifically asked him to do so. However, if the Y.E.O. considers that the placing prospects of a young person would be substantially improved by explaining the position to an employer, for example, to one who had no previous experience of immigrant workers, he may do so on those grounds alone.[2]

The verdict of the Hunt Committee (1967)[3] on the basis of the evidence it heard was that:

. . . the Youth Employment Service, in cooperation with the secondary schools, has addressed itself actively to the many problems of enabling immigrant boys and girls to obtain employment appropriate to their abilities and on equal terms with other school-leavers.

At the same time the Committee stressed the need to strengthen and support the Y.E.O.s in their work.

Several official reports have addressed themselves to the special problems of those coloured school-leavers who have spent a relatively short time in British schools. In 1964 the Commonwealth Immigrants Advisory Council[4] recommended that greater stress be placed in the schools on teaching immigrants spoken English, and it proposed that research be undertaken into this question. In 1966, the Plowden

1. 714 H. C. Deb. cols. 8–9 (14 June 1965)
2. 737 H.C. Deb. col. 1723 (9 December 1966). For earlier directions to the Y.E.O.s on this subject see: 714 H.C. Deb. cols 8–9 (14 June 1965) and 720 H.C. Deb. cols. 3–4 (11 November 1965)
3. *Immigrants and the Youth Service*, paras. 110–23
4. Third Report (Cmnd 2458), paras. 11, 12, 26

Report[1] proposed that schools with special language problems should be generously staffed and there should be expanded opportunities for teachers to train in teaching English to immigrants. The Hunt Committee asked others to consider the example of Slough where young immigrant workers are encouraged to make social contacts, to join youth organizations and to take up further education, through the association of firms with youth and community centres. Local youth employment committees and officers have been encouraged by the Central Youth Employment Executive to stress the importance of spoken English and to cooperate with schools in advice about employment opportunities.

If carried out, these proposals will go a long way towards enabling coloured school-leavers to compete fairly with their white counterparts. The problem which will remain is that revealed by the P.E.P. Report: no less than 70 per cent of those with English school-leaving or trade qualifications claimed that they had been refused jobs because of race or colour.[2]

DISCRIMINATORY ADVERTISEMENTS AND INQUIRIES

An incident of discriminatory recruitment policies is the appearance of 'anti-coloured' tags in advertisements for vacant jobs. In 1960 it was thought 'unthinkable' that such tags might appear since 'public opinion would not allow it.'[3] However, in the period 1961–5 several 'No coloureds' advertisements, and 'Coloured Quota Full' signs on factory gates, were reported. Statements like 'No overseas applicants' are used to cloak a colour bar. Some private fee-charging employment agencies make pre-employment inquiries on their standard application forms such as 'Country of origin?' or 'Place of birth?' which can be used to discover the probable race or colour of the applicant. Ministry of Labour exchanges ask immigrants signing on to state their country of origin, but Ministry officials explain that this is done solely for information purposes and not with the intention of discriminating.

ROLE OF EMPLOYMENT EXCHANGES

Coloured work-seekers find jobs in a variety of ways. The most important is through direct application to employers (76 per cent of those interviewed in the P.E.P. Survey had used this method). In the case of recent immigrants, relatives and other contacts from home often act as

1. *Children and their Primary Schools,* vol. I, para. 199
2. P.E.P., op. cit., p. 25
3. Ruth Glass, *Newcomers,* p. 66

intermediaries. This results in immigrants being confined to those industries in which there are already immigrants and it places the intermediary in a powerful position over his fellow-countrymen. A few get their jobs in reply to advertisements (only 5 per cent in the P.E.P. sample). The other way is through Ministry of Labour exchanges and private fee-charging agencies.

In the P.E.P. Survey, only 8 per cent of those interviewed had used the Ministry's exchanges. In a small sample of Jamaican immigrants whose experience is recorded by Dr R. B. Davison,[1] only 18 per cent of the men and 26 per cent of the women used this method in their first year in Britain and this declined to 15 per cent and 7 per cent respectively in the second year. The Ministry itself publishes no figures about the number of coloured immigrants using its employment services, but officials believe that the samples are untypical and that considerably more use is made of the exchanges by immigrants than the figures indicate. At any rate, it is important to remember that the exchanges are in a position to set standards to an extent which is far beyond the precise numbers of persons who use their facilities.

A former Permanent Secretary to the Ministry of Labour has said that:

the basic principle governing the selection of persons for submission to a vacancy is that the best qualified persons on the register should be submitted without regard to irrelevant considerations such as race, colour, sex or belief.[2]

It has not always been easy for employment officers to carry out this basic policy. The employment services are judged according to their placement record and as a result officers are under pressure to offer employers the best possible selection of applicants for any job within the limits imposed by the employers themselves. In the past, there has also been a widely held belief that employment officers must protect coloured workers from exposure to discriminatory employers. This attitude was endorsed by the Association of Officers of the Ministry of Labour in May 1964 in a resolution which stated:

it is not in the interests of those subjected to discrimination to ignore the expressed wishes of employers when submitting applicants to vacancies even when these wishes are discriminatory.

The actual policy and practice of the Ministry has shown some vacillation. In the early 1950s Dr Banton found that at an exchange in

1. *Black British*, p. 78
2. Sir Godfrey Ince, *The Ministry of Labour and National Service* (London 1960), p. 64. A similar statement was made by the U.K. Government in its Report to the I.L.O. Committee of Experts, loc. cit., Part Two, p. 53

East London one group of clerks had been made responsible for interviewing coloured Commonwealth and colonial work-seekers, a practice which was discontinued once its segregated character became apparent.[1] General Ministry policy before 1954 was, in fact, expectedly vague: any order for workers which put 'unreasonable restrictions' on the kind of worker wanted (no more precisely defined) was to be refused. Then for ten years, from 1954 to 1964, exchanges were told to accept 'no coloured' orders in those cases where the officer was unable to persuade the employer concerned to change his mind and accept coloured workers. In August 1964, the Ministry announced a new directive which allowed exchange facilities to be withdrawn from firms which 'continually discriminated' against coloured applicants. Before this drastic action could be taken the matter had to be referred to a regional office, then Head Office and finally to the Minister himself. A qualification to this policy was described by the Minister of Labour when he said that:

a distinction has to be drawn between employers who may have personal prejudices . . . and employers who have difficulties which they cannot overcome because of the feelings of their workers or their customers.[2]

In cases where the employer was 'personally prejudiced' the exchange was bound to take all the measures, up to and including withdrawal of facilities, to persuade the employer to change his attitude. The effect of this refinement must have been to reduce the efficacy of Ministry policy, because, as has already been pointed out, personal prejudice on the part of employers rarely comes to the surface. In effect, the Ministry opted out of those situations in which employers discriminated because of fears of adverse reactions by customers and employers.

Late in 1966 the Ministry tightened up its policy and account is now taken of all the reasons given by an employer for a discriminatory request. These are gone into individually and considered on their merits. The policy of withdrawing exchange facilities from an employer who practises discrimination is still the ultimate sanction. Up to the end of November 1967, this sanction had to be used only once. Where an employer applies a quota and already employs what the Ministry considers to be a 'reasonable proportion' of coloured workers any stipulations designed to maintain his quota are ordinarily regarded as acceptable. Employment officers are directed, however, to try to overcome the objections of an employer who seems unwilling to employ more than

1. *Coloured Quarter* (London 1955), p. 134
2. 710 H.C. Deb. cols. 923–5 (12 April 1965)

a relatively small number of coloured workers. Even where an employer has a high quota of coloured workers he might be persuaded to consider a coloured worker who is well qualified for the job.

The amount of public attention which has been given to the policy of the Ministry's exchanges during recent years, and the more active anti-discriminatory policy of the employment services, must account for the decline in the number of reported instances of overtly discriminatory job referrals. In 1961, the Manager of a London employment exchange considered it perfectly proper for his officers to volunteer the question to every employer: 'Will you accept a C.W.?' [meaning coloured worker].[1] In 1968, such an inquiry would result in an immediate reproof.

Private fee-charging agencies are rarely used by coloured workers in the provinces, but in the London area some private bureaux stated during the P.E.P. Survey that 15 to 40 per cent of their clients were coloured persons. The discrimination practised by private agencies is widespread and takes two forms. The first is to comply with discriminatory requests from the employer/client to supply only white workers. The second is the self-imposed one of refusing to cater for coloured job applicants even where the employer/client makes no such stipulation. The major difference between these agencies and the Ministry's exchanges is that the former are at the mercy of their employer/clients, whilst the latter are under official and Parliamentary pressure to refuse to accede to discriminatory requests.

One consequence of the difficulties which coloured work-seekers experience is the bribery and corruption of those who might be able to find them places. There have been several reported prosecutions of Asian go-betweens and white managers and foremen who are alleged to have abused their positions by demanding money from Asian workers in return for jobs or other favours. Occasionally, coloured workers are the victims of 'protection rackets', as in a recent case in which two white youths, aged 15 and 17 respectively, were fined for demanding five shillings weekly from three Indian workers who were told that failure to pay would result in a 'bashing and kicks'.[2]

VOCATIONAL TRAINING

The discrimination which bars coloured workers from skilled jobs is not always racial. In many crafts there are barriers erected in a bygone age which still operate so as to exclude West Indians as effectively as they bar most Englishmen.

1. See Appendix I, case 19, p. 205   2. *The Times*, 21 September 1966

It is perhaps significant that 10 of the 103 trade unions who replied to the author's questionnaire volunteered the information that although they impose no restrictions against coloured or foreign labour, there are no coloured or immigrant workers in their trade because of the apprenticeship or other training required. There are several reasons for this. Most recent immigrants arrive too late in life to be considered for apprenticeships which are in short supply throughout the country. The Commonwealth Immigrants Advisory Council therefore asked the Ministry of Labour in 1964 to press both sides of industry to make it easier for late entrants to obtain apprenticeships.[1] This was still under discussion in 1967.

Another reason is that some unions insist on preference in apprentice selection being given to the relatives and friends of existing craftsmen. Where the union also insists on a fixed proportion of apprentices to trained craftsmen the chances of an outsider getting an apprenticeship becomes even more remote. This reflects itself in the composition of the union which is restricted to trained craftsmen whose control over apprentice selection becomes self-perpetuating. The discrimination they practise is against all strangers, not only coloured workers. There have been reports of stirrings among some craft workers when rumours have circulated that there were to be coloured trainees. But just as much suspicion might have been aroused by the training of a Yorkshireman.

Ministry of Labour policy is to accept immigrants on the same basis as other persons for industrial training. An impression formed at one Government training centre was that about 20 per cent of the trainees were immigrants, but there is no way of knowing whether or not this is typical because of the absence of published statistics. There is no evidence of a planned training policy to cater for the special needs of immigrants, although individual employers are known to have evolved special training techniques – such as the use of instructors who speak the immigrant's language and the modification of certain jobs. The real barrier to advancement seems to be that employers will encourage and promote the training of immigrants only for those jobs which long-established local labour does not want. So far, the Government has not acted upon the suggestion by a Transport and General Workers' Union official that training grants (made under the Industrial Training Act 1964) should be withheld from employers who discriminate against coloured workers in respect of training facilities.[2]

1. Third Report (Cmnd 2458, 1964), paras. 16 and 26
2. *The Observer*, 20 February 1966

WORK ALLOCATION AND PROMOTION

Frequent allegations are made that Indian university graduates have to sweep floors in British factories. More generally, many newcomers complain that they have had to move down the ladder of occupational prestige since coming to Britain. In some cases this downgrading is more apparent than real, for example, a man might earn more as an industrial worker than as a clerk. But it is said that there are coloured immigrants who have had to accept positions very much inferior to the skilled manual or white-collar jobs they had at home. Among the explanations offered for this are that (a) certain types of skill are not readily transferable from one country to another; and (b) there is colour discrimination.

Any assessment of the extent of downgrading must depend on accurate information about the level of skills of immigrants prior to coming to Britain, and their occupations in Britain. As we have seen, information on both these vital matters is lacking. Different methods of gathering information on skills have led to widely divergent statistics. For example, Mrs Ruth Glass found that of the 236 male West Indian migrants in her sample, 54 per cent had a lower status in London than in the West Indies, while only 5 per cent had a higher status. The remaining 41 per cent had the same status.[1] She found that managerial and black-coated workers found it especially difficult to continue their previous occupations. On the other hand, in a survey of migrants in Croydon industry Mrs Sheila Patterson found no great evidence of genuine downgrading.[2] A survey conducted among 2,956 Commonwealth immigrants for the Economist Intelligence Unit in 1961 showed that the number of immigrants, from all territories, engaged in skilled and semi-skilled work *rose* after arrival in England.[3] The P.E.P. Report indicated continuity of skill level among those immigrants who were manual workers, about two thirds of whom stayed at the same level they occupied before emigrating. But in the case of those in non-manual occupations, only 7 per cent had remained at a comparable level and one half were in unskilled occupations.[4] The evidence is too unsatisfactory for any definite conclusion to be drawn about downgrading. All that can be said is that the British assessment of migrants' abilities is generally lower than the migrants' own evaluation.

Discrimination is most likely to occur over the promotion of suitably

1. Op. cit., p. 31
2. *Immigrants in Industry* (London 1968)
3. E.I.U., *Studies on Immigration from the Commonwealth*, no. 4, p. 9
4. Op. cit., pp. 19–20

qualified coloured workers. The problem is illustrated by the situation at Euston station, where a coloured West Indian was refused promotion to the job of passenger guard in July 1966. He claimed that this was because a local department committee, composed of members of the National Union of Railwaymen (N.U.R.), objected to the promotion of coloured workers. The N.U.R. itself is on record against all forms of colour bar and white railway-men interviewed by the Press denied that they were discriminating. After the case had received considerable publicity the man was promoted. A Divisional manager of British Rail was reported to have said that if this had been a 'real' colour bar 'we would not have done it this way. We would have found some excuse to show he was not suitable for the job'.[1] There are other reported instances of upgrading of coloured workers leading to strike threats from white workers.

The most acute problem arises when coloured workers are appointed to supervisory posts above white workers. The P.E.P. Report showed that it was unusual for coloured immigrants to rise to such positions. In a survey of attitudes among white people, Clifford S. Hill found that 83 per cent who were asked 'Would you object to working under a coloured person?' answered yes, while only 17 per cent answered no. None of these men had any experience of working under a coloured man.[2] In many cases, disputes about upgrading are settled by a compromise. This was the case in a Lancashire firm in 1965 when eight night-shift workers were dismissed for refusing to take orders from a 'stand-in' foreman because he was a Pakistani. Seven of the eight were later reinstated with a promise by the management that the Pakistani would in future only 'transmit' orders from the production or shift manager and he would remain in his position as a mechanic.[3]

WAGES

It has already been suggested[4] that job-for-job West Indian workers are not underpaid in comparison with British workers. Whether this generalization can be applied outside the East Midlands and Greater London (where research bears it out) or to other groups of coloured workers is an open question. Allegations are made from time to time that coloured workers are being employed in certain factories for longer hours and at lower rates than white workers. Moreover, it is

1. *Daily Telegraph*, 12, 15 and 16 July 1966
2. *How Colour Prejudiced is Britain?* (London 1965), pp. 124–8
3. Appendix I, Case 45, p. 209
4. Above, p. 59

occasionally alleged that white workers see to it that coloured workers do not get their fair share of overtime and this reduces coloured workers' earnings.

In those collective agreements which regulate the employment of European workers there is usually a special provision that 'foreign labour shall be employed on terms and conditions not less favourable than those applicable to local labour'. The Heating and Domestic Engineers' Union has negotiated agreements in most industries for which it caters containing a provision along these lines in relation to coloured workers – the only ones of their kind to be found. This protects the position of both coloured and white workers.[1] Once again, the shipping industry stands in a special position. The National Maritime Board's agreement regarding deck and engine-room ratings provides:

National standard rates apply to coloured men and Asians on European articles forming part of the mixed manning of the deck, engine-room or stokehold departments, except in cases where a distinction in rates has hitherto been made, which cases are to be separately considered. In cases where it has hitherto been customary to pay whole or part crews of coloured ratings on European articles the same wages as whites, the custom shall continue, it being understood that such custom must be of pre-1914 origin.

This indicates that there may be cases in which white and coloured men on European articles are paid at different rates.

SEGREGATION: (a) THE SEPARATION OF FACILITIES

Language difficulties, cultural antipathies and colour prejudice may be jointly or severally responsible when groups of workers voluntarily avoid each other at work. Patterns of segregation have most frequently emerged in relation to separate toilet and canteen facilities. At least eight of the employers interviewed in the P.E.P. Survey had arranged for coloured workers to have separate toilets. Some had segregated canteens, and one, separate showers.[2] Dr R. Desai has recorded how these situations typically develop.[3] A few white workers complain that Asians are dirtying the lavatories. The management is then persuaded to introduce separate toilets for Asians. In one instance, after Asian workers had voluntarily used their own toilet for a month, white workers were forced to concede that the Asian toilet was cleaner than their own and the practice was discontinued. In other cases segregated

1. See below, Chapter 7, p. 113, regarding the legal effect of these and related provisions
2. P.E.P., op. cit., p. 45
3. *Indian Immigrants in Britain* (London 1963), p. 85

facilities have been dropped after protests from union officials and immigrant organizations.

Friction occasionally occurs when living quarters have to be shared by different groups. When this happened recently on board a trawler three offending white deckhands were sentenced to two months' imprisonment and fines of £20 and £10 respectively for unlawfully combining to disobey lawful commands.[1]

(b) ETHNIC WORK-UNITS

Work gangs of foreign labourers are not new in Britain. Irish navvies not infrequently band together under one of their fellow-countrymen who, in turn, agrees to supply their labour to a building contractor. The latter is saved the bother of recruiting and controlling individual workers. The navvies, however, are unprotected against the negligence or dishonesty of the gang-leader. During the hard winter of 1962–3 several cases were reported to Irish welfare officers in Britain of Irish labourers who had lost their unemployment benefits because subcontractors had failed to deduct or had misappropriated national insurance contributions.

The ethnic grouping of coloured workers is a more recent development. This has happened primarily in the North and Midlands where employers in a number of factories have set up work-units of Asians under English-speaking go-betweens ('straw-boss' in the American parlance, 'boss-boy' in South Africa). The immediate reason for this has been the language problem. But once an ethnic unit is established contact with other workers in the establishment is cut down to a minimum, there is little incentive to learn the English language and, in consequence, the group tends to be self-perpetuating. The employer comes to regard the segregation of the work force as a permanent way in which to accommodate coloured workers in his factory system.

Strikes involving ethnic units at a Preston mill in May 1965 and at a Middlesex rubber firm in December 1965 have emphasized the dangers inherent in this type of segregation. In the Preston strike almost all the 610 Asian and 120 West Indian production workers out of a total work force of 2,400 were employed in the Tyre Cord Spinning Department and the Box Spinning Department in ethnic work teams under English-speaking go-betweens. The management, an official of the Transport and General Workers' Union and four shop stewards representing the

1. (Presumably) under s. 376 of the Merchant Shipping Act 1894. See Appendix I, case 52, p. 210

Tyre Cord Spinning Department, came to an agreement that each man in the Department should in future work one and a half machines instead of one for a bonus increase of 10s. a week. The Asian workers were confused about this agreement because they did not attend union branch meetings and the shop stewards had little contact with them. The management tried to implement the agreement by ordering men in the Department to work one and a half machines immediately. The men refused to obey and went on a sit-down strike inside the factory. After seventeen hours almost all the coloured workers in the factory walked out, but European workers and supervisors continued to man the machines. During the three-week strike that followed the Europeans kept the Department working at 85 per cent of capacity. The vice-chairman of the shop stewards declared the strike 'unofficial' and is reported to have said: 'The issues involved in this strike appear to be entirely racial.' Later, organizers of the Racial Adjustment Action Society appeared and proposed without success the setting up of a 'coloured' trade union. This led to the response from the secretary of the local Trades Council: 'If they don't like it here there are plenty of trains, boats and planes to take them back. . . .' Eventually almost all the workers returned to work. The management agreed not to victimize the strikers. Subsequently the European workers at the mill were themselves compelled to accept the increased work load originally given only to the 'coloured' Department.

So a strike which might otherwise have been an everyday industrial dispute became a racial conflict with adverse consequences for both white and coloured workers.[1] The trouble started because contact broke down between those in the ethnic work units and union officials and shop stewards. The management, for its part, might not have introduced the new working arrangements so promptly had the workers been English. Once the strike had started other workers were hesitant about supporting it because it appeared to be a dispute between 'them' (the identifiable strangers) and the management, and not one between 'us' (all the employees) and the management. Union officials, for their part, faced with unofficial action and unable to communicate effectively with the ethnic work groups, used the racial factor as a big stick to settle the dispute. Finally, the acceptance of dual standards by white workers was to their own disadvantage. All of these consequences arose more easily because the workers were clustered together in ethnic work groups.

1. Paul Foot, 'The Strike at Courtaulds, Preston', Supplement to I.R.R. *News Letter,* July 1965, on whose account I have drawn extensively

Some of these lessons also emerged from the dispute at Woolf's Solar Works, Southall, which employed about 800 workers, the unskilled labour being done by Punjabis, Pakistanis, West Indians, a small group of local women and a handful of Irishmen. The Punjabis were by far the largest ethnic group in the factory. As one commentator said,[1] this was 'a source of both strength and weakness'. Large numbers meant that they were able, through the intervention of the Indian Workers' Association (Southall), to use ethnic solidarity as a basis for rebuilding trade union organization which had earlier broken up at the factory due to non-recognition by the management. But, at the same time, small groups of Pakistanis, West Indians and English women held aloof because they considered that an 'Indians' union' was being organized. When a long-standing dispute with the management about pay, conditions and trade union recognition erupted into a six-week strike from 30 November 1965 to 12 January 1966, many national newspapers laid special stress on the racial aspects of the situation because the majority of the 600 strikers were Punjabis. From the beginning of the strike there were misunderstandings between the strikers and the administrative wing of the T.G.W.U. about 'official support': poor communications were accentuated by the fact that most of the strikers were not articulate in English or in the subtleties of trade union practice. During the stoppage the men were sustained by their community in money and goods, and after it had ended the union recommended that a lump sum should be paid to those who were paid-up members at the time of the strike. A year after the strike had ended, however, it was reported that there was not one shop steward left in the factory, and 'the large body of inarticulate Punjabi workers remain leaderless and impotent, and in the present economic situation unwilling to take any further initiative'. It seems that the concentration of one group of recent immigrants in a factory does not in the long run lead to effective trade union organization; instead it may insulate that group from free association with other workers.

CULTURAL DISTINCTIONS

One of the most celebrated controversies of recent years has been over the right of Sikhs, who are enjoined by their religion to display five symbols of their faith, to wear beards and turbans when employed as

1. Peter Marsh, 'Southall Part III', Supplement to I. R. R. *News Letter*, January 1967, on whose account I have drawn extensively. A fuller version has since been published by the same author: *Anatomy of a Strike* (London 1967)

bus drivers and conductors. Those English workers who object to this concession to the religious beliefs of Sikhs argue that it is wrong to grant special privileges to any one group of workers or to recognize religious practices in industrial relations. One local official of the T.G.W.U., Mr J. Povey, is reported to have said:

Now that religion has been introduced into industrial relations [by allowing Sikhs to wear turbans] there are many sects who work at the transport department who would be concerned about equal rights. For instance, some people might want Saturday off while others would want Friday off.[1]

It ought to be noted that a limited religious concession in favour of Jewish employees has existed for nearly a century. Several poorer Jews were subjected to heavy fines by Manchester magistrates in the late 1860s for working on Sundays. Parliament intervened in 1871[2] by passing an Act (to which there does not appear to have been any Parliamentary opposition) permitting Sunday labour in the case of young persons and women professing the Jewish religion who were employed in workshops occupied by Jews, so that they could observe their own Sabbath. A similar provision is to be found in section 109 of the present Factories Act 1961. Although this indicates that there is nothing novel in tolerating minority beliefs in industry so long as they do not interfere with the performance of work, workers adhering to non-Christian beliefs would generally acknowledge that over-emphasis on cultural distinctiveness is likely to be divisive and is undesirable.

The regulations of municipal transport departments usually require transport employees to report for work 'clean and tidy' and to wear standard uniform including peaked caps. Where the officials have given in to the objections of English workers they have supported their decision by referring to such regulations. In 1963, a Pakistani, who was dismissed as a trainee bus conductor because he would not shave off his beard, successfully sued the Bradford Corporation in a county court for wrongful dismissal.[3] The trainee, who said he wore his beard for religious reasons, was awarded £21 1s. 10d. damages and costs after Judge Stansfield had held that the beard was not scruffy or unsightly but 'of a neat and rather distinguished variety of which many Englishmen would be delighted to be the proud possessor'. The Judge described the dismissal as 'an unwarrantable interference with the freedom

1. *The Times,* 31 December 1966
2. 34 & 35 Vict., c. 19
3. Appendix I, Case 56, p. 211

of the individual'. Increasingly, municipal corporations are abandoning their former over-rigid interpretations of the regulations and are allowing Sikh busmen to wear turbans and beards. This is often accompanied by fierce opposition. A decision by the Manchester Corporation to allow turbans was reached in October 1966 only after a heated debate in which members of both parties walked out and a Conservative councillor had to be escorted out of the council chamber by two police officers for continually interrupting a speaker. The decision, carried by 71 votes to 23, was opposed by local representatives of the Transport and General Workers' Union who said that it would anger busmen.[1]

REDUNDANCY AND ARBITRARY DISMISSAL

Discrimination in respect of loss of employment assumes two forms. The first is selection agreements between unions and employers that in the event of redundancy foreign labour will be the first to go. A variant of this is the kind of agreement negotiated between the Amalgamated Union of Foundry Workers and engineering employers in 1946 (not at present in operation) that Italian workers were 'to be returned to their homes as and when the position [could] be met by the employment of British labour'. Apart from formal agreements there appear to be informal understandings in several firms along these lines in respect of coloured workers. Where this informal system operates the employer usually draws up a provisional list of redundant workers with the names of immigrant workers at the top. Shop stewards may then either adopt the attitude that *all* redundancies will be opposed, or they may accept the inevitability of some dismissals and thereupon insist on the maintenance of agreed principles such as 'foreign [or coloured] labour first to go'.

These practices are at variance with the usual redundancy rule which is 'last in, first out'. Even the latter can work unfavourably to immigrant workers who are usually not of as long standing in a firm as local labour. The way in which the ordinary rule comes into operation was explained in a report by Sir William Carron to the Executive Council of the Amalgamated Engineering Union in January 1957 on a survey of redundancy practices through a questionnaire to A.E.U. district secretaries. He said:

In a number of firms foreign nationals and dilutees are . . . given top priority

1. *The Times*, 6 October and 31 December 1966

for redundancy notices and it is usually at this stage of the laying-off procedure that [the] principle 'last in, first out' is adopted

More recently, all employers and unions interviewed during the P.E.P. Survey, denied redundancy agreements discriminating against coloured workers.[1]

The second form of discrimination occurs where there is no redundancy agreement, and an employer unilaterally decides to dismiss a worker on racial grounds. Provided that the worker is given due notice to terminate his employment, such a dismissal will not be unlawful. Unless other workers are prepared to support the dismissed worker, there will be no redress. It is rare for individual dismissals to be subjected to agreements which lay down the procedure to be followed in the settlement of disputes, and no cases have been found in which dismissals on racial grounds have been settled in this way.

TRADE UNION PRACTICES

The official policy of all Britain's trade unions is racial equality. The Trades Union Congress was in conference in 1958 when racial disturbances broke out at Nottingham and Notting Hill. The Conference unanimously adopted a resolution urging trade unionists to 'ensure that all who live and work in Britain understand the rights and observe the obligations of citizenship'.[2] The next year a Congress resolution, moved by the Chemical Workers' Union, supported the need for legislation to prevent racial discrimination but added that the real need was for 'progressive education in school and on television in all aspects of this problem'.[3] In its 1959 Report the T.U.C. General Council said it would continue to keep the problem under review, but no discussion took place either then or at the 1960 or 1961 Conferences. In 1962 the Congress criticized the Commonwealth Immigrants Bill for being weighted against coloured Commonwealth citizens. In 1964, a memorandum was submitted by the General Council to the Commonwealth Immigrants Advisory Council saying:

The most serious social problems facing immigrants to Britain are those which have faced working people for many years and have caused hardship to substantial sections of the British public as a whole. But there is a need for

1. P.E.P., op. cit., p. 50
2. T.U.C., *Report of Proceedings at the 90th Annual Trades Union Congress*, p. 458. The T.U.C. represents about 8 million of Britain's 10 million organized workers. Racial discrimination was expressly condemned at the 1955 and 1966 Conferences
3. T.U.C., *Report of Proceedings at the 91st Annual Trades Union Congress*, pp. 425–8, p. 527

special action to deal with special problems which arise because some immigrants are ignorant of the English language while others lack knowledge of the conditions of entry into skilled employment.

Beyond this, the General Council did not recommend that the Government should make any special provision for immigrants. It had no evidence that trade unions provided special services for immigrants nor did it consider that these were necessary or desirable.

The General Council's attitude is that of most unions: while regarding it as legitimate to take action in regard to difficulties of language and skills, they believe that it would be wrong to allow immigrants any special treatment which might savour of privilege. Some unions, however, have gone further than the General Council's memorandum suggests. For example, the Nottingham Trades Council helped found a liaison committee to aid integration and paid the cost of a booklet issued by the committee to immigrants, including a section 'Why You Should Join a Trade Union'. The Electrical Trades Union has educational conferences at which questions of immigration and discrimination are discussed. The Transport and General Workers' Union has tried to ensure that every applicant for full-time office with the union is questioned on his views about integration. The former Union of Foundry Workers has sent a prominent Indian trade unionist round its branches not only to recruit coloured workers but to improve relationships between white and coloured labour. The examples could be multiplied: they all indicate a growing preoccupation in unions with the need to formulate positive integrative techniques.

A resolution to the 1967 T.U.C. Conference from the Tobacco Workers' Union called for union rule books to be altered to state clearly that membership is available irrespective of race or colour and that equal opportunity is the aim of all unions. Strictly speaking, this resolution was unnecessary. The doors of the unions appear to be open to all workers,[1] although an investigation of union rule books by the author during 1966 revealed only one – the Amalgamated Engineering Union – expressly prohibiting racial discrimination (this led to the breakaway of its South African section). In practice, objections to coloured workers joining unions have been rapidly quashed by the intervention of regional or national officials. In one case, an objection was raised against transient workers belonging to a union, but that this was not a colour bar was proved by the fact that 20 of the 75 members of the branch were coloured workers.

1. See above, p. 34, regarding discrimination on grounds of nationality

Trade unionists claim that coloured immigrant membership of unions catering for general and semi-skilled workers is relatively high, but it is relatively low in the case of supervisory, white-collar and heavy industry unions. A real difficulty is that many of the industries in which they are employed, such as construction, woollens and catering, suffer from weak trade union organization. In those industries immigrant organizations have aided unionization by encouraging immigrant workers to join their unions. In practice, very few coloured workers are found in craft unions. This is because their qualifications do not satisfy the unions' strict membership requirements.

The closed shop operated by some craft unions, described earlier,[1] operates to exclude coloured workers from apprenticeships as much as it excludes white workers. Apart from that particular form of restriction on entry into the trade there is no evidence that other kinds of closed-shop arrangement result in discrimination against coloured workers. In fact, once coloured workers join their unions objections by white workers to their employment tend to evaporate.[2] Where the closed shop takes the form of the union operating as the sole or main source of labour (the 'labour-supply' shop) it is not the discriminatory admissions policy of the unions which prevents coloured workers from getting jobs but factors such as the absence of positive steps to recruit coloured workers and a corresponding negative attitude to trade union membership on the part of coloured workers.

There are coloured shop stewards in a number of unions. A limited study in various parts of the country by Beryl Radin[3] revealed the election of such stewards by predominantly white sections in fourteen national unions and, no doubt, there are a number of others. There are also coloured branch chairmen and secretaries, members of branch committees and other governing bodies. Coloured workers participate in leadership training courses and have been nominated by unions for full-time educational courses. The evidence supports Miss Radin's conclusion that 'there would seem to be very few overt obstructions to stop the coloured immigrant from taking part in the activities of his union'.

Nevertheless there are indications of lack of communication between

1. Above, p. 73
2. Several collective agreements make trade union membership by 'foreign' workers a condition of employment or else require the employer to 'encourage' such membership. No such agreements relating to 'coloured' or 'immigrant' workers have been found
3. 'Coloured Workers and British Trade Unions' *Race* VIII, 2 (1966), p. 157 and 168. The suggestion by a speaker at the 1965 Trades Union Congress that it was impossible for a coloured man to become a delegate to the Congress was greeted with cries of 'Rubbish!' (*Report of Proceedings of the 97th Annual Trades Union Congress*, p. 542)

trade union leaders and coloured rank and file in several unions. Immigrants from non-industrial backgrounds are often unfamiliar with union conventions and practice, and unions do not bother to explain the established procedures to them. Some unions, it is true, have issued organizing leaflets and other printed matter in immigrant languages like Hindi and Urdu but this is frequently out-balanced by other factors which reduce contact, such as the toleration of ethnic work-units.

The real testing point of union policies comes when some white members decide to resist the employment of a coloured worker on racial grounds. Officials and shop stewards have been found to react in several ways. They might actively or tacitly support the objectors; they might do nothing about the situation; they might limit themselves to pronouncements that the objections are 'unofficial'; or they might actively attempt to persuade members to drop their objections. Two factors, apart from the personal foibles of the official concerned, seem to play a decisive role in determining which of these stances is taken. The first is the extent to which the official is prepared to encroach on regional or branch autonomy, a delicate matter in most unions. The second is whether the official is prepared to risk his own position by offending the majority of members. Branch officials and shop stewards, in particular, are beset by this 'constituency' problem.

Britain has not so far suffered from the aberration of 'coloured only' trade unions. Only once – during the Preston strike in May 1965[1] – has the proposal that coloured workers should set up their own union gained prominence. The fact that nothing came of the suggestion may have been due more to lack of organization on the part of the proponents of the idea, than to any inherent objections to it by coloured workers. Yet, so long as they are able to join and participate in the general trade union movement there seems little danger that any sizeable number of coloured workers will lend support to such divisive and harmful manœuvres.

It is interesting to compare the absence of separate coloured unions with the rapid growth at the turn of the century of Jewish trade unions.[2] But these, as the Webbs point out, did not represent 'a religious or even primarily a racial cleavage, but merely sectional organization, usually

1. Above, p. 78. A former vice-president of the Racial Adjustment Action Society (the organization involved in the Preston strike) attempted to gather support for another racial organization, the Universal Coloured Peoples' Union, during a strike of Pakistani mill-workers at Bradford in September 1967, but again without success (*The Guardian*, 20–29 September, 1967)
2. Only one of these – the Jewish Bakers' Union with twenty-eight members all over the age of fifty — is still in existence

transient, among particular branches of industry which happen to be principally carried on by Jews'.[1] Today the emphasis is on industrial rather then sectional unionism, and the policy of immigrant organizations has been to encourage membership in the general trade union movement rather than to foster separatism. In this respect the attitude of Commonwealth immigrants seems to differ from that of Poles who settled in Britain after the war. In 1953 there were no less than twelve Polish occupational organizations with about 15,000 members. The most important of these, the Union of Polish Craftsmen and Workers in Great Britain with 9,500 members in seventy-eight branches, affiliated itself to the National Union of General and Municipal Workers. The existence of separate ethnic unions discouraged Poles from seeking membership in British trade unions, reduced the frequency of contact between Poles and British people and was a barrier to the full participation of Poles in British social and political life.[2] Happily, coloured workers have avoided the temptation to segregate themselves from the rest of the trade union movement in this way.

SOME CONCLUSIONS

In this complex picture of discrimination several strands of social conflict are interwoven. In the case of the first generation what often appears at first sight to be discrimination is in reality the result of inequality of social background. Different standards of skill assessment lead to allegations of downgrading, language barriers result in ethnic work-units, quota systems are implemented to ease the stresses of accommodating men of a non-industrial background into the modern factory system. Local British workers fearing dilution erect barriers to keep out the foreigners. Sometimes these are informal understandings marking an uneasy peace with management, sometimes they become institutionalized in collective agreements between unions and management requiring 'consultation', spelling out quotas and laying down that foreign labour shall be the first to go. These are all defensive mechanisms by which British workers believe they can protect themselves against undercutting and job insecurity by limiting competition for available jobs. This reflects not racial antipathy but more deep-rooted conflicts between British workers and their employers and between British workers and recently industrialized newcomers of mainly peasant origin.

1. S. & B. Webb, *The History of Trade Unionism* (London rev. ed. 1920), p. 478 n.
2. Jerzy Zubrzycki, *Polish Immigrants in Britain* (The Hague 1956), pp. 108, 115, 119

In these conflicts, however, the element of colour does influence the situation. A work-unit of Asians, established for the best of language reasons, rapidly assumes the form of racial segregation. Fears of competition may lead local workers to base their objections on spurious grounds such as the wearing of turbans, and when the newcomer is easily identifiable by the colour of his skin it is an easy step to translate 'no foreigners' into 'no coloureds'. Underlying the opposition to coloured workers by individual managers and workers may also be well-concealed racial prejudices. These elements tend to remain latent until industrial conflict reaches an acute stage in a strike or in a time of mass unemployment. Then half-spoken, suppressed murmurs about colour erupt into sharp racial conflict. A grievance against management is turned against coloured scapegoats, and racial rivalries are exploited. Unemployment may be seen not as the consequence of general economic conditions but will be blamed on the 'flooding' of the labour market by coloured workers.

In the case of the second generation of coloured British citizens, evidence is appearing of how far the responses of managers and workers to immigrants have become identified with colour rather than with the strangeness of the newcomers. The British-born or almost wholly British educated school-leaver encounters a measure of discrimination which is racial in character. To the extent that this discrimination is allowed to continue, British workers and their employers will have sought a *modus vivendi* in which white workers feel a sense of security and the employers have a reserve of second-class coloured workers. But from both their points of view, as well as that of the coloured workers themselves, this can represent no more than a temporary arrangement. In the long run, white workers are likely to find their own standards threatened by the existence of a reserve of underprivileged workers and so their interests must lie in securing equal opportunities regardless of race for all workers. Employers, under pressure to modernize and in need of skilled labour, may find that a system which deprives a section of the labour force of the opportunity to become properly trained is unproductive and unprofitable.

One further factor complicates the position of coloured workers. Ancient industrial practices, such as the outdated apprentice-selection system, work a double injustice against them. The need of immigrants for training, to bring them up to the industrial level of British workers, is urgent. Yet they are likely to fall under the axe of existing procedures even more readily than Englishmen. Similarly the old master and servant approach which allows an employer to dismiss a worker without rhyme or reason, on giving as little as a week's notice, is a convenient smokescreen for dismissals on grounds of colour. The examples can be multiplied, but the point simply is that many of the grievances of coloured workers cannot be resolved without tackling the wider problems of social inequality.

Part Two

THE NATURE OF
LEGAL CONTROL

6. The Common Law Approach

The victim of job discrimination who seeks redress in the courts of law is likely to be frustrated. The major reason for this is that the judge-made common law does not recognize racial discrimination as a distinct legal wrong in itself. The discriminator will not be punished for his behaviour through the processes of the criminal law, nor will he have to pay damages in a civil action, nor will a court restrain him by way of injunction from discriminating in the future. The victim who may have lost his livelihood and suffered a most serious assault on his dignity will come away empty-handed and disgruntled. His only hope of success will be to rely on the ingenuity of his lawyers to convince a court that racial discrimination was the *way* in which some recognized wrong was committed, for example that racial objections to his employment by a group of persons amounted to the vaguely defined civil wrong of 'conspiracy to injure'. Only rarely will he succeed in remedying the injury to himself in this *indirect* fashion, as will be seen in the next chapter. In this chapter I shall discuss why the English common law[1] has failed to evolve a legal remedy specifically against racial discrimination.

No less than five reasons can be found: (1) the absence of any constitutional guarantee against racial discrimination; (2) the traditional treatment of racial incidents as matters relating primarily to the maintenance of public order rather than as wrongs to particular individuals; (3) judicial reluctance to extend the doctrine of public policy to racial discrimination; (4) the practical difficulties in proving discrimination to the satisfaction of a court of law; and (5) the unsuitability of ordinary legal remedies to redress racial discrimination.

ABSENCE OF CONSTITUTIONAL GUARANTEES

In most modern states the first place one would look for a clear state-

1. Most of the general observations made here could be applied to Scots law as well, and the labour legislation considered in the next chapter extends to Scotland. But the reader is warned that there are important differences not considered in this discussion in the detailed legal and procedural rules of the two countries

ment in legal terms about equal rights, regardless of race, creed or colour is in the Constitution, which in those countries is regarded as a fundamental law against which the validity of all other laws and executive acts must be tested. In Britain, however, there is no *written* Constitution in this sense. Whatever basic rights the individual has are secured not by a formal code but as a result of the ordinary law of the land. The principal safeguard of 'human rights' is thought to lie in the free access of all persons to the independent courts of justice. This is neatly summed up in the expression that with us there is 'equality before the law'.

This belief is reflected in Mr Justice Phillimore's remarks to a Sheffield jury that 'Whatever their views on immigration may be, an English jury can always be trusted to hold the scales fairly quite regardless of colour.'[1] English courts have a reputation for ensuring a fair trial without regard to racial matters. For example, when a coloured barrister and schoolteacher recently brought an action for damages for false imprisonment and malicious prosecution against two police officers, Mr Justice Marshall told the jury he was quite certain that colour prejudice would not figure in their deliberations. The jury found for the plaintiffs awarding £5,000 damages.[2] In the reverse situation, where persons are on trial for their alleged racialistic activities the courts similarly do their utmost to ensure a fair trial. For example, when a leader of the neo-Fascist Greater Britain Movement was charged before Marylebone magistrates and a Jewish solicitor was appointed to defend him, the solicitor was granted leave to withdraw from the case after stating: 'Not only as a Jew could I not represent him, but it would not be in the interests of justice.'[3] Exceptionally one encounters a feeling among coloured immigrants that they receive a raw deal at the hands of magistrates. Certainly there is evidence that in the early years of coloured immigration some lay magistrates made disparaging remarks about immigrants, in much the same way that severe sentences for assault are sometimes imposed on Irishmen on the grounds that they are by habit unsober and prone to brawling. Conventional stereotypes of this kind are bound to influence lay magistrates and jurymen, even if only unconsciously. Apart from this, however, the Englishman's pride in the ability of the courts to provide a fair trial is justified.[4]

1. *Sheffield Telegraph*, 1 December 1965
2. *Allum and Hislop* v. *Weller and Jackson*, *The Times* 24, 25 February 1966
3. *The Times*, 14 April 1966
4. A fair trial might be prejudiced by improper police behaviour and there have been some allegations of this kind which have been denied by the police authorities: see e.g.

This emphasis on just procedures has, unfortunately, had one negative result, namely that little attention has been devoted to developing any substantive right of 'freedom from discrimination'. It is one thing to allow everyone into the Ritz Hotel, as Anatole France might have said, but quite another for them to find that once inside there is no wine to drink.

Does the cure lie in a formal Bill of Rights guaranteeing, among other things, equal opportunity for all in Britain regardless of race, colour or creed? Merely writing down high-sounding principles does not make them effective safeguards of individual freedom. White-ruled Rhodesia has a Declaration of Rights which prohibits discrimination (with widely drafted exceptions) yet the protection which this purports to afford to the African majority has proved to be worthless. In the U.S.A. the Fourteenth Amendment to the Constitution guaranteeing the 'equal protection of the laws' to all citizens was emasculated for more than seventy years by judicial interpretations which placed private acts of discrimination beyond the reach of the Amendment. The Supreme Court found that the legal requirements were satisfied in the case of discriminatory state action provided Negroes were afforded 'separate but equal' treatment. Only after 1941, in an increasingly liberal climate of public and judicial opinion, was the 'separate but equal' doctrine rejected and, in the employment field, was the 'equal protection' clause interpreted to mean that labour unions, which by statute are given exclusive authority to represent all employees when elected as collective bargaining agents, may not discriminate against Negroes.

Before Britain could adopt a meaningful Bill of Rights basic assumptions about Parliamentary sovereignty would have to be re-examined. In a system like that of the U.S.A. the Constitution is a basic law which can be altered only by following special procedures, which themselves cannot be easily changed. In Britain, however, sovereignty is taken to mean that Parliament can alter any law, however fundamental it may appear to be, by the ordinary process. If a 'freedom from discrimination' were to be enacted, Parliament could change it as readily as it can re-introduce the death penalty for murder. An added difficulty would be that British judges, unlike their American counterparts, are not equipped by their training and background to interpret written Con-

Derrick Sington, 'The Policeman and the Immigrant', *New Society*, 24 February 1966; J. A. Hunt, *Nigger-Hunting in England?* (West Indian Standing Conference, London 1965) and reply by the Police Federation, *The Times*, 28 April 1966. On the advice of the Home Secretary, many authorities now provide recruits with special instructions on how to maintain good relations with immigrants: *Report of Chief Inspector of the Constabulary for 1966*, p. 9

stitutions. The British conception of the judge is as an umpire, sitting above the dust of the arena, scrupulously avoiding overt consideration of political, economic and social matters. Basic human rights, particularly those of an economic nature (such as the 'right to work'), cannot be interpreted in such an atmosphere. Indeed, it was only by paying express attention to the social and educational position of Negroes that the Supreme Court of the United States was able to cast aside the 'separate but equal' formula and open up a new vista for desegregation.

The value of a Bill of Rights in the present state of politics and law would be limited to a not unimportant emotional function. In the U.S.A. the Fourteenth Amendment has given the movement against racial discrimination a distinctive 'civil rights' flavour. Society has been put down on record in favour of equal opportunity and those who complain of continuing discrimination may justifiably say that they are upholding and implementing the Constitution. Public opinion is effectively mobilized around the Bill of Rights. In addition, the constitutional provisions provide a basis *in law* for a sustained attack on discrimination. In Britain, on the contrary, those who campaign against discrimination are unable to point to any unifying legal principle.

RACIAL CONFLICT AND PUBLIC ORDER

Relatively few cases in which racial incitement or discrimination have been directly in issue have come before the courts, and when they have this has most often been in the context of racial disturbances constituting a threat to public order. This feature of the cases has had a distorting effect on legal attitudes to matters of race relations. Viewing the questions in issue simply as matters of public order has led the courts to believe that it is beyond their function to provide remedies to individual victims of discrimination.

'The long arm of the common law', it has been said, 'can deal very adequately with . . . racial disturbances. Offences can be brought which would bring [the wrongdoers] before an Assize court. . . . And [there] the law . . . can be applied very hard indeed.'[1] Severe sentences have been imposed on those assaulting coloured people. After the Notting Hill riots in 1958 'nigger-hunting' youths were each sentenced to four years' imprisonment, Mr Justice Salmon commenting:

Everyone, irrespective of the colour of their skin, is entitled to walk through

1. Mr Justice Lawton, *The Times*, 23 October 1962

our streets in peace, with their heads erect, and free from fear. That is a right which these courts will always unfailingly uphold.[1]

A different approach has been displayed by the courts in relation to racial incitement where no actual violence has followed. The vaguely defined common law offences of sedition and causing a public mischief, which in theory might cover many of these cases, have rarely been relied upon, and no attempt has been made to invoke the offence of conspiring to corrupt public morals. The judges have often seemed to echo Gladstone's sentiment that 'in this country there is a great and just unwillingness to interfere with the expression of any opinion that is not attended with danger to the public peace'.[2]

In the case of words likely to cause a breach of the peace, effective use has been made of section 5 of the Public Order Act 1936, for example the conviction of Colin Jordan for his 'Hitler was right' speech in Trafalgar Square in 1962.[3] But it was not until 1965 that incitement to racial hatred became an offence in its own right, irrespective of the fact that no breach of the peace is likely to be occasioned in the circumstances in which the words are spoken or published. Section 6 of the Race Relations Act 1965, renders the accused liable to conviction if he had the intention of stirring up racial hatred and the written matter he published or the words he spoke were *likely* to stir up such hatred. This is a controversial provision. On the one hand, there is a danger in placing too much discretion in the hands of the police about the *content* of what is said, over and above the effect of the words on the audience.[4] On the other hand, doubts have been expressed about the adequacy of the new provision to deal with the kinds of racialist literature at present being distributed.[5]

This aspect of section 6 need not be pursued here. What must be noted is that the offence of 'incitement to racial hatred' retains a strong

1. *R.* v. *Hunt and others, The Times,* 16 September 1958. The principal charges were assault and wounding with intent to do grievous bodily harm. A similarly firm attitude has been taken in other cases of racial violence where the charges have been causing an affray (*R.* v. *Taylor, The Times,* 31 March 1965) and arson (setting fire to two London synagogues: *The Times,* 16 February 1966)
2. *Hansard's Parliamentary Debates,* 3rd series, vol. 205, cols. 574–5 (24 March 1871). See generally, D. Williams, *Keeping the Peace: The police and public order* (London 1967) pp. 153–78
3. *Jordan* v. *Burgoyne* [1963] 2 Q.B. 744
4. An application by Colin Jordan for legal aid to apply for a writ of habeas corpus, after he had been sentenced to eighteen months' imprisonment following his conviction under section 6, on the ground that the Act was invalid as being a curtailment of free speech was dismissed since the courts cannot question the validity of Acts of Parliament: *R.* v. *Jordan* (1967) 9 J.P. Supp. 48
5. For examples see David Shipper, 'Britain's Hate-Makers', *Tribune,* 21 January 1966; Paul Rose, 'How we should change the Race Relations Act', *Tribune,* 10 June 1966

association with the problems of public order (in the Act it appears under the heading 'Public Order') and it has not introduced a remedy in favour of individual victims of racial incitement. This was shown when Dr Carl-Theo Thorne, a German doctor of laws resident in Britain, sought an injunction against the B.B.C. to discontinue the television series 'Rat Patrol' and certain other broadcasts on the alleged (and unproven) ground that these constituted 'a continuous propaganda of racial hatred against the Germans living in Britain'. The Court of Appeal held that his action must fail because section 6 creates a criminal offence and prosecutions require the consent of the Attorney-General, which Dr Thorne did not have. The Court left open for future consideration whether the Attorney-General could himself seek an injunction or whether an individual, with the Attorney-General's consent, could do so: it seems most unlikely, however, that any civil remedy is given to an individual by section 6.[1] A further indication that the section is preoccupied with public order is the requirement that the words in question must be used in a public place or at a public meeting and, in the case of written matter, this must be distributed to the public at large or to any section of the public not consisting exclusively of an association of which the person publishing or distributing is a member. This led the Court of Appeal to quash the conviction of a seventeen-year-old youth who left a pamphlet bearing the words 'Blacks not wanted here' on the door of a Labour M.P. and four or five similar pamphlets on his porch. The M.P. and his family were not, for the purposes of this section, treated as a 'section of the public'.[2]

In other words, the public order approach underlies the new offence of incitement to racial hatred. This approach, as the reader will see later,[3] also had a decisive effect on the form of the legislation first introduced in 1965 to control racial discrimination. In this, Parliament was asked to perpetuate a common law tradition.

RACIAL DISCRIMINATION AND PUBLIC POLICY

English judges do not lay down general principles. They decide individual cases and, in doing so, they consider themselves bound by earlier precedent. At the same time the judges have for long believed that the community which they represent possesses a basic morality which they

---

1. *Thorne* v. *B.B.C.* [1967] 1 W.L.R. 1104 (C.A.)
2. *R.* v. *Britton* [1967] 2 Q.B. 51 (C.A.). In any event, said the Court, leaving a pamphlet with an M.P. with the object of persuading him to change his mind about immigration could not be regarded as a distribution intended 'to stir up' hatred
3. Below, Chapter 8, p. 133

must uphold through rules of public policy. 'Whatever is injurious to the public is void' declared a nineteenth-century judge,[1] and this ambiguous formula has been flexible enough to enable courts to declare combinations of workmen to improve wages contrary to public policy because in restraint of trade, and to refuse to uphold agreements regarded as sexually immoral. However, no English case has expressly declared racial discrimination to be contrary to public policy. In 1949 the then Attorney-General (Sir Hartley Shawcross) opined that

a clause in a lease or other agreement discriminating between different classes of His Majesty's subjects on the ground of colour may well be void under the existing law as being contrary to the rules of public policy upheld by the English courts.[2]

Since then, although racial and religious provisions in wills and similar documents have had to be considered by the courts on several occasions, the Attorney-General's view has not been adopted. Indeed, in 1965 when Mr Justice Buckley had to decide whether a provision in a trust to establish studentships was void because one of the qualifications to become a student was that the person should not be of 'the Jewish or Roman Catholic faith', his Lordship specifically held that this was not contrary to public policy.

I accept that racial and religious discrimination is nowadays widely regarded as deplorable in many respects [he said] but I think it is going much too far to say that the endowment of a charity, the beneficiaries of which are to be drawn from a particular faith, or to exclude adherents to a particular faith, is contrary to public policy. . . . It is undesirable but it is not, I think, contrary to public policy.[3]

The Judge was not dealing with a case of colour discrimination but there is little comfort in his remarks for those expecting a clear judicial statement against racial discrimination.

Rather than state a policy of this kind the judges have preferred to use indirect techniques to strike down particular types of racial covenants. For example the House of Lords has held that a provision in a will that a legacy is to be forfeited if the beneficiary marries a person 'not of Jewish parentage', is 'void for uncertainty' because it is impossible to decide what degree of 'Hebraic blood' a permissible spouse would have to possess.[4] In several other cases, however, courts have

1. Tindal C. J., in *Horner* v. *Graves* (1831) 7 Bing. 735, 743
2. 470 H. C. Deb. cols. 2–3 (21 November 1949)
3. *Re Lysaght, Hill v. Royal College of Surgeons* [1965] 3 W.L.R. 391,402
4. *Clayton* v. *Ramsden* [1943] A. C. 320 (H.L.); *Re Tarnpolsk, Barclays Bank* v. *Hyer* [1958] 1 W.L.R. 1157

refused to declare racial or religious qualifications for taking a benefit void for uncertainty, holding in these cases that simply because someone may have difficulty in demonstrating that he falls within a prescribed racial category does not invalidate the provision.[1] In one case, where there was a condition that London House, a students' hostel, should be restricted to 'dominion students of European origin', the court authorized the deletion of the colour bar provision on the ground that were it to stand it would be 'impossible' to fulfil the main object of the charitable scheme which was to foster goodwill and community of citizenship among all members of the Commonwealth.[2]

The judges have been less ambivalent in dealing with other peoples' racial laws. In cases involving a foreign element the English courts have rules for deciding whether to apply English law to the facts in issue, or to apply some relevant foreign legal rule. And in this context it is well established that the courts will not apply a foreign law which is penal in nature. On this basis the English courts will usually refuse to apply foreign laws which confiscate property or impose an under-privileged status on individuals because of their race. For example, when the Nazis in pursuance of their racial policies confiscated a Leipzig Jewish music publishing business and transferred 'Rustle of Spring' and certain other musical works belonging to it to Ivor Novello & Company Limited, an English court refused to hold that the Company had acquired the copyright in these works.[3] Another case in which policy clearly played an important part was that in which the manager of the London branch of a German company was dismissed in 1936 on the grounds that he was a Jew. He instituted proceedings in an English court claiming damages for breach of contract. The Company wanted the matter tried before a German court and argued that as both parties were German and the contract would have to be construed according to German law, the German court was the most convenient forum. The manager pointed out that if he went back to Germany he would not be allowed, as a Jew, to be represented by an advocate, would have to conduct his own case before a special Labour court and ran a real risk of being put into a concentration camp. His counsel managed to per-

---

1. *Re Lysaght* (above); *Re Selby's Will Trusts, Donn* v. *Selby* [1966] 1 W.L.R. 43
2. *Re Dominion Students' Hall Trust* [1947] Ch. 183
3. *Novello & Co. Ltd.* v. *Hinrichsen Edition* [1951] Ch. 595; aff. [1951] Ch. 1026 (C.A.). In some later cases in which Czechoslovakian Jews had been compelled by the Nazis to transfer their property the point was not taken that the racial nature of the confiscations in itself rendered the transfers invalid in the eyes of English law: see F. A. Mann 'Nazi Spoliation in Czechoslovakia' (1950) 13 M.L.R. 206; and S. W. D. Rowson 'Some Private International Law Problems arising out of European Racial Legislation, 1933–45' (1947) 10 M.L.R. 345

suade the Court of Appeal (overruling an order made by Mr Justice Talbot) that the breach of contract had occurred in London and that Germany was not the best place for the matter to be tried. The Court of Appeal was obviously loathe to see a person oppressed in a foreign court for racial reasons.[1]

In the field of labour law the problem of racial agreements and rules has rarely come before the courts. The matter is, however, potentially of great importance because of the proposals which have been made by several influential bodies that collective agreements should be made legally enforceable. At the present time the orthodox view is that these agreements are binding in honour only. They are not regarded as contracts which may be legally enforced between the trade unions and employers' associations. For this reason no problem has ever arisen about the legal validity of racial provisions in collective agreements of the kind described in Part One. The Confederation of British Industries and others who have proposed making agreements legally enforceable have not spelt out how control is to be exercised over the terms of these agreements and it must therefore be assumed that the courts will be left to apply the ordinary rules of the law of contract. If the proposals are implemented in this way, the courts may soon have to say whether or not provisions imposing a racial quota on recruitment or stipulating a racial selection process on redundancy are contrary to public policy and therefore void.

The real dispute in these cases might turn out to be about the legal interpretation of terms like 'foreign labour', 'non-European' and 'consultation' which are inherently vague. As a general rule, contracts cannot be upheld if their terms are indefinite but the courts usually do their utmost to find out what the parties intended and give effect to this. The courts would, no doubt, have regard to the custom of the shipping industry to decide what is meant by the term 'non-European' in the manning agreement between the National Union of Seamen and the Shipping Federation. In other contexts the courts might have the unenviable task of deciding whether a Commonwealth citizen is a 'foreigner' and which persons are 'coloured'. In highly race-conscious societies such problems do not alarm the legal mind. In South Africa the judges have devised numerous criteria by which to define racial categories, such as 'blood', 'repute', 'general acceptance', 'mode of living' and, most recently, 'the ordinary experience of everyday life of the layman'. Even the Judicial Committee of the Privy Council has managed to give a meaning to the words 'British subjects of the

1. *Oppenheimer* v. *Louis Rosenthal & Co., A.G.* [1937] 1 All. E.R. 23 (C.A.)

Japanese race' in a Canadian Order-in-Council.[1] But if an English court found itself able to say what the parties meant by terms such as 'coloured immigrants' it would mean that vague and fluid social groupings had begun to acquire more definite and rigid legal recognition. One result of making collective agreements enforceable might be to increase the use of precise lawyer-like language which would make it all the easier for the court to interpret and enforce such provisions.

The general question, whether the courts will regard racial provisions in collective agreements as void on grounds of public policy, remains an open one. One straw in the wind is a decision of the Judicial Committee of the Privy Council (comprising five eminent British Law Lords) on an appeal from the Supreme Court of Canada in 1923.[2] A company held a special timber licence containing the stipulation authorized by an Act of the British Columbia Legislature: 'N.B. – This licence is issued and accepted on the understanding that no Chinese or Japanese shall be employed in connexion therewith.' In defiance of this provision the Company employed Chinese and Japanese labour and the courts were called upon to decide whether or not the stipulation was valid. In the Canadian Supreme Court it was argued that it was against public policy to enter into a racial stipulation of this kind, reliance being placed on U.S. decisions to this effect. The Court brusquely dismissed the contention on the simple ground that a provincial legislature could dictate its own public policy unless and until the Dominion Parliament declared otherwise. The matter was not raised again before the Judicial Committee which upheld the stipulation on the ground that the British Columbia legislature was free to settle the conditions on which timber licences could be enjoyed. The decision may readily be distinguished from any case that might arise in the future in an English court on the ground that the real question in issue before the Privy Council was whether the British North America Act entitled a provincial legislature to prevent Chinese and Japanese earning a living in that province. But it is indicative of the juristic approach to these questions that the public policy argument was of no relevance. Rather than argue that discrimination is in itself contrary to public policy, therefore, it might be more fruitful to contend that racial stipulations are void as contrary to public policy on the somewhat different ground that they are in restraint of trade. This will be discussed in the next chapter.

Why have English judges failed to enunciate an unequivocal public

---

1. *Co-operative Committee on Japanese Canadians* v. *A.G. for Canada* [1947] A.C. 87 (P.C.) at 109
2. *Brooks-Bidlake and Whittall Ltd.* v. *A.G. for British Columbia* [1923] A.C. 450 (P.C.)

policy against racial discrimination? Two reasons may be suggested, one doctrinal, the other practical. The first is that courts traditionally take the view that they cannot today create new heads of public policy. It follows that as racial discrimination did not arise as a crisp legal problem in the formative years of the law of contract in the nineteenth century, it cannot now be subjected to those rules. Underlying this narrow view of public policy is the economic and social outlook of *laissez faire*, above all the still firmly entrenched concept of 'freedom of contract'. When this freedom comes into conflict with the post-Second World War concept of 'freedom from discrimination' it is hardly surprising that the older and better appreciated freedom has prevailed. In the words of the Ontario High Court: 'The principle of freedom of contract . . . represents a paramount public policy which is to be preferred against an alleged public policy of freedom from discrimination.'[1] Similarly the freedom of choice or association which is implicit in discrimination has been preferred above any hypothetical right to equal treatment regardless of race. The high-water-mark of this approach was the decision of an Irish judge that 'genuine and deep-rooted' anti-semitic feelings were a reasonable excuse for a landlady's refusal to consent to the assignment of a lease.[2]

The practical reason for judicial caution in stating a public policy against discrimination is the difficulty which judges experience in ascertaining current public policy. They will not listen to any evidence as to what this policy is. Indeed no English judge is likely to follow the lead from Ontario given by Mr Justice Mackay who looked at the United Nations and Atlantic Charters, anti-discrimination legislation, the Constitution of the U.S.S.R., speeches by Roosevelt, Churchill and de Gaulle and the resolutions of the London World Trade Union Congress to determine whether there was a public policy against discrimination. By doing this, he believed he could 'use the doctrine of public policy as an active agent in the promotion of the public weal'.[3]

The general attitude of the courts is summed up in Lord Reid's statement that 'public policy is essentially a matter for Parliament'.[4]

1. Headnote in *Re Noble and Wolf* [1948] 4 D.L.R. 123 (Ontario H.C.) approved in the Ontario Court of Appeal ([1949] 4 D.L.R. 375) where Hope J. A. regarded the freedom to refuse to associate with certain races as an absolute, implicit in the freedom of the individual under a democracy (at 391). On a further appeal a majority in the Supreme Court of Canada expressed no disapproval of these statements: ([1951] 1 D.L.R. 321.)
2. Gavan, Duffy J. in *Schlegel* v. *Corcoran and Gross* [1942] I.R. 19. An English judge has held otherwise: *Mills* v. *Cannon Brewery Co. Ltd.* [1920] 2 Ch. 38. The Race Relations Act 1659, s. 5, now deems all such refusals on racial grounds to be unreasonable.
3. *Re Drummond Wren* [1945] 4 D.L.R. 675 (Ont. H.C.) at 679. But this was disapproved in the later case of *Re Noble and Wolf* [above]
4. *Rumping* v. *D.P.P.* [1964] A.C. 814 at 835

This means that if racial discrimination is considered so immoral that it ought to be treated as unlawful it is for Parliament and not the courts to say so. Had Parliament not intervened with extensive legislation, it is possible that in time the conservative judicial approach would have been discarded and a distinct head of public policy against racial discrimination created, so as to give effect to Lord Denning's declaration that:

it is a cardinal principle of our law that [persons of all races] shall not suffer any disability or prejudice by reason of their race and shall have equal freedom under the law. . . . [1]

THE PROBLEM OF PROOF

At the heart of objections to providing a legal remedy against racial discrimination often lies the belief that the problems of proving discrimination are insuperable. It is argued that making discrimination unlawful gives birth to a dilemma since those who wish to discriminate will resort to subterfuge in order to evade the law so rendering it all the more difficult to eradicate discrimination. Illegalizing discrimination, it is said, will drive it underground and make it **intransigent**.

The argument is *not* about weighing 'one man's word against another's' which laymen tend to believe prevents a court from coming to a decision on the facts. In this respect cases of discrimination are no different from any other kind of case. For example, in 1943 Mr (now Sir) Learie Constantine alleged that he had been refused accommodation at the Imperial Hotel, London, because of his skin colour. There was no doubt that at common law a hotel-keeper has a duty to provide accommodation to all bona fide travellers. There was, however, a dispute about what had happened. Constantine's witnesses testified that the manageress had said 'We won't have niggers in this Hotel.' She denied using the word 'nigger' and said she had taken particular care not to be offensive, but after effective cross-examination by Sir Patrick Hastings, K.C., Mr Justice Birkett accepted 'without hesitation' the evidence given on behalf of Constantine.[2] It was a simple question of deciding who were the most credible witnesses, a task which courts have daily to perform.

The real problem lies in identifying the mental processes of the alleged discriminator. In cases of employment discrimination, for

1. *Freedom Under the Law* (London 1949), p. 51; G. Treitel, *The Law of Contract*, 2nd ed., (London 1966), p. 333 suggests such a development.
2. *Constantine* v. *Imperial Hotels Ltd.* [1944] K.B. 693. The references to the evidence are from H. Montgomery Hyde, *Norman Birkett* (London 1964), pp. 487–91

example, it is usually admitted that the complainant has been refused a job, or discharged, is being paid lower wages than other employees, or has not been promoted. The crucial issue is whether this act or omission was racially inspired. Because those who discriminate rarely concede that their reasons are racial, the lawyer is faced with difficulties which are common to all cases in which a specific intent has to be proved by indirect, circumstantial evidence. Proof has to be by inference from other proved facts.

Take a hypothetical case. X who is coloured is refused employment at a factory which employs 200 workers in the manufacture of soft drinks. The factory has never employed coloured persons although it is situated in an area in which 5 per cent of the population is coloured. The employer claims that X was refused work because 'he does not understand English'. The evidence on which X might wish to rely in order to prove that this was a case of racial discrimination can be divided into three categories: (a) evidence that the employer has never employed coloured workers; (b) evidence that X's spoken and written English is at least as good as that of other workers in the factory; and (c) evidence that the employer's reasons were a mere pretext and were unsubstantiated.

Evidence in the first category, that is to prove general employment patterns or practices in the factory, would not be admissible in evidence in order to prove the likelihood of discrimination against X. 'Habit' evidence to show bad character, or the probability that the present act took place is not allowed. But it is arguable that evidence of the number of coloured work-seekers in the area, how many had applied unsuccessfully for jobs in the past and the labour turnover of the factory would be admissible to prove the racial intent, motive or design of the employer. The question after all is not whether X was refused a job, but whether the *reason* was a racial one. This kind of evidence is likely to lie buried in the employer's filing cabinets, and provided he can be compelled to produce his records, it would seem that their production would not be subject to the general exclusion of hearsay evidence because they fit into the well-recognized exception which allows evidence of business-entries.

Evidence in the second category, to show that the complainant is well-qualified for the job in question, is not difficult if the standard is an objective one. For example, if a trade test is a condition of job entry it would be a simple matter to prove whether or not the complainant has passed that test. Proof of subjective qualifications, such as honesty, personal cleanliness (and possibly in this category, ability to understand

English to the employer's satisfaction) is linked with showing that the employer's reasons are bogus. In this context the question is partly one of credibility. For example, if the employer has given different reasons on different occasions this would raise an inference that he is not telling the truth. The most difficult problem, however, arises from the fact that the employer is not bound to state reasons at all. This is illustrated by a case decided in the House of Lords in 1919.[1] Hugo Weinberger was born in Bavaria but became a naturalized British subject at the age of twenty-six. He was a member of the London Stock Exchange for twenty-two years but as a result of anti-German hysteria during the First World War the General Purposes Committee of the Exchange was prevailed upon to refuse to renew his annual membership and that of a number of other members because of their 'enemy' origin. Weinberger's 'patriotism' could not have been in doubt. His sons were in the Officer's Training Corps, his English-born wife and daughters were active on the Home Front and he had given his brothers-in-law financial help so that they could join up. He asked the Court to declare that the Committee's refusal to accept him was invalid. All the nine judges who heard the matter at various stages were agreed that the re-election of Exchange members was a matter in the 'wide and absolute' discretion of the Committee. But Weinberger contended that the Committee had acted 'arbitrarily and capriciously' and invited the Court to interfere with the exercise of discretion on that ground. This made it relevant to know what the ground was on which the Committee had turned down Weinberger. The Committee had wisely kept quiet about its reasons and this placed the judges in some difficulty. Four of them found that enemy birth was the sole reason upon which Weinberger was not re-elected, two thought that there were other reasons as well, while the remaining three considered that it was not possible to speculate what the reasons were. In any event, they all agreed that the action must fail, a decision whose consequences will be discussed in the next chapter. In the present context the case shows the great advantages enjoyed by a person who does not state reasons for his actions. He will be presumed to have acted honestly and in good faith until the contrary is proved. The way around this difficulty would be to place the burden on the employer to prove that the reasons for his actions were not racial. But this is not a solution which is possible at common law. Were the courts to treat racial discrimination as a civil wrong the burden of proof

1. *Weinberger* v. *Inglis* [1919] A.C. 606 (H.L.), affirming [1918] 1 Ch. 517. In *Cassel* v. *Inglis* [1916] 2 Ch. 211, in similar circumstances, Astbury J. emphasized that if the Stock Exchange Committee failed to give reasons he was bound to assume that they had acted for good and sufficient reasons

would be on the person alleging discrimination as is the case with other civil actions. The standard of proof would be the somewhat mystical balance of probabilities. The difficulty in satisfying this standard is illustrated by a Scottish case[1] in which a man described as 'a Jewish money-lender of German origin' sought relief in the Court of Session against the proprietors of the North British Station Hotel, Edinburgh, whom he alleged had refused him accommodation at a time of widespread anti-German feeling in 1918, on the grounds that he was an 'unsuitable guest'. While affirming that his national origin was not a lawful ground for refusing him accommodation, the Court dismissed the action because he had failed to prove that this was the reason for the refusal.

If racial discrimination was a criminal offence the prosecution would have to prove its case beyond reasonable doubt, making it all the less likely that the allegations would be brought home.

Thus to some extent the strict rules of evidence which obtain in courts of law might constitute a real obstacle to success were legal action to be allowed in respect of discrimination. This has largely been overcome in the United States and Canada by entrusting the enforcement of anti-discrimination laws to administrative agencies which do not have to observe all the forensic niceties. This, and the way in which the Race Relations Act affects the problem of proof, will be discussed in later chapters.[2] Here, it ought to be noted that the courts by their nature are concerned with redressing individual complaints, rather than altering general patterns of behaviour. This case by case orientation imposes the limits indicated on the means of proof. On the other hand sociologists are concerned with general patterns of employment discrimination. They collect individual cases only to determine those general patterns, concluding by inductive process that discrimination is racial if race is the single element which always accompanies individual acts of discrimination. A consequence of this is that a great deal of evidence which is highly relevant to the trained sociologist is of little value in a court of law. It is important to remember this when discussing the nature of the powers which ought to be possessed by any statutory body set up to alter *patterns* of discrimination and not simply to adjust individual complaints.

INADEQUACY OF REMEDIES

Fines and imprisonment have been imposed in cases of racial violence

1. *Rothfield* v. *North British Railway Co.* 1920 S.C. 805, 813, 820, 828
2. See below, p. 149

and incitement. These penalties of the criminal law seem appropriate in cases where the maintenance of public order is imperilled. Would criminal sentences be equally appropriate in cases of discrimination? If the aim of the law is to redress the injury inflicted on the individual victim, then sending the discriminator to jail seems hamfisted since it deprives the victim of any real chance of obtaining compensation. If a fine were imposed it would mean that the right to equal treatment would depend on the size of the fine and the wrongdoer's willingness to pay it. The smaller the fine and the wealthier the accused person, the greater would be the chances of his repeating his discriminatory conduct. In any event the courts are likely to be reluctant (as they have been in the U.S.A.) to send persons to jail or impose heavy fines for discrimination since the element of violence or danger to public safety is entirely absent. Above all, the aim of the law ought to be the eradication of discrimination and not retribution or punishment, which are traditional objectives of the criminal law.

If discrimination were to become a civil wrong the major remedy which the courts could grant would be an award of damages. The amount which the plaintiff would recover would probably be only nominal. This is indicated by what happened to Constantine in the case referred to earlier. Mr Justice Birkett held that he was entitled to nominal damages of five guineas and costs, but he rejected the argument by Sir Patrick Hastings that substantial damages ought to be awarded because of the deep humiliation and indignity to which the West Indian cricketer had been subjected. The decision on this point was probably wrong because a hotel-keeper's improper refusal to lodge a traveller is one of those torts[1] in which the court is free to award substantial damages although the interest protected is incapable of precise monetary estimation, and it is well established that where the plaintiff suffers unjustfiable distress in addition to some other harm a special award (known as 'parasitic' damages) should be made even though this is not the interest primarily protected by the tort. The most serious weakness in the award of nominal damages is that it gives the discriminator the option either of recognizing the victim's right or of paying a small sum for the privilege of disregarding that right.

If racial discrimination in refusing a man a job or promotion were to become a tort it is by no means clear what the measure of damages would be. In all probability recovery by the plaintiff would be limited to his actual loss, such as bus fares wasted on his fruitless journey for

---

1. A tort (in simple terms) is a civil wrong, arising otherwise than out of a breach of contract, which gives rise to a claim for compensation

an interview, and he would be denied any claim in respect of prospective advantage such as the wages he might have earned had he been taken on. Similarly if dismissal from employment on racial grounds was to become unlawful the common law approach would be to limit the dismissed employee's claim to the wages he would have earned had he received due notice of dismissal. He would not be permitted to add to this a claim for damages in respect of his injured feelings or humiliation at being unjustifiably dismissed. A rule of this kind exists in respect of other forms of unjustifiable dismissal and it seems likely that it would be extended to racial dismissals were the remedies to be left in the discretion of the courts.

The real interest of the complainant in a case of racial discrimination in employment is in getting something done: he wants the employer to take him on, or to promote him, or to reinstate him. It is here that the fundamental weakness of the ordinary legal remedies is manifest. Even assuming that the common law was to admit a right of freedom from discrimination the courts lack the necessary powers to make this effective. In particular, reinstatement of a dismissed employee will not, as a rule, be ordered. This stems from the reluctance of equity

to compel persons who are not desirous of maintaining continuous personal relations with one another, to continue those personal relations . . . lest they should turn contracts of service into contracts of slavery.[1]

Thus no one would force an unwilling employee to continue working for his employer (though sometimes the courts have come close to doing so by drawing a distinction between 'compelling' a defendant to perform his contract and 'tempting' him to do so by granting an injunction to restrain the breach of a negative stipulation not to work for another). Correspondingly, the employer will not be made to accept an employee because that would violate the notion that the obligations of the parties are reciprocal and equal. This was a perfectly natural attitude for the courts to adopt at a time when the law was freeing itself from the old conceptions of serfdom and villeinage; it was an inevitable part of the movement from 'status to contract' which led to the buyer and seller of labour power being regarded as voluntary and equal contracting parties. But pressures are now developing in Britain against this classic liberal position and towards the recognition of the interest which the employee has in his job. The effect of the new concept of job security on the question of arbitrary dismissal from employment will be considered in the next chapter.[2] At this point, it needs to

1. *De Francesco* v. *Barnum* (1870) 45 Ch. D. 430 at 438 *per* Fry, L. J.
2. Below, p. 116

be observed that in the case of an ordinary contract of employment with a private employer, the employee cannot legally obtain reinstatement, which is the corollary of job security.

Inroads are constantly being made, however, on the classic position. In wartime, the Essential Works Regulations[1] laid down that the employer in certain undertakings should not terminate the employment of specified persons (except for serious misconduct) without the permission of a National Service Officer. Dismissal contrary to the regulation was a nullity, that is to say, the employee was entitled to reinstatement and back pay. The National Service Act 1948, together with the Reinstatement in Civil Employment Act 1950 (still in force), provides that if an employee is called up for military service, the employer must re-employ him for not less than twenty-six weeks; or, if he had fifty-two weeks' consecutive service before he was called up, for not less than fifty-two weeks; or for not less than thirteen weeks if his previous service was less than thirteen weeks. Disputes go to a Reinstatement Committee which can order the reinstatement of the employee or award him compensation not exceeding the amount of remuneration that would have been paid to the employee had he been reinstated. Even the courts have afforded certain classes of employee – principally those with a statutory status such as registered dockworkers under the Dock Labour Scheme and National Health Service doctors – a measure of protection against arbitrary dismissal. This has been done by the development of the remedy of granting a declaration (which declares the rights of the parties but does not order their fulfilment).

These exceptions indicate that there is nothing particularly novel in advocating a power to order the reinstatement of a wrongly dismissed employee. Nor are there any insuperable barriers to the enforcement of such a remedy, as is also shown by the position in the United States where both at common law and under various statutory powers reinstatement has freely been ordered. At the same time it has to be recognized that the English courts still labour under the old conceptions. Despite the expansion of the remedy of declaration, the legal means do not yet exist to make 'freedom from discrimination' a meaningful right protected by the courts. Only legislation can provide the necessary remedies.

---

1. 1942, S.R. & O. No. 1594

7. Remedies for a Rebuffed Worker?

The fact that there is no common law remedy against racial discrimination does not mean that the aggrieved member of a racial minority is entirely without legal protection. The question to be discussed in this chapter is whether the victim of discrimination in employment may rely on any established legal rules in order to remedy indirectly the harm he has suffered.

One word of caution must be issued. 'Most employers would be appalled at the idea of issuing writs against their workers; and most workers would go first not to a solicitor but to their shop steward.'[1] This truism applies to the coloured victim of discrimination no less than to any other worker who feels himself wronged. Traditionally, disputes between workers and management are settled by collective bargaining backed by economic and social sanctions. Differences between workers are settled on the shop-floor or at the union meeting. Reliance on legal sanctions is normally a last resort, an admission by the parties that the voluntary system has broken down. For this reason, the present discussion is bound to take the shape of a nightmare view of what life would be like were the lawyers allowed to rule industrial relations. In apology, it may be pleaded that this review is essential if the extent of protection against discrimination is to be accurately defined.

ENGAGEMENT FOR EMPLOYMENT

May a worker bring an action against an employer who refuses him employment on racial grounds? The answer is no.

1. K. W. Wedderburn, *The Worker and the Law* (Harmondsworth: Penguin 1965), p. 11. Readers who experience difficulty with this chapter because of their unfamiliarity with labour law would be well advised to consult Professor Wedderburn's book or some other introductory account such as O. Kahn-Freund, 'The Legal Framework' in *The System of Industrial Relations in Great Britain* (eds. Flanders & Clegg London 1954), pp. 42–127

An employer [said Lord Davey in a famous speech][1] may refuse to employ [a workman] from the most mistaken, capricious, malicious or morally reprehensible motives that can be conceived, but the workman has no right of action against him. . . . A man has no right to be employed by any particular employer, and has no right to any particular employment if it depends on the will of another.

Basic here is the notion of contractual freedom which implies an absolute right on the part of the employer to discriminate in the choice of his employees. Such restrictions as are imposed on this freedom are either statutory or by collective agreement. An example of the former kind is the Disabled Persons Employment Act 1944, which obliges employers who have twenty or more employees to employ a quota of 3 per cent registered handicapped persons, and which reserves all vacancies of lift and car park attendants for the disabled.

As regards racial restrictions in collective agreements, there are two ways in which an individual worker who is discriminated against because of such an agreement may obtain legal redress: (1) an action for damages arising out of the tort of conspiracy, which will be considered later;[2] or (2) an action for a declaration that the agreement is void as contrary to public policy. Until recently, it was by no means clear that an individual worker who was prevented from working because of the terms of an agreement to which he was not a party had any legal remedy where the elements of the tort of conspiracy were absent. But in 1963, George Eastham, a professional footballer, was granted a declaration against the Football Association and Football League that their rules relating to the retention and transfer of players were not binding on him because they were in unreasonable restraint of trade. Mr Justice Wilberforce said:

The employees' liberty of action in seeking employment is threatened just as much as the liberty of the employers to give them employment, and their liberty to seek employment is considered by the law to be an important public interest.[3]

It would be unjust, he thought, to leave the defence of that interest exclusively in the hands of the employers who had shown every intention of maintaining the restraint as long as they could. Consequently, he held, the 'persons whose rights [were] vitally affected' were entitled to a declaratory judgement. This decision might be a useful precedent

1. *Allen* v. *Flood* [1898] A.C. 1 (H.L.) at 172–3
2. Below, p. 122
3. *Eastham* v. *Newcastle United F.C. Ltd.* [1964] Ch. 413 at 442–3

for a worker who seeks a declaration that a racial restriction in an agreement is void. The weakness of this remedy is that it has no coercive effect. A declaration will not prevent the parties from continuing to act in accordance with their agreement if they so wish. Indeed, as has been mentioned earlier, the parties to collective agreements usually observe their conditions although they believe that these agreements have no legal effect and are binding in 'honour' alone. So a declaration, it would seem, is unlikely to cause them to change their practices.

The other difficulty which the plaintiff in such an action would have to surmount is to establish that the agreement runs contrary to public policy. In the last chapter the hesitation of the common law about creating a new head of policy against racial discrimination was explained.[1] It is also clear that a restrictive practice is not void as contrary to public policy simply because a court considers it to be 'unreasonable': something more is required, namely an unlawful restraint of trade. All restraints which purport to restrict a person's economic activity are prima facie void, but they can be justified in certain circumstances. The onus would be on the party seeking to uphold a racial agreement to show circumstances from which the court might conclude that it was reasonable in the interests of the parties. In times of full employment this might be difficult, but the actual decision would depend on factors such as the time limit on the agreement, and the nature and size of the restricted group.

Even if the agreement was held to be reasonable to protect the parties' interests, circumstances could be proved from which the court might conclude that the restraint was injurious to the public interest. Recently, Mr Justice Thesiger held a pension fund rule void on this ground where the rule provided that a pension could be discontinued in the event of certain skilled work being undertaken by the pensioner.[2] On the face of it, this decision lends support to the view that a contractual restriction on the use of immigrant labour may in future be treated as a restraint contrary to the public interest. But Mr Justice Thesiger specifically referred to Lord Reid's approach to questions of policy[3] and noted that Parliament has 'discussed Commonwealth immigration from the point of view of the labour market'. Exactly what this implies for judicial policy-making is far from clear. It is, however,

1. Above, p. 96
2. *Bull* v. *Pitney-Bowes Ltd.* [1967] 1 W.L.R. 273, following *Wyatt* v. *Kreglinger and Fernau* [1933] 1 K.B. 793 (enforced retirement of sixty-year-old woolbroker held contrary to public interest, even though in times of widespread unemployment) and rejecting the academic criticisms of the latter decision, at least in modern conditions of full employment
3. Above, p. 101

now a fact that legislation against racial discrimination in employment has been introduced and the courts may seek guidance from Parliament in deciding whether racial restraints are contrary to the public interest.[1] Two important practical limitations on this are, first that the doctrines of restraint of trade are not applicable if the agreement is concerned only with what is to happen *whilst* a particular employee is employed by an employer. As a result, an agreement restricting promotion on racial grounds could not be declared void as in restraint of trade. Secondly, where a trade union operates a closed shop in conjunction with a colour bar, section 3 of the Trade Union Act 1871 will effectively prevent the agreement being declared void.[2]

EMPLOYMENT EXCHANGES

If a worker is not referred to a particular employer by an employment officer at a Ministry of Labour employment exchange because the employer refuses to accept coloured workers, the work-seeker has no legal redress. The powers of the Minister of Labour to establish and run the exchanges derive from the Employment and Training Act 1948 which contains no prohibition on racial discrimination. It would be a relatively simple matter to amend the Act by providing that no person shall be disqualified or otherwise prejudiced in respect of exchange facilities because of his race, colour, ethnic or national origin, and that notification of vacancies is not to be accepted from any employer who insists on racial stipulations. However, as we have seen,[3] the Ministry prefers to rely on persuasion with the ultimate sanction of withdrawal of facilities.

A Private Members' Bill introduced by Mr Hugh Jenkins (Labour) in 1966 sought to bring private fee-charging employment agencies under legal regulation. This had the distinction of almost becoming the first legislative measure to deal specifically with discrimination by employment agencies. Under its provisions no person was to carry on a fee-charging employment agency unless he held an annual licence or an authorization from the Minister of Labour certifying that the agency was not carried on with a view to profit. One of the grounds on which a licence or authorization might be refused was 'that discrimination on the ground of colour, race or ethnic or national origins has been

1. *Cf. Nagle* v. *Feilden* [1966] 2 Q.B. 633, in which Danckwerts, L. J. was prepared to look at the Sex Disqualification (Removal) Act 1919, to show the 'position of present-day thought on the question of [sex] discrimination'
2. Discussed below, p. 125
3. Above, p. 71

improperly practised in the conduct of the agency'. The Minister was empowered to secure the proper conduct of these agencies and to regulate the services they render with a view to the employment in the United Kingdom of persons from abroad. The Bill specifically covered 'information' provided by the agencies so that discriminatory job advertisements displayed by an agency (but not by tobacconists and others who do not carry on the business of an employment agency) would have been a ground for putting it out of business.

Although the Bill excluded from its scope those trade unions and professional associations which make no charge beyond membership subscriptions for employment services, it would have provided a useful lever against discrimination by private agencies. Unfortunately, the Bill lapsed at the end of the 1966–7 Parliamentary session, having progressed no further than the committee stage in the Commons.

TERMS AND CONDITIONS OF EMPLOYMENT

The starting point of the legal relationship between employer and employee is the individual contract of employment. There would be nothing in law to prevent the parties agreeing expressly that the employee shall suffer no discrimination in regard to the terms of his employment or dismissal. But this is not what happens in practice. Can a term be *implied* in the employment contract of a coloured worker that the employer will not discriminate against him? This is not one of those matters which the Contracts of Employment Act 1963 requires the employer to include in the written statement of terms of employment which he must give every employee. Nor is it one of those terms which is 'so obvious that it goes without saying'.[1] The courts would need very compelling evidence before implying a term as novel as this and which has not yet been recognized in any decided case.

This does not mean that a coloured worker is entirely unprotected. There are three ways in which the existing law might operate to bring an employer who discriminates in regard to terms of employment up to scratch. The first is by the use of section 4 (5) of the Contracts of Employment Act 1963. This provides that the written particulars of employment which have to be supplied to each employee may refer to 'some document' accessible to the employee, such as a collective agreement. If this is done then the coloured worker will be legally entitled to enjoy the same terms as all other employees who are subject to that agreement.

1. *Shirlaw* v. *Southern Foundries (1926) Ltd.* [1939] 2 K.B. 206,227

Secondly, collective agreements may have a normative effect in relation to individual contracts of employment. For example if the union-employer agreement provides that foreign labour shall enjoy 'recognized' terms and conditions of employment or terms 'not less favourable' than those enjoyed by British workers, the collectively bargained terms might be implied into the individual contract of each foreign worker. Of course this could happen only if these terms do not conflict with *express* terms of the individual's contract, so that if the latter are *less* favourable terms than those in the collective agreement, the agreement provides no protection.

The third and most useful legal weapon is the Terms and Conditions of Employment Act 1959, section 8 of which enables a trade union or employers' association representing a 'substantial proportion' of workers or employers in an industry to report a 'claim' to the Minister of Labour that an employer is not observing the 'recognized terms and conditions'. If the Minister fails to settle the matter by negotiation, he must refer it to the Industrial Court. If the Court finds that the employer is observing terms and conditions 'less favourable' than the 'recognized' terms it will make an award compelling him to observe the better terms in the employment of all his workers. The Court's decision becomes a compulsory implied term in the contract of employment of each worker. From the point of view of the discriminated worker, however, this procedure suffers from the disadvantage that complaints can be initiated only by his union. While this may provide an impetus to increased union participation by coloured workers, it leaves them remediless if a white majority abuses its position and refuses to sanction the complaint. Fortunately, the interests of the majority would normally lie in ensuring equal terms for all.

Can the terms of a collective agreement which discriminates *against* foreign labour be imported into the individual contract of employment? For example the agreement between the National Union of Railwaymen and British Rail dated 20 May 1959, provides that if a foreign national is placed in a vacancy in step 2 or higher he may remain there for two years after which (if he is not by then naturalized) the post must be re-advertised. Does this mean that after two years the individual's contract automatically terminates or that he is then subject to demotion? The better view must surely be that this is one of those collective terms which is not appropriate for incorporation into the individual's contract of employment. Of course it would be open to British Rail to make it an express term of the foreign national's contract that he would be employed in the grade for the fixed period of two years only, but if it does not do so then it would seem that reasonable notice would have to be given to terminate the job. Collective terms of this kind are intended to regulate the relations between unions and management rather than to affect the contracts of individual workers. A similar problem arises in relation to terms such as 'in the event of redundancy foreign labour must be the first to be dispensed with'.[1] Could a British worker who is made redundant before a foreign worker in an industry where there is a long-standing collective agreement to this effect claim that he has been wrongly dismissed? A decision of the Judicial Committee of the Privy Council (on appeal from Canada) is persuasive authority that he could not do so. In that case a collective agreement included a 'first in last out' redundancy rule. A dismissed worker claimed that contrary to this seniority rule the firm had retained men junior to him. Lord Russell of Killowen thought that the effective sequel of this refusal to observe collective terms 'would be not an action by any employee . . . but the calling of a strike until the grievance was remedied'.[2] If this reasoning is accepted by an English court the 'foreign labour first to go' rule could not be implied into the individual's contract. From a purely legal standpoint, therefore, the job security promised to British workers by these clauses is illusory.

SEGREGATION AT WORK

It is quite clear that no legal sanction exists against the deployment of labour within a factory into ethnic work-units. Can the practice[3] of separating toilet and other on-job facilities be subjected to legal control?

The usual statutory obligation in regard to factories, shops and offices is that 'sufficient and suitable' sanitary conveniences must be provided for persons employed there. These provisions must be enforced by local authorities, and in most cases they would not require much prodding to forestall the establishment of segregated facilities. If they failed to do so the most sensible approach would be through the factories inspectorate of the Ministry of Labour which has statutory powers to enforce the provisions of the Factories Act in default of action by local authorities.

If the employer refused to alter the segregated facilities a prosecution could be instituted, and it would then be open to the magistrates to say

---

1. See above, Chapter 3, p. 50 and Appendix II, p. 218
2. *Young* v. *Canadian Northern Railway Co.* [1931] A.C. 83, 89 (P.C.)
3. Described above, Chapter 5, p. 76

that such facilities are inherently unequal in their operation as between different classes and for that reason unsatisfactory and unsuitable. The existing law, provided it is flexibly interpreted and speedily enforced, provides an adequate safeguard against this particular type of discrimination.

TERMINATION OF EMPLOYMENT

It is fashionable these days to refer to the worker's 'right of property' in his job.[1] Implicit in this concept is the recognition that the employee ought to be protected against involuntary dismissal. In Britain the first two hesitant steps in this direction are the Contracts of Employment Act 1963, laying down minimum periods of notice of dismissal, and the Redundancy Payments Act 1965, which creates positive legal rights to payments for redundant workers. These measures protect employees belonging to minority groups as effectively as they help all other employees.

The view that employees should be specially protected from dismissal on racial grounds is, in effect, an assertion of the job-property concept. At present the law affords no such protection. It is important to bear in mind that an employer may dismiss a worker either by giving him the period of notice required by statute or the longer period required in the contract, or summarily (without notice) for misconduct. We have seen that when an employer wants to dismiss an employee for racial reasons he ordinarily gives him notice or, what amounts to the same thing, pays him wages in lieu of notice. The employee is wholly unprotected in this situation because the *motives* of the employer in giving notice are irrelevant in the eyes of the law. An exception to this exists in the case of dismissals by statutory public authorities, which are not allowed to act in bad faith or from corrupt motives or upon irrelevant considerations. Lord Justice Warrington once suggested that if a local education authority were to dismiss a teacher 'because she had red hair or for some equally frivolous and foolish reason, the court would declare the attempted dismissal void'.[2]

In the case of summary dismissal the employee faces the considerable difficulty that the employer does not have to inform him of his reasons. As long as it turns out at the trial of the employee's action for damages

1. The leading study (of Britain, the U.S.A. and Mexico) is by Frederic Meyers, *Ownership of Jobs: a Comparative Study* (California 1964)
2. *Short* v. *Poole Corporation* [1926] Ch. 66, 91 (in which the dismissal of married women teachers on the ground that they were unfairly competing with unmarried women instead of looking after their domestic concerns was held by the Court of Appeal to be lawful)

that the dismissal was justified, it does not matter that at the time of the dismissal the employer did not actually know of any misconduct. So, for example, if an employee is summarily dismissed because of his dark skin colour this would be unjustifiable and he would be entitled to damages. But if it transpired that he had, unknown to the employer at the time, also been guilty of some form of recognized misconduct – such as wilful disobedience – the original dismissal would stand justified. Even where damages are recovered, it has been seen that these will be limited and reinstatement will not be ordered.[1]

Unsatisfactory as the present state of the law is for any employee threatened with dismissal, it is even more so for the coloured worker. Not only is he vulnerable to arbitrary[2] dismissal on grounds of his colour, but he is also less likely than other workers to enjoy the protection of collective action on his behalf. In practice employers are often forced to accept that workers cannot be dismissed without good cause because of the fear of labour unrest. However, a white majority may not be prepared to offer its collective support to coloured brethren. *A fortiori*, if the employer has been induced to dismiss the worker because of pressure from the white majority, or in pursuance of a collective agreement, the coloured worker is defenceless.

The United Kingdom Government is committed to wider job security measures by reason of its adoption (with certain reservations) of the I.L.O. Recommendation No. 119 of June 1963 which recommends that dismissal must always require a valid reason related either to the conduct or capacity of the workers or the needs of the firm. Reasons which are not valid include the worker's race, colour, sex and social origin. In the discussions which the Government has promised to have with employers and trade unions[3] to devise effective safeguards against arbitrary dismissal a close look ought to be taken at the discriminatory selection procedures in existing collective agreements which are clearly inconsistent with the I.L.O. Recommendation. Any legal code relating to dismissals ought to oblige the employer to state his reasons at the time of the dismissal, and place the burden of proving just cause on the employer. Where the employee disputes the reasons he should have a right of appeal to an industrial tribunal, which should have powers to order reinstatement where the dismissal is for invalid

1. Above Chapter 6, p. 107. One case in which damages were awarded was that of the bearded Bradford bus conductor: above, p. 80
2. 'Arbitrary' is used in this context to connote a dismissal which might be after due notice but which is without adequate moral or economic foundation. Professor O. Kahn-Freund calls this 'unfair' dismissal
3. Cmnd. 2548, 1964, p. 7

reasons such as his race. A remedy of this kind is essential if recognition is to be given to the employee's 'property' in his job. It will be seen later that this remedy works in other legal systems and, in particular, in the context of redressing discrimination in employment in the U.S.A.[1] In addition the tribunals should have the right to award a lump sum for loss of the job, the amount being based on an assessment of the *value* of the job to the worker, depending on factors such as the prevailing labour situation. Such a general change in the law would be significant in alleviating the specific problem of racial dismissals.

Another example of the general law providing a shield to employees against whom there is discrimination is the position in relation to the payment of unemployment benefits. The National Insurance Act 1965, and its predecessors, do not distinguish between contributors on racial grounds. But a question which might arise is whether a coloured worker is to be disentitled from receiving a benefit because he has refused an offer of employment at a firm which employs coloured workers in conditions which are inferior to those enjoyed by other employees. The Act is careful to state that a vacancy is not to be deemed 'suitable' if it is at worse wages or conditions than he might expect to earn in his own district or, if it is in some other district, it is on less favourable wages and conditions than those observed in collective agreements with unions or generally recognized by 'good employers'. In this indirect way, therefore, the Act shields a coloured worker from an employer who discriminates in regard to terms and conditions of employment by allowing the worker to continue receiving benefits until 'suitable' employment is found.

The reverse situation arises when an employee loses his employment because he refuses to work alongside workers of other racial groups. The Act disqualifies a person who participates in a 'trade dispute' from receiving benefits throughout the period of the stoppage and in the next section we shall discuss whether racial conflicts in industry can be

1. Below, Chapter 8, p. 150. In his Memorandum of Evidence to the Royal Commission on Trade Union and Employers' Associations (January 1966) s. 21, Professor K. W. Wedderburn suggested that a reinstatement order in such circumstances should protect the employee from dismissal for six months, except for misconduct, subject to discharge of the order on the employer's application, the worker then being paid six months' wages. The proposals made here in relation to dismissal are substantially the same as those made by Professor Wedderburn. See, too, the Memorandum to the Commission by the Industrial Law Society, and the article by G. de N. Clark 'How wrong is wrongful dismissal?' (1966) 63 *Law Society's Gazette* 255. A Report of the National Joint Advisory Council Committee on Dismissal Procedures (1967) recommended that if statutory tribunals are set up to deal with dismissals their function should be one of conciliation rather than adjudication; for this reason the dispute should go first to a Ministry of Labour official whose job it would be to establish the facts and act as conciliator, and then to an impartial tribunal other than the industrial tribunals set up under the Industrial Training Act 1964

classed as 'trade disputes'. If they can, then the discriminating employee will lose benefits. The Act also disqualifies a person who loses his job through 'misconduct' or who voluntarily leaves his employment without just cause. The National Insurance Commissioners have said that 'misconduct' implies an element of blameworthiness and includes behaviour which causes offence to fellow workers. It remains an open question whether the Commissioners would treat racial discrimination as offensive behaviour of this kind. There can be little doubt that a coloured worker who is driven to leave his job because of the offensive racial behaviour of his work-fellows does so for 'good cause' and is entitled to benefits.

RACIAL CONFLICT IN INDUSTRY

When one looks at Ministry of Labour statistics about work stoppages, it is noticeable that no reference is made to strikes caused by racial antagonisms. Not only is this due to the comparative rarity of such disputes, but it also reflects the difficulty in getting to the root of any conflict in which there is a racial element. For example, the strike at a Middlesex Rubber Company described earlier[1] is correctly described in the official statistics[2] as having been in support of a demand for 'the complete settlement of a wage claim, that trade union membership be made a condition of employment and in protest against the suspension of a worker. . . .' This was basically a labour dispute, and strikes of this kind need not engage our attention in this chapter because they are not aimed against racial minorities, nor are they in support of demands peculiar to a particular racial group. Our concern is with two contrasting situations: first those in which white workers object to the employment or promotion of coloured workers; and secondly, picketing and strikes against colour bars in industry.

Labour law provides a growing armoury of strike-breaking weapons fashioned by the courts, in particular such civil wrongs as conspiracy, intimidation and inducing or procuring breaches of contract. Those who engage in picketing may find themselves sued for wrongs such as trespass to the highway and nuisance. Broadly speaking, however, if the strike leaders or rank and file workers are sued they have the foundation for a complete defence, under the Trade Disputes Acts 1906–65, if they can show that their actions were taken 'in contemplation or furtherance of a trade dispute'.

1. Above, p. 77
2. *Ministry of Labour Gazette*, vol. LXXIV no. 6 (June 1966), p. 289

Section 5 (3) of the Trade Disputes Act 1906 defines a 'trade dispute' as

any dispute between employers and workmen, or between workmen and workmen, which is connected with the employment or non-employment, or the terms of employment, or with the conditions of labour, of any person.

The courts have never had to decide whether those involved in a racial dispute can claim to fall within this 'golden formula', but there are indications that a dispute which might otherwise appear to be a trade dispute will not be treated as one if its predominant purpose is racial or religious discrimination. This follows from those cases in which it has been held that there is no statutory protection if what is being asserted is not a 'trade right' but a 'personal matter' or 'private animosity'. A useful analogy here is the tort of conspiracy in which combinations to do acts resulting in economic injury are actionable provided only that the true or predominant motive was to injure the plaintiff. In that context Viscount Maugham once instanced as an example of what would be unlawful the case in which 'the object of the combination [is] a dislike of the religious views or the politics or the race or the colour of the plaintiff. . . .'[1] Similar reasoning can be applied to find out whether a dispute is protected by the statutes. The mere fact that the dispute is at first sight 'connected with the employment or non-employment' of a person does not make it a 'trade dispute' if the dominant element is racial malevolence. It is erroneous to argue, as counsel did in a case in 1921,[2] that simply because there is a 'trade dispute' if workmen object to a person on grounds of his membership of a particular union, it must necessarily follow that it is also a trade dispute if they base their objection on his colour, religion or politics.

The suggested distinction between racial and 'trade' disputes is, however, subject to certain limitations. The first was stated by the National Insurance Commissioner in connexion with a claim for unemployment benefit. A dispute 'which arises out of a purely personal matter, such as (say) . . . opinions as to race and colour', he has said, '*may develop into a trade dispute.*'[3] The claim in question arose out of a dispute aboard a fishing vessel. The skipper was a member of the Close Brethren sect and he ordered non-members of the sect to have their meals at separate tables from members. The claimant (the cook) was prepared to carry out his normal duties but was not prepared to accept

1. *Crofter Hand Woven Harris Tweed Co.* v. *Veitch* [1942] A.C. 435 at 451
2. *White* v. *Riley* [1921] 1 Ch. 1 at 9
3. Decisions of the National Insurance Commissioner R(U) 12/62. Italics added

the new condition of employment about separate tables, and this resulted in a two-day stoppage. The Commissioner (overruling a local tribunal) held that this was a trade dispute because the skipper had carried the question of religious beliefs to the point where it had become a 'condition of employment' that the other crew members had to comply with his views. Consequently the cook was not entitled to unemployment benefits. It might be argued, with respect, that the Commissioner's reasoning was unsound because the skipper's predominant purpose was to introduce new and undesirable conditions of service on extraneous religious grounds, and the cook therefore had just cause for voluntarily leaving his employment. In any event, it must be remembered that the Commissioner's interpretation as to what constitutes a 'trade dispute' for the purposes of social security law may not be the same as that of the judges interpreting the Trade Disputes Acts.

The second factor which might bring a case of racial discrimination under the protective umbrella of the golden formula is that some symptom of animosity against particular individuals seems to be required before the courts will say that no trade interest was involved. One writer[1] has suggested that if resistance to immigrant labour is based on a 'justified' fear of wage-cutting or redundancy of indigenous labour this involves a trade purpose. This would mean that racial *prejudice* would have to be shown before the existence of a trade dispute could be negatived. Not only is this virtually impossible to prove in an individual case, but, as has been shown earlier, many instances of discrimination are not simply the outcome of prejudice but are usually complex manifestations of economic insecurity, traditional mores and other factors. The still uncertain sixty-year-old concept of a 'trade dispute' seems to be inadequate for the purpose of drawing the proper distinctions between those disputes in which racial discrimination is intended (from whatever motive) and those in which it is not.

An anti-colour bar dispute in industry would also have to run the gauntlet of the golden formula. If the aim was simply to convince the government to adopt a certain policy, such as to refuse to contract with employers who discriminate, those involved would not be protected. On the other hand a dispute between an employer and workmen about the refusal of the employer to engage coloured workers or his decision to dismiss a coloured worker would seem to relate to the 'employment or non-employment of any person'. A difficulty here is that it has been urged that the employer's right to hire and fire is within 'the exclusive

1. Cyril Grunfeld, *Modern Trade Union Law* (London 1966), p. 361

province of management' and that workmen have no right under the Trade Disputes Acts to intervene in such matters. But it would be a curious result if those taking action against a colour bar were not protected while those discriminating on racial grounds were. Where the dispute is about the physical or psychological conditions under which coloured workers are employed this would clearly be a 'trade dispute'.

Those not protected by the Trade Disputes Acts might incur liability under the ordinary law. It has already been pointed out that when two or more combine so as to inflict damage on a third party they commit the tort of conspiracy if their predominant purpose is a dislike of the race or colour of that person. This is so even if the means used by the conspirators are perfectly lawful. However, there is one important limitation. If the 'predominant purpose' of the conspirators was to advance their 'legitimate interests' the action for conspiracy will fail. The courts have already had to consider what this qualification means in the context of anti-colour bar action by a trade union. In 1958 the Musicians' Union asked its members not to perform at the Scala Ballroom, Wolverhampton, until the proprietors lifted a colour bar which they had imposed against coloured persons using their ballroom. The proprietors issued a writ for damages for conspiracy and sought an interlocutory injunction to restrain the officials of the Union from continuing with their boycott. The Court of Appeal held that there was no actionable conspiracy, since the defendants honestly believed they were advancing the welfare of their members. The Court was led to this conclusion by the affidavit of one of the officials who stated that the Union had a great number of coloured members and the imposition of a colour bar on dancers had its effect on the musicians since it was impossible for them to insulate themselves from their audience.[1] It must follow from this decision that if the colour bar had been imposed against the Union members themselves, then their 'legitimate interest' in opposing it would have been even stronger. Unfortunately, some of the remarks made by their Lordships in the Court of Appeal in this case are wide enough for it to be argued that trade union officials seeking to *enforce* a colour bar are not to be held liable if they 'honestly believe that it is the wish of their members that such a policy should prevail'. But there is, as Professor Kahn-Freund has said,[2] a 'world of difference between enforcing a policy of non-discrimination and . . . an expression of a dislike of the political views or the race or colour of an individual' and as much as the Scala Ballroom decision is to be

1. *Scala Ballroom (Wolverhampton) Ltd.* v. *Ratcliffe* [1958] 1 W.L.R. 1057
2. 'Attacking the Colour Bar – A Lawful Purpose' (1959) 22 M.L.R. 69

welcomed one would feel quite differently were the judgements to be used to protect discriminators.

If the means used by those seeking to oppose a colour bar are unlawful in themselves – for example they induce trade suppliers of the discriminating employer to break their contracts with him – they will be held liable for conspiracy and it will be of no avail for them to say that they were furthering their legitimate interests. Good intentions are not allowed by the common law to excuse unlawful methods. By judicial interpretation in 1964 it was determined that the Trade Disputes Act 1906 does not protect conspiracy in this so-called 'narrow' form, so that those who use unlawful means against a colour bar will not escape liability even though there is a 'trade dispute'. Exactly what constitutes 'unlawful' means in this context is debateable. Since the Trade Disputes Act 1965 the threat to break a contract of employment is no longer regarded as unlawful. But if the threat is to break a commercial contract, or if no trade dispute is contemplated or being furthered, the anti-colour bar confederates will be open to legal attack.

In the other principal torts connected with industrial conflict – inducing or procuring breaches of contract – the motives or purposes of the defendant are usually irrelevant and cases of racial discrimination or, on the other hand, anti-colour bar action, would be treated no differently from other conflicts in which breaches of contract are knowingly induced or procured. Given the existence of these torts, however, the defendant may be able to refer by way of defence to his purposes in 'justification' of his action. The courts have never had to determine whether racial reasons constitute a justification in this context. There are isolated judicial remarks that religion or moral factors may justify the actions of defendants. The ultimate question is one of public policy; and racial discrimination can hardly be *justified* on this ground. More debateable is whether the judges would regard action against a colour bar in the same light. In 1924 Mr Justice Russell regarded as justifiable the action of trade union officials who induced chorus girls to break contracts under which their wages were so low that they were compelled to resort to prostitution. The case against racialism might be thought to be just as deserving of the 'sympathy and support of decent men and women'.[1]

Peaceful picketing 'in furtherance or contemplation of a trade dispute' has been lawful since 1906. Where the dispute falls beyond the reach of this formula, the law is more concerned with the *way* in which the picketing was conducted than the objectives of the picketers, and

---

1. *Brimelow* v. *Casson* [1924] 1 Ch. 302 *per* Russell, J.

in this respect those who picket for racial reasons or, on the other hand, those who picket against an employer who practises a colour bar are in no different position from any other pickets. In disputes outside the scope of the 1906 Act the common law tort of 'nuisance' is the one most likely to be relied upon by those seeking to break a picket line. In a leading case in 1899[1] Lord Justice Lindley said that persuasion not to work was an actionable nuisance for 'such conduct seriously interferes with the ordinary comfort of human existence and ordinary enjoyment of the [premises] beset. . . .' This view was vigorously applied in a series of decisions in 1899 concerning the actions of pickets against the importation of 'free' (non-union) labour from Ireland. A consequence of the unlawfulness of such picketing was that the courts regarded the conduct of the pickets as constituting the criminal offence of 'watching and besetting' contrary to the Conspiracy and Protection of Property Act 1875.

More recently the courts have held that not every act of peaceful picketing is a common law nuisance. In 1963, Mr G. Raphael, Marylebone magistrate, dismissed charges against eleven people arising from picketing a public house in Herne Hill which was alleged to be practising a colour bar. The accused had written to the licensee to stop this practice but he had ignored their letter.

What else could these people do but demonstrate? [asked Mr Raphael]. They wanted to hold pickets outside the public house and if it is proper for strikers to hold pickets outside their places of employment, then it is eminently proper for pickets to be put outside the public house in these circumstances.[2]

On the other hand, it might still be open to a court which disliked the pickets' behaviour to rely on the earlier case law to declare those not protected by the 1906 Act liable for nuisance and statutory watching and besetting. Pickets who carry placards or distribute written material of a racialistic nature might in any event be prosecuted under section 6 of the Race Relations Act 1965.[3]

---

1. *Lyons* v. *Wilkins* [1899] 1 Ch. 255. See too, *Tynan* v. *Balmer* [1967] 1 Q.B. 91
2. *The Times*, 7 December 1963. The offences charged included the use of threatening behaviour and, in one case, obstructing a police officer. Mass picketing (even in a trade dispute) which obstructs the general use of the highway will render the participants liable criminally for obstructing the public highway and for public nuisance
3. See above, p. 95

THE CLOSED SHOP AND DISCRIMINATION

Racial discrimination in regard to admission to and expulsion from trade unions is so rare that it does not warrant detailed legal consideration.

If the courts were ever confronted with a union rule barring coloured workers from membership it is most unlikely that they would strike down the rule simply because it appears to be 'unreasonable', or 'contrary to natural justice'. On the other hand, unless the rules expressly provide for this, an expulsion from membership on racial grounds would be invalid.[1]

A more tangible problem arises when a union's rule book provides for the operation of a closed-shop arrangement and the union objects to the employment of a coloured worker on racial grounds. It has been seen that in most closed-shop cases the coloured worker can avoid antagonism by taking out a union card before applying for the job. If, despite this, racial objections persist the employer would be within his rights under the closed-shop agreement if he hired the card-carrying coloured worker. On the other hand, the objectors might (despite the colour-blind nature of the membership rules) make it impossible for the coloured worker to get into the union because of their initial objections to his employment. In this situation would the courts be prepared to hold that the closed-shop purposes of the union taken in conjunction with the racial objections constitute an unreasonable restraint of trade and for that reason are unlawful?

The answer is to be found in section 3 of the Trade Union Act 1871, which provides that 'the purposes of any trade union shall not, merely by reason that they are in restraint of trade, be unlawful so as to render void or voidable any agreement or trust'. Recently it has been said in the House of Lords that a union with closed-shop purposes is manifestly unlawful at common law and were it not for section 3 the courts

---

1. On the analogy of *Judge* v. *T.G.W.U.*, *The Times*, 9 December 1937, where an expulsion for political reasons was held to be invalid. In California, the Supreme Court in 1944 found a basis in the common law for preventing a union from using the closed shop provisions of a collective agreement to compel the discharge of a Negro employee who was eligible only for membership of an auxiliary Negro local but who refused to be relegated to this second-class membership, insisting, instead, on his right to join the white local: *James* v. *Marinship Corp.* 25 Cal. 2d. 721; 155 P. 2d. 329 (1944), and *Williams* v. *International Brotherhood* 27 Cal. 2d. 586; 165 P. 2d. 903 (1946). *Justice* (British section of the International Commission of Jurists) has proposed legal safeguards in regard to eligibility tests for union membership (Memorandum of Evidence to the Royal Commission on Trade Unions and Employers' Associations, 1965). See generally, R. W. Rideout, *The Right to Membership of a Trade Union* (London 1963), pp. 12, 22

would intervene on grounds of unreasonable restraint of trade.[1]

In the case of monopoly professional associations (such as the Inns of Court, the Stock Exchange and the Jockey Club) there is no such statutory protection and one would therefore expect judicial intervention to protect individuals deprived of their living because of apparently unreasonable membership rules. None of these bodies practises any kind of racial discrimination[2] today so that the problem is academic. In *Weinberger's* case[3] even those of their Lordships who were prepared to find that he had been refused membership on grounds of his German origin declared that there was nothing 'arbitrary or capricious' in this, provided that the Committee had acted 'honestly and in good faith'. Their Lordships thought it perfectly proper for the Committee to consider Weinberger's German origin because, as Lord Atkinson put it,

political or social . . . prejudice, whether just or unjust, affecting a considerable section of the members of the Stock Exchange might render the presence of Weinberger and others . . . a danger . . . to the proper conduct of the business of the Stock Exchange.

Some of their Lordships went even further in supporting the Committee for resisting what Swinfen Eady L.J. described as the 'German method of peaceful penetration'. The almost unlimited freedom of action allowed the Stock Exchange in this case contrasts strangely with the common law objections to trade union closed shops.

However, a recent case indicates, in Lord Justice Danckwerts' words, that 'the wind of change' is blowing on the doctrine of public policy. Mrs Florence Nagle asked in 1966 for a ruling that the practice of the stewards of the Jockey Club (which claims a monopoly over horse-racing on the flat) in refusing to grant licences to women trainers was void as against public policy. The matter came before the Court as a procedural application and the issue was simply whether she had an arguable case. The Court of Appeal held she did and ordered the action to proceed.[4] Lord Denning, Master of the Rolls, described the Jockey Club's alleged rule as 'arbitrary and capricious', Lord Justice Danck-

1. *Faramus* v. *Film Artistes' Association* [1964] A. C. 925 (H.L.)
2. A resolution of the Society of Lincoln's Inn dated 4 November 1437, stated that no person born in Ireland should be admitted as a member (V. T. H. Delaney, 'The History of Legal Education in Ireland' (1959–60) 12 *Journal of Legal Education* 396)
3. See above, p. 104
4. *Nagle* v. *Feilden* [1966] 2 Q.B. 633 (C.A.). The action was subsequently settled on the basis that Mrs Nagle was granted a licence but acknowledged that the stewards retained their 'absolute and unfettered' discretion to grant or refuse a licence to a woman: *The Times*, 29 July 1966. See, too, *Dickson* v. *Pharmaceutical Society of G.B.* [1967] 2 Ch. 708 (C.A.)

werts said it was 'restrictive and nonsensical' and '. . . entirely out of touch with the present state of society in Britain' and Lord Justice Salmon went so far as to say that the exclusion of women was 'as capricious as to refuse a man a licence simply because of the colour of his hair'. However, it has already been pointed out that a rule will not be treated as contrary to public policy and void simply because it is 'unreasonable'. There has to be something more and here the additional factor was supplied by the monopoly position of the Jockey Club. This is stretching things rather far because at common law adhering to a restraint of trade is not in itself a cause of action. But here Lord Denning said that he could *declare* the unwritten rule to be void, although Mrs Nagle might not be entitled to any other form of relief.

THE 'RIGHT TO WORK'

The real basis of Lord Denning's judgement was his belief that

A man's right to work at his trade or profession is just as important to him as, perhaps more important than, his rights of property. Just as the courts will intervene to protect his rights of property, they will also intervene to protect his right to work.

A narrow interpretation of this statement would be that a closed shop cannot be operated so as to deprive a man of his livelihood on capricious grounds. But it seems to be impossible to reconcile this view with what the House of Lords laid down in *Weinberger's* case and, in any event, section 3 of the Trade Union Act renders it nugatory in relation to trade unions.

Lord Denning's statement is also capable of a far wider interpretation as laying down a legally protected right to earn a living. Such a 'right' would entail a corresponding 'duty' on the part of an employer to enter into a contract of employment with a particular man and not to break that contract in an arbitrary fashion. But this cannot be what his Lordship intended because the freedom *not* to contract is an essential part of received judicial doctrine. If Lord Davey's view that an employer can refuse to employ a man for the most malicious of reasons still represents the law (and it is believed that it does) then the so-called 'right to work' is meaningless. If (as is also believed) an employer who observes the formality of paying wages in lieu of notice can dismiss workers for the most arbitrary reasons, then the 'right' is a hollow one for it can be forfeited at any time. To invoke a 'right to work' against closed shops, which often fulfil important social and economic functions,[1] but not

1. See W. E. J. McCarthy, *The Closed Shop in Britain* (London 1964) esp. pp. 107 et seq.

against discriminatory employers is both inconsistent and intolerable.

In any event, it remains a basic tenet of modern jurisprudence that a plaintiff who wishes to establish the commission of a civil wrong must prove either that a contract has been broken, or that there has been a breach of some duty owed to him by the defendant or, at least, that he enjoys a status (for example by virtue of a statute) which would entitle the court to grant a declaration in his favour. None of these circumstances existed in Mrs Nagle's case, and welcome as the decision is in supporting a woman's demand to be treated on an equal basis with men, it rests on shaky legal foundations. For this reason, the judicial concept of a 'right to work' does not seem to be an appropriate basis on which to stake the future development of legal protection against racial discrimination.

In a competitive and acquisitive society it is cynical to tell an employee who has to take his chances of being hired at will or fired at short notice that he has a 'right to work'. This concept is best confined to its traditional role as a trade union demand for full employment policies and job security. The former rests primarily on economic, social and political factors, while the latter may be developed through legal measures. In particular, protection against arbitrary dismissal will give some substance to vague 'property-in-the-job' notions.

Such developments will leave untouched large areas of employer/employee relations in which Britain's industrial laws have been shown to be hopelessly inadequate in protecting victims of discrimination. Some minor blemishes could easily be remedied. The Employment and Training Act could follow the excellent example of the Employment Agencies Bill by proscribing discriminatory job referrals. The definittion of 'trade dispute' could be clarified so as to exclude those disputes in which the aim is racial discrimination, while protecting those who take industrial action against a colour bar. The major problems, however, are discrimination in engagement, promotion and terms of employment, and for these no simple reform of labour law will provide the solution.

8. The Race Relations Act

The first attempt to legislate against racial discrimination in public places in Britain was made in a Private Member's Bill introduced in 1951 by a Labour M.P., Mr Reginald (now Lord) Sorensen, and this was followed a few months later by a Bill introduced by Mr Fenner (now Lord) Brockway, with the support of eleven other Labour M.P.s 'to establish a standard of human rights and freedom in the U.K. and colonies'. But even before then the publicity given to instances of discrimination in the late forties had led to questions in Parliament, which were invariably met with the reply that existing law and practice were adequate to deal with the situation.

In the eleven years between 1953 and 1964 Fenner Brockway made nine further attempts to persuade Parliament to legislate on the subject, and Bills were also introduced by two other Labour M.P.s, Mr J. Baird (1958) and Sir Leslie Plummer (1960).[1] In the early years these Bills had only Labour support, but from December 1960 the Brockway Bills included amongst their sponsors M.P.s of all parties. The Labour Party's Commonwealth sub-committee had the benefit of a memorandum in the early 1950s from Dr Kenneth Little, one of the earliest researchers in this field, who advised that there was 'a good case both in principle and in fact for the enactment . . . of . . . legislation . . . as a means of stirring the national conscience and of creating a new standard of public behaviour in relation to coloured people'.[2] He proposed legislation similar to the Fair Employment Practice laws in the United States. Sir Lynn Ungoed-Thomas M.P. (later a judge) examined the legal aspects of this memorandum and advised that any Bill should deal with specific issues such as clauses in leases, and discrimination in inns, lodging-houses, dance-halls and in the sphere of employ-

---

1. The Baird Bill arose out of a colour bar at a Wolverhampton dance-hall and aimed at discrimination in lodging-houses, dance-halls and similar establishments. The Plummer Bill was aimed at racial and religious insults and arose out of a rash of swastika-daubings.

2. As quoted by Keith Hindell, 'The Genesis of the Race Relations Bill' (1965) 36 *Political Quarterly*, pp. 390–405

ment. But the Labour Party did not act upon this and it was left to individual M.P.s to take the initiative. After the racial disturbances of 1958, however, the Labour Party issued a statement urging the Conservative Government to illegalize 'the public practice of discrimination' and pledging the next Labour Government to take an early opportunity to introduce such legislation.[1] After the Brockway Bill had been unsuccessfully brought up for second reading in February 1964, Mr Harold Wilson promised that the Bill would be taken over as a Government measure when Labour came to power,[2] and the pledge was repeated in Labour's election manifesto that October.

Only once did any of these Bills enjoy a second reading debate and and that was on three Fridays early in 1957 for a total of sixty minutes, after which the Bill in question was counted out, there being less than forty Members present.[3] A measure following the lines of the Brockway Bill, introduced by Lord Walston, was rejected by 41 votes against to 21 in favour on its second reading in the House of Lords in May 1962.[4] There was thus little opportunity for the opposition to emerge clearly. Individual conservative M.P.s appear to have had three major objections. The first was that the existing law was adequate[5] and that legislation would introduce the concept of race and colour into the law for the first time;[6] secondly, in the words of Lord Chesham '[an] Act[7] ... would run a risk of recognizing the existence of discrimination in a way which might draw attention to it and would tend rather to foster it than do away with it'; and finally, there was the ground put forward by Mr Henry Brooke (then Home Secretary) that legislation would be neither effective nor enforceable.[8] Consequently he believed that the eradication of discrimination could 'come about only through the education of public opinion, not by changes in the law'.

The first mention of employment discrimination in the proposed

1. Labour Party, *Statement on Racial Discrimination*, 1958, p. 4. On 7 December 1959, Mr James Callaghan (Labour) moved a motion expressing disapproval of racial intolerance and discrimination: 615 H.C. Deb., col. 177
2. *The Times*, 17 February 1964
3. 567 H.C. Deb., col. 1582; 569 H.C. Deb., cols. 1425–6; 570 H.C. Deb., cols. 1602–8
4. 240 H.L. Deb., cols. 439–522
5. Sir Winston Churchill (as Prime Minister) said on 18 February 1954, that he would not take steps to instruct Ministers to prevent the operation of a colour bar since 'the laws and custom of this country upon the subject are well known and I am advised there is no need for new instructions': 523 H.C. Deb., cols. 2154–5
6. Mr R. Bell, 569 H.C. Deb., col. 1427 (10 May 1957) – a rather surprising contention in the light of the shipping legislation referred to in Chapter 3 above, p. 42
7. 212 H.L. Deb., col. 718 (19 November 1958)
8. *Jewish Chronicle* 14 February 1964. Another leading Conservative, Mr Selwyn Lloyd, had told representatives of all denominations a month earlier that he hoped that legislation against racial discrimination would be possible after the election

legislation came in Mr Brockway's Bill of 12 June 1956, clause 4 of which provided that

No person who employs fifty or more persons in any industry, trade or business shall be entitled on [ground of colour, race or religion] to refuse to employ or to promote or to terminate the employment or promotion of any person, and no persons shall be entitled on any such ground to act in concert to refuse to consent to such employment or promotion or to terminate the same.

This was repeated in his later Bills, except that in April 1958 the exclusion of persons employing less than fifty employees was dropped and a provision was added prohibiting the employment of any person at less than the standard rate of wages and conditions for his grade of work on racial and religious grounds. In the Bill introduced by Mr Brockway on 7 December 1960, the provisions relating to employment discrimination were abandoned and the measure was confined to discrimination in public places and housing. A racial incitement clause was added in December 1961. The decision to remove the employment provisions of the Bill was apparently taken as a result of pressure by the trade union group of Labour M.P.s. These provisions were never resuscitated.

Early in 1964 three members of Labour's shadow Cabinet (Sir Frank Soskice and Messrs D. Houghton and G. Mitchison) drafted a Race Relations Bill covering racial incitement, discrimination in public places and leases. About the same time the Society of Labour Lawyers set up a sub-committee on Race Relations (under the chairmanship of Professor Andrew Martin, Q.C., later one of the Law Commissioners) which reported in July 1964 recommending that all places of public resort including employment exchanges be covered by the proposed law. Although this report, like the Soskice Bill, proposed criminal penalties for such types of discrimination it also referred to the American practice of dealing with discrimination by administrative means.

Soon after Labour's victory in the 1964 election a group of lawyers under the chairmanship of Mr Anthony Lester studied the U.S. and Canadian experience and came to two conclusions which were later embodied in the proposals made to the Government by the Campaign Against Racial Discrimination.[1] These were that legislation must (1) deal with the worst problems namely housing and employment and (2) be enforceable. The latter objective, it was argued, could not be

---

1. C.A.R.D. engaged in intensive lobbying among M.P.s and won wide support for the Lester committee's proposals

achieved through the ordinary criminal law making it an offence to discriminate on racial grounds, because of the possible reluctance of the authorities to prosecute, the heavy burden of proving the case beyond reasonable doubt, and the possible lack of sympathy of juries for such legislation. The right approach, it was thought, would be to create administrative machinery along the lines of F.E.P. Commissions in the U.S.A. and Canada, which would rely on education and private conciliation and only in the last resort upon compulsory enforcement. In view of the difficult problems involved it was thought that a special division of the proposed Commission could deal with employment. The procedure of the Commission, it was suggested, would be that an aggrieved person or any person on his behalf could initiate a complaint to the commission; the complaint would be investigated by members of the commission's conciliation staff who would attempt in private by mediation, persuasion and conciliation to achieve compliance with the law; failing mediation the commission would be able to hold a formal inquiry with powers to subpoena witnesses and documents and to take evidence on oath; the commission might then either dismiss the complaint, or order the respondent to cease and desist from discrimination, where necessary adding to this an award of damages in favour of the individual complainant; the commission could then register its order in the county court as an order of that court; in the event of non-compliance the commission could bring proceedings in the county court, where the order could be enforced by way of injunction. In addition, it was proposed that the commission have powers to investigate the nature and extent of discrimination and to carry on a programme of public education.

The advantages which were seen in this administrative approach were manifold. The vast majority of cases would, as in the U.S.A., be settled voluntarily without recourse to the courts or even to public hearings.[1] Secondly, the members of the proposed commission would become experts and being independent of the government would not be subject to variations of policy on a change of government. They would deal with all aspects of discrimination rather than taking the limited standpoint of a single government department. Thirdly, the

1. This is confirmed by the experience of the New York Commission. Of 9,214 complaints in respect of all types of discrimination received between 1945–62, 3,709 (39.1 per cent) were adjusted by conciliation and 104 (1.1 per cent) settled by consent at hearing, while 4,411 (47.9 per cent) were dismissed for lack of probable cause, in 835 (9.1 per cent) there was no jurisdiction and in 255 (2.8 per cent) the complaint was withdrawn. The Massachusetts Commission against Discrimination received 3,897 complaints of employment discrimination between 1946–64. Of these 2,860 (71 per cent) were successfully conciliated and in only 2 (0.5 per cent) was a final order necessary

procedure would offer a remedy to the individual who would himself be able to initiate proceedings rather than leaving it to the police or the Director of Public Prosecutions. Proof would be on a balance of probabilities. The expense would fall on the state. Finally, the commissioners would be able to use their flexible powers in an attempt to alter conduct rather than to punish the wrongdoer.

A month after a C.A.R.D. delegation had put these proposals to the Home Office, the Soskice Bill was read a second time in Parliament. As Home Secretary, Sir Frank justified the limitation of the Bill's scope on the ground that it was concerned 'basically . . . with public order'.[1] His Bill followed the penal approach which is traditional in legislation relating to the maintenance of public order. It provided a maximum fine of £50 on conviction for a first offence and £100 for subsequent offences.

Prosecutions for what was otherwise treated as a minor offence were made unusually difficult by requiring the consent of the Director of Public Prosecutions to a prosecution in England and Wales.[2] Sir Frank explained that

if the Bill had been intended to deal with . . . employment . . . sanctions of a different character would have been obviously more appropriate, possibly civil sanctions such as are made applicable in the United States and Canadian legislation. . . . Probably, however, completely informal conciliation processes would have been more acceptable to our way of thinking about such matters.[3]

For the Conservative Opposition Mr Peter Thorneycroft moved an amendment declining to give a second reading to a Bill 'which introduces criminal sanctions into a field more appropriate to conciliation and the encouragement of fair employment practices'.[4] Labour backbenchers expressed their concern that employment discrimination was not covered, and supported the setting up of a statutory commission. The second reading was carried by 258 votes in favour to 249 against. Then a surprising volte-face took place. In the three weeks between the second reading and the committee stage Sir Frank, who had earlier rejected conciliation procedures because of 'serious difficulties in the way to their adoption'[5] drafted far-reaching amendments to his own

1. 711 H. C. Deb., cols. 926–7 (3 May 1965)
2. The Private Members' Bills had also provided for criminal prosecutions, sometimes adding a right to claim actual damages in a civil action
3. 711 H.C. Deb., col. 928 (3 May 1965)
4. ibid, col. 943
5. ibid., col 929. During the second-reading debate Sir Frank had indicated that he was about to yield on this matter by saying: 'We will take careful note of what is proposed . . . in argument.'

Bill to substitute them for criminal sanctions. The result was to win Opposition support for the measure, but the legislation itself was far removed from the proposals of the C.A.R.D. lobby.

The Act which emerged was confined to discrimination in specified places of public resort (e.g. hotels, restaurants, public-houses, theatres, cinemas, dance-halls, sports grounds, swimming pools and public transport services). An amendment moved by Labour backbenchers to extend its provisions to 'any shop, office, agency or similar place where goods or services are customarily available to members of the public' was rejected. Among the oddities[1] arising from this were that a man could be unlawfully refused a drink in a public-house on the ground of his colour, but it was still perfectly lawful to refuse him service on the same ground in an off-licence shop next door. Another anomaly was revealed in a case in which the Attorney-General refused to take proceedings under the Act against a 'private' hotel at Great Yarmouth which was alleged to be practising discrimination, because of doubts whether the place was an hotel or a boarding-house, the latter not being covered by the provisions of the Act.[2] Related to these anomalies was the fact that the Act did not bind the Crown. It did apply to 'places of public resort maintained by a local authority or other public authority' but a public authority could only fall within the scope of the Act if it was independent of the Crown. As a result, employment exchanges maintained by the Ministry of Labour were not subject to the provisions of the Act; those maintained by local authorities were. In the result, the Act not only omitted the most important areas of discrimination – employment and housing – but it failed to cover many places commonly regarded as places of public resort.

Perhaps most curious of all the features of the Act is the twist which was given to the proposals for conciliation procedures. According to Lord Stonham, a Government spokesman, the change to these was made 'to avoid bringing the flavour of criminality in to the delicate question of race relations'.[3] This is a rather different reason from that which led to the transition from criminal penalties to administrative remedies in the United States, the nominal source of the conciliation technique. There the case for conciliation was simply utilitarian: this

1. Standing Committee B, 23 June 1965, cols. 251–64
2. 741 H.C. Deb., cols. 25–6 (27 February 1967). For further examples see Race Relations Board Report for 1966–7, p. 14 and p. 29 Case A
3. 268 H. L. Deb. col. 1006 (26 July 1965)

was the most productive and effective means to achieve desired results. Criminal proceedings do not work on the other side of the Atlantic largely because trial by jury, required in criminal prosecutions, often results in an alleged discriminator being judged by a group of men as prejudiced or out of sympathy with the objects of civil rights legislation as he is himself. District attorneys cannot always be relied upon to prosecute and judges are reluctant to imprison or fine the wrongdoer. Admittedly the criminal law which aims in part at retribution does not seem particularly appropriate to deal with discrimination, but in relation to public places where the primary problem, according to the Home Secretary, is one of public order, something can be said for the psychological value of a criminal sanction. In reality discrimination in places of public resort is infrequent and it is unlikely that any significant problems of proving discrimination in public would arise, even on the strict standard of the criminal law.

The confused motives which led to the late introduction of conciliation procedures must also explain the failure to heed yet another primary lesson from the North American experience. American experts are unanimous in the view that statutes prohibiting discrimination are relatively useless unless an adequate scheme of enforcement is provided. In the words of a Columbia Law School professor:

while an impotent commission can, on occasion, function effectively as mediator or educator, an administrative agency, to be truly effective, must possess the power to compel offenders to mend their ways.[1]

A striking example of the difference made by having enforceable laws is afforded by the experience of the Kansas Anti-Discrimination Commission. Between 1953 and 1961 Kansas had a law which in effect declared a public policy against employment discrimination, but provided no means for enforcing the law. In that eight-year period only eighty-nine complaints were filed with the Kansas Commission, no doubt reflecting the lack of confidence among Negroes in the Commission's effectiveness. Only thirty-three of these complaints were successfully settled and in twenty-three cases the respondents refused to cooperate with the Commission. As a result the Commission recommended the enactment of a fully enforceable law. Since this was enacted by the Kansas legislature there has been a striking improvement. In the two-year period 1961–3, eighty complaints were filed, and of these thirty-four were satisfactorily adjusted, in twenty-five there was no

1. Michael I. Sovern, *Legal Restraints on Racial Discrimination in Employment* (New York 1966), p. 56

'probable cause' (i.e. the complaint was dismissed), sixteen were still in process and in five there was no jurisdiction. This has led the Commission to the view that the twenty-three outstanding complaints under the non-enforceable 1953 legislation would have been resolved had the Commission then had the enforcement powers it obtained under the 1961 law.[1]

The procedure laid down by the 1965 Act was unnecessarily complicated while at the same time being toothless. The Act is administered by a Race Relations Board, whose first members were Mr Mark Bonham Carter (chairman), Sir Learie Constantine and Alderman B. S. Langton. The Board was empowered to set up local conciliation committees for such areas as it considered necessary and this has been done for Greater London (July 1966), the North-West – Manchester and District (July 1966), the West Midlands (December 1966), Yorkshire – East and West Ridings (January 1967), the East Midlands (April 1967) and Berkshire, Buckinghamshire and Oxfordshire (September 1967). Each of these committees has been authorized to receive complaints from certain additional areas, in effect covering the whole of England and Wales, for which there may ultimately be eleven committees. A separate committee for Scotland was set up in August 1967. Before appointing a committee, the Board members have made it a practice to visit the area concerned and consult informally with local political leaders, chief officials and others, the appointment of each committee usually requiring at least four visits to the area which it was to serve.

The Board has initially appointed between six and nine members to each committee. Members are appointed for one year in the first instance; subsequently they are to serve for three-year terms, one third retiring each year, but eligible for re-appointment. Although committee members, who serve on a voluntary basis, are appointed in a personal capacity, they represent a fairly wide range of interests. Among the first thirty-five appointments, the best-represented occupation is university teaching (seven, of whom two are lawyers) social work (six, including two housewives) and schoolteachers (five). Five may be classed as employers (one of these is an advertising consultant) and four are trade union officers (one of whom is attached to the Prices and Incomes Board). For the rest, there are two practising lawyers, two doctors, a retired police superintendent, a cricket coach, a clergyman and a Pakistani community leader.

The first stage in the procedure laid down by the Act of 1965 is that a person who claims that he has been discriminated against, or someone

1. Kansas Commission on Civil Rights, 1963 *Report of Progress*, p. 12

else acting on his written authority, may complain either orally or in writing to a local conciliation committee which is then obliged to make such inquiries as it thinks necessary. A source of confusion in the wording of the Act is that while section 1 (1) makes it unlawful 'to practise discrimination' (this having been substituted for the expression 'to discriminate' at the committee stage of the Bill), section 2 (2) requires conciliation committees 'to receive and consider any complaint of discrimination in contravention of section 1 of [the] Act'. On the one hand, therefore, discrimination can be unlawful only if there is a practice, i.e. more than one act of discrimination. On the other hand, it seems so unlikely that a single person could be the victim of more than one act of discrimination by the same person that the only reasonable interpretation to give to section 2 (2) is that one act of discrimination is enough to bring the machinery into operation. The Board recommended, in its first report, that this ambiguity be resolved. In practice, committees have been prepared to receive and investigate complaints of a single act of discrimination; but, as will be shown below, the absence of a 'course of conduct' may bar further proceedings.

On receipt of the complaint, one of the professional conciliation officers appointed by the Board and attached to particular local committees, interviews the complainant and any witnesses named by him. He may also endeavour to interview the respondent and any other witnesses. He then reports his investigations either to a meeting of the full committee or (the more usual practice) to two members of the conciliation committee assigned to supervise the case. (The precise procedure adopted appears to depend on the forcefulness of the local chairman, the experience of the committee and the conciliation officer and similar factors.) The committee or the two members assigned to the case then decide, on the evidence before them, whether there is a prima facie case. In some instances one or more of the committee members may accompany the conciliation officer when he sees the parties; the deliberations of the committee take place in private and the respondent is not confronted with the complainant nor does he have any opportunity to cross-examine him at this investigatory stage of the proceedings.

If the two members decide that there is no prima facie case, the complainant is informed of their decision and is told that he may dispute it before a meeting of the committee. In practice, very few objections have been heard from complainants whose complaints have been dismissed. If a dissatisfied complainant were to report the matter to the Board the latter would make inquiries but would, no doubt, be reluctant to intervene. Indeed, it seems clear that once it has created the committee, the Board has no legal power to interfere in its proceedings. In the United States the courts have power to review the proceedings of anti-discrimination commissions, but it seems unlikely that any basis could be found in English law for judicial review of the findings of the local committees or, for that matter, of the Board itself. Nor do the Board and its committees fall under the purview of the Council on Tribunals (set up in 1958 to watch over the work of some administrative tribunals) or the Parliamentary Commissioner (Ombudsman).

If the two members (or the full committee, as the case may be) decide that there is a prima facie case, the committee is then under a duty 'to use their best endeavours by communication with the parties or otherwise to secure a settlement of any difference between them and a satisfactory assurance against further discrimination'. The Board regards as the *minimum* requirement for a 'satisfactory settlement' a written assurance against further discrimination and, in the case of hotels (but not public houses in the complainant's own area) a written apology to the complainant.

Two features of this investigation and conciliation process ought to be specially noted. The committees have no self-initiating powers: they must await a formal complaint before they can act. Now, a traveller refused overnight accommodation at an hotel is unlikely to want to go to the trouble and out-of-pocket expense of lodging a complaint, particularly where no direct benefit will accrue to himself, unless he is an unusually public-spirited individual. This reluctance is likely to be increased once complainants realize that the delays will be considerable. (There was at least one pending case, not yet settled by July 1967 because of the hard-headedness of the discriminator, in which the complaint had been made over a year before.) The Board commented in its first report that 'it calls for considerable courage to complain about humiliation'. It also takes considerable patience.

The second point is that the committees lack any power to subpoena witnesses and documents or to take testimony under oath. In some cases, persons against whom discrimination has been alleged have refused to meet representatives of the conciliation committee. The Board, in its first report, accordingly asked the Government to consider whether, with appropriate safeguards, there should be a power to compel attendance before the committee, or the disclosure of information to it. The Board reported that, despite doubts expressed when the Bill was being debated in Parliament, it had not proved difficult to establish whether or not discrimination had taken place in those areas where the law was unambiguous. In public houses, for example, there is a simple preliminary test: does the establishment normally serve coloured people? The committees have experienced little difficulty in such cases. On the other hand, where the law was ambiguous, the problems were found to be considerable. For example, in at least two cases where it was doubtful whether certain hotels fell within the scope of the Act, the respondents simply refused to talk with the conciliation officer concerned or members of the committee. Their silence could be construed as a sufficient admission of discriminatory conduct to establish a prima facie case against them; but conciliation as envisaged by the Act is rendered impossible without powers to compel the attendance of the parties and witnesses.

In the absence of these powers, the ability to reach a settlement depends primarily on the tact and persuasiveness of the conciliation officers and committee members. Of the five officers attached to local committees, two are ex-probation officers, one is a former civil servant, one was previously in child welfare work and the other is an ex-chief superintendent of police. Their success is shown by the fact that up to 30 November, 1967, of 220 cases falling within the scope of the Act, 62 had been settled by conciliation.[1]

If the committee is unable to secure a settlement, or if it appears to the committee that an assurance is not being complied with, the committee must report the matter to the Race Relations Board. If it appears to the Board that there has been a 'course of discrimination' which is likely to continue it must report the matter to the Attorney-General (or the Lord Advocate in Scotland). Up to 30 November 1967, four cases had been so referred. Only at this stage does the possibility of a legal sanction arise. The Attorney-General may institute civil proceedings in England and Wales in either a county court or the High Court (the former is likely to be preferred for reasons of convenience and expense). The court, if satisfied that there has been a course of discrimination contrary to the statute in which the defendant is likely to persist, may grant an injunction restraining further acts of discrimination. If the defendant defies the order he will be subject to further proceedings for contempt of court which could, in theory, result in a fine or imprisonment.

A series of anomalies in this procedure have revealed themselves. The first is that the Board can refer a matter to the Attorney-General

1. Of the remainder, 103 were not substantiated and 51 were still under investigation. Statistics of the number of complaints received in the first year of the Act's operation are given in the Introduction above, p. 3

only if there is a 'course of conduct'. But (as was indicated earlier) the committees are apparently competent to intervene where there is only a single act and if they fail to secure a settlement they must make a report to the Board. Unless a single act is to be construed as a 'course of conduct' for the purposes of the Act (even lawyers would have difficulty in stretching words that far!) there may be cases which cannot go beyond the Board, which has no power to impose any type of sanction. Secondly, in addition to a 'course of conduct' there must be a likelihood that that conduct will continue before the matter may be referred to the Attorney-General. The Board has had cases in which discrimination has been admitted but the discriminator has refused to give an acceptable assurance against further discrimination. But without a likelihood of continuance there is no action the Board can take.

Finally, the Attorney-General is not able to seek an injunction unless there is a 'course of conduct' and a likelihood of continuance. In proving this, the Attorney-General not only faces the difficulties of proof discussed in Chapter 6,[1] but is further limited by section 3 (2) of the 1965 Act which provides that in such proceedings:

evidence of any communication made to the Race Relations Board, a local conciliation committee, or any officer or servant of the Board or of such a committee . . . shall not be admitted except with the consent of the party by whom it was made.

The purpose of this provision is to preserve the confidentiality of the conciliation process so as not to inhibit the respondent at that stage. However, the section is so worded that it excludes from evidence an assurance against further discrimination where it is subsequently alleged that there has been a breach of the assurance. It also excludes communications made in the course of investigation of complaints, before an attempt at conciliation has been made. Apart from this, the Board has pointed out that the delay inherent in the intervention of the Attorney-General, and the fact that both the Attorney-General and the judge who hears the case must exercise their discretion may 'reduce the effectiveness of the sanction of the law'. The significance of this, in the Board's experience, was that 'conciliation would have been virtually impossible were it not for the sanctions provided by the Act'. It can be added that in other legal contexts (for example actions by ratepayers to challenge the legality of local authorities' expenditure) actions brought

1. Above, p. 102. In three cases referred to him during the first eighteen months of the Act's operation, the Attorney-General decided that, on the evidence available to him, he would not be justified in taking court proceedings, although in each case the Board was satisfied that there was a course of discriminatory conduct which was likely to continue

by the Attorney-General at the instance of some other person are on the decline, the practice increasingly being to allow the aggrieved person to bring the action on his own behalf. There seems little justification for reverting to the old practice in the case of racial discrimination.

To some extent the lack of solicitude which the 1965 Act reveals for the complainant is related to the inadequacy of the remedies provided. Section 1 (4) provides that apart from the proceedings for an injunction, no other civil or criminal proceedings may be brought in respect of unlawful discrimination. To this there is one exception: if the discrimination was already unlawful at common law the aggrieved person may pursue both his common law remedies and those provided under the Act. In all other cases he must content himself with making a complaint to the local committee. The absurdity to which this leads is that a person refused accommodation at a hotel or refused the services of a common carrier on racial grounds has both a civil remedy for damages and an administrative remedy because these types of discrimination were unlawful at common law. But a person refused service in a restaurant or barred from a dance-hall on racial grounds has only the administrative remedy. Either the Act ought to have abandoned the common law remedies entirely or it ought to have been consistent and allowed all those discriminated against a civil remedy. In the U.S.A. many states have retained the private action for damages in addition to the administrative remedy for discrimination. This has the advantage of affording the injured party pecuniary redress where appropriate and of keeping the administrative commission on its toes. Less satisfactory has been the practice in some states of requiring the complainant to elect between the civil and administrative remedies. Where he chooses the former the state is deprived of the opportunity of following up an instance of discrimination which might be part of a larger pattern in a particular place which the commission is investigating. Most satisfactory of all appears to be the practice of empowering the commission itself to make an award of damages. This serves the dual purpose of affording compensation to the victim and providing a monetary deterrent against discrimination.

Ultimately, the success of any anti-discrimination agency, within the limits imposed by the law, will depend upon the amount of money spent upon it, and the judicious use of its funds. In the financial year 1966–7 (up to 28 February 1967) the Board's expenditure was £16,951 14s. 3d., of which most (around £14,000) went on Board members' fees (only the chairman is employed on a full-time basis) and staff salaries (including legal adviser's fees). Expense on publications was included in a figure for 'miscellaneous' items (including, as well, press cutting services, hospitality, etc.) of £442 16s. 7d. Publications during that year consisted mainly of a pamphlet explaining how to make a complaint of discrimination. (Arrangements were made to display copies of this in post offices, employment exchanges, town halls and elsewhere.) However, in the year 1967–8 the Board's budget is much greater and it is expanding its publicity considerably, in particular by the publication of a quarterly bulletin. Another useful form of publicity has been the visits of Board members to various areas where they drew the attention of local politicians and officers and the general public (through the local press) to the work of the Board.

Despite its obvious successes in a limited field of operation, there was by the summer of 1967 a growing sense of frustration among those administering the Act at the inadequacy of its sanctions, the complicated nature of its machinery and, above all, the fact that it covered only the periphery of racial discrimination. Perhaps the most important of all the work done by the Board in this early period of its existence was its commissioning (with the N.C.C.I.) of the P.E.P. Report and a study of foreign legislation and the form that amending legislation could take.[1] Instead of becoming, as some critics had feared, a mere postman for complaints of discrimination, the Board succeeded, by means of these two reports and intensive lobbying, in lifting itself by its own bootstraps.

EMPLOYMENT DISCRIMINATION: THE ALTERNATIVES

What alternative forms of legislation were available to the Government when it decided that racial discrimination in employment[2] should be illegalized? The basic feature of the 1965 Act, namely the stress on conciliation, was obviously destined to become the nucleus of any fresh legislation. But there were several possibilities for the precise way in which each stage of the proceedings could be shaped.

1. *The Race Relations Board and local conciliation committees.* The advantages of entrusting the administration of the law to an independent Board rather than a Government department are that (a) decisions in individual cases are not subject to political controversy; (b) a body of expertise dedicated to the eradication of discrimination can be built up; and (c) complaints against Government organs can be independently

1. See above, Introduction, p. 6
2. The scope of the proposed law, the areas of employment it could cover and possible exemptions were discussed above, p. 30

investigated. For these reasons, the Street Report proposed that the present structure of the Board and its local conciliation committees should be retained, but that they should be considerably expanded and strengthened (in particular by giving Board members full-time tenure for at least five years). Local conciliation committees would continue to be responsible for handling complaints in the first instance and the precise work given to the professional conciliation officers would be a matter of administrative convenience. The query which this prompts is whether even a relatively large number of voluntary committee members will be able to cope with their added responsibilities. An increasing case load and novel problems of proof will surely demand more professionalism in the work of conciliation and investigation, so enabling the committees to concentrate on their important educational and publicity functions.

2. *The complaint.* A major defect of complaint-based procedures is that individuals are able to allocate the Board's resources. For example, if an individual lodges a complaint against a small bakery this will take precedence over the public interest in investigating a large banking institution which, there is reason to believe, practises a discriminatory policy but against which no specific complaint has been filed. The investigation of the bank's employment policies is likely to yield far more employment opportunities for coloured people than the inquiry into the small bakery, but it is the latter which will have to be investigated.

There are three ways out of this dilemma. The first is to confer self-initiating powers on the Board. This would enable committees to investigate without a formal complaint and, when evidence of discrimination is found, to set the conciliation and enforcement process into operation. A second way is to enable, if not encourage, outside bodies such as trade unions and organizations of ethnic minorities to report discrimination. The third and most controversial solution is to require reports from employers and unions giving details of employees and members classified according to race. This is tied up with the first proposal, because if the returns disclose possible discrimination, the Board would be expected to use its self-initiating powers to launch an investigation. Title VII of the Civil Rights Act 1964 has such a requirement and the form in current use by the Equal Employment Opportunity Commission inquires about the number of members of minority groups employed in the various departments of the firm and their grades and responsibilities. This represents a drastic change from earlier American practice. In the early years of state anti-discrimination laws it was believed that to permit a person's race to be recorded would facilitate discrimination, and elaborate rulings were issued prohibiting many varieties of pre-employment inquiry designed to reveal an applicant's racial group. Today, the official view in the U.S.A. is that the keeping of records facilitates the proof, and hence elimination of discrimination.

The Street Report proposed that current American practice be followed in a limited form, namely by making it a term of conciliation agreements that employers should make periodic reports about the racial distribution of their labour force. This would assist the Board in checking-up whether agreements were being complied with. The proposal goes far beyond present administrative practice (although prior to 1962 a tally was kept of the number of *coloured* persons employed[1]) by which persons may be classified according to citizenship and birthplace but not race or colour. The innovation could be justified on the grounds that discrimination does occur against certain social categories on racial pretexts and it is impossible to alter entrenched discriminatory practices without knowing their extent and location. Against this it may be argued that the very task of collecting racial statistics compels people to become conscious of race, whereas the aim should be to lessen racial awareness. There is always a danger that a vast collection of computerized data about racial origins will be used in a discriminatory fashion. Many practical administrative problems present themselves: is the individual to be asked what his racial group is (a question which many would find offensive and suggestive of a discriminatory intent)? Or is the employer to judge by appearances (which may be deceptive)? Or is the nefarious South African practice of subjecting individuals to racial classification by a quasi-judicial process to be emulated? No doubt it is desirable that official statistics should be collected on a more realistic basis than at present, but the wisdom of making employers keep racial statistics in the present phase of British race relations may be doubted.

3. *Investigation.* This cannot be separated entirely from the stage of conciliation because efficient fact-finding may clarify issues and so hasten agreement. But it should be remembered that without adequate preliminary investigation (is there a prima facie case?) conciliation cannot get off the ground.

Who should investigate complaints of job discrimination? The Street Report proposed that, as would be the case with other types of racial discrimination, the local conciliation committees should be empowered to make the necessary inquiries on receipt of a complaint. A special provision in respect of employment cases would be that the committee would be required to hear evidence of attempts to settle the dispute

1. See above, p. 57

through trade channels. This was aimed at encouraging the growth and improvement of procedures for dealing with grievances at factory, plant and office level. It was hoped that employers would realize that the best way to contest complaints would be to show that the matter had been competently handled by a works committee.

A number of alternative proposals were made by practitioners of industrial relations. First, the T.U.C. favoured the use of the Ministry of Labour's conciliation officers as a means of relating racial integration to broader industrial issues. Against this a working party set up by the Labour Party's National Executive Committee (July 1967) argued that these officers are experienced in handling disputes between the two sides of industry but not individual complaints of this kind, that some complaints might be made against the Ministry itself, and that job discrimination may be closely connected with other forms of racial discrimination (e.g. in housing). It was felt to be more likely that the Race Relations Board would succeed in incorporating experience of industrial relations into its work than that the Ministry would succeed in bringing the experience of race relations into its conciliation service. The Street Report took the view that the administrative confusion which would result from referring one stage of the proceedings in respect of one kind of discrimination to these officers, who would have to be specially trained and recruited for the task, would not be offset by the compensating advantage of utilizing their skill and experience in industrial relations. At the heart of these objections was probably a fear that the Ministry might not take affirmative action against discrimination. The essential feature of the Ministry's conciliation work is that it avoids interfering in a dispute until agreed industrial procedures have been exhausted. The conciliator's task (in the words of the Ministry) is 'to bridge the gap between the two points of view'. The race relations conciliation officer, on the other hand, is primarily concerned to obtain an agreement which signifies the acceptance of a particular policy, that of non-discrimination.[1]

A second proposal was that Ministry of Labour employment exchanges, possibly with the assistance of local employment committees, should investigate complaints of discrimination in relation to recruitment. This was prompted by the knowledge that voluntary industrial procedures are rarely designed to handle this kind of grievance. The objections to the suggestion were: (a) a substantial proportion of immigrants do not find work through the exchanges;[2] (b) those who do not

1. See below, p. 159, for further elaboration of this point
2. See above, p. 70

would generally be unaware of the facilities offered by the exchanges to investigate complaints; (c) some complaints might be made against the exchanges themselves; (d) the exchanges would find it difficult to act impartially (and just as important, they would not *appear* to act impartially) because they are under conflicting pressures to ensure equal opportunity while at the same time satisfying the requirements of employers.

A third proposal, originally suggested by Mr Oscar Hahn (chairman of the West Midlands conciliation committee of the Race Relations Board), was that a complaint made to a local conciliation committee should be referred to a 'fair employment practices committee' that the firm, against which a complaint had been made, would be required to set up. It would then be the statutory duty of the firm's committee to investigate the matter and try to satisfy the complainant. If no satisfactory settlement was reached the local committeee could require further investigation or could investigate the matter itself. The Street Report rejected this proposal on several obvious grounds: (a) it would take some time in each case to set up a committee after receipt of a complaint; (b) there would be no opportunity to subject its constitution and procedures to outside scrutiny; (c) the mechanism of the local conciliation committee would be at a standstill until the firm's committee had reported; and (d) the lengthy delays inevitable under this system would discourage complainants and so frustrate the law's purposes.

A final alternative was that the law could require all complaints to be investigated in the first instance by appropriate voluntary industrial procedures. The Street Report rejected this on the grounds that large segments of industry had no effective machinery, that a substantial section of the labour force is non-unionized and that even if special committees were set up they would not be able to deal adequately with recruitment, nor would they be in a position to impose effective sanctions. Unfortunately, the Street Committee took insufficient account of the way in which the boundaries of the law in industrial relations have been fixed historically and how these boundaries are now being changed. Fairness, speed and effectiveness – the criteria adopted by the Street Committee – are not the only considerations in the framing of industrial legislation. Broader social issues have always predominated in this field. For example, the war-time Conditions of Employment and National Arbitration Order No. 1305 of 1940, and its modified postwar successor, Order No. 1376 of 1951, obliged the Minister to refer trade disputes which came to him to voluntary machinery of negotiation and arbitration, where he was of the opinion that suitable machin-

ery existed and all practicable means of reaching a settlement through
it had not been exhausted. Settlements under the voluntary machinery
were treated as final, but where a dispute could not be so settled, the
Minister had to refer it to a tribunal. A current example is the Industrial
Courts Act 1919 which empowers the Minister to refer a 'trade dispute'
(which by definition might exclude those inspired by racial motives)[1]
for settlement by the Industrial Court but only *after* failure to obtain a
settlement by voluntary means. The Conciliation Act 1896 allows the
Minister to intervene at an earlier stage, but he is still required to take
into consideration the existence and adequacy of available voluntary
means of conciliation. These precedents could be adapted to an anti-
discrimination statute, although there might be controversy about
whether the Minister or the Race Relations Board should exercise control over the proceedings. The crucial issue of the relation between
legal intervention and voluntary control will be discussed at length in
the next chapter.[2]

4. *Conciliation.* The 1965 Act merely requires a local conciliation
committee to attempt conciliation 'where appropriate' and this means,
in theory if not in practice, that the committee is not bound to seek
conciliation even where they find that discrimination has occurred. To
remedy this defect, the Street Report proposed that a committee should
be obliged to attempt conciliation if in its opinion there was 'reasonable
cause' to believe that discrimination had taken place. Their decision on
'reasonable cause' would be final and not appealable: at this stage it is the
calibre of the committee and the influence of the Board which must
provide the guarantee of the fair exercise of discretion rather than judicial review which might enable frivolous complainants and obdurate
respondents to hold up the work of conciliation.

Conciliation would take place in private and evidence obtained
during the process of conciliation (but not that obtained in the investigation stage nor the conciliation agreement itself) would be inadmissible in further proceedings without the consent of the parties. The
terms of conciliation agreements would be in the discretion of local
committees and might go far beyond an assurance against future discrimination.

5. *Hearings to determine the facts.* If conciliation fails because the
parties cannot agree on the facts (e.g. the respondent denies discrimination) definitive fact-finding becomes necessary. As we have seen, the
1965 Act provides no effective means for doing this until an injunction

1. See above, p. 120
2. See below, p. 155

is sought by the Attorney-General. Apart from the courts, either the anti-discrimination commission itself (as in the U.S.A.) or an independent tribunal (as in Ontario) might be entrusted with this task. The advantages of an independent tribunal are that fact-finding is separated from conciliation and the policing of agreements, and public confidence in the law is enhanced by the knowledge that hearings will be speedily, thoroughly and impartially conducted by persons of independent judicial standing. This led the Street Committee to propose the setting up of a race relations tribunal to determine whether unlawful discrimination has taken place. The tribunal would be selected from a panel of members such as county court judges and others appointed by the Lord Chancellor. In employment cases, it suggested, the tribunal could include chairmen of existing industrial tribunals and lay members with industrial experience.

A strong case can be made out for entrusting employment cases to the industrial tribunals rather than the proposed race relations tribunal. The former at present determine appeals by persons assessed to a levy imposed by a training board, deal with references and appeals under the Redundancy Payments Act 1965, and settle disputes in regard to the written statements of their main terms of employment which the Contracts of Employment Act 1963 requires to be given to employees, and disputes about compensation under certain statutory provisions. The Ministry of Labour, in its evidence to the Royal Commission on Trade Unions and Employers' Associations, saw in these tribunals the nucleus of a future system of labour courts in Britain to deal with individual grievances such as unfair dismissals; it is more questionable whether they would be suited to dealing with conciliation in labour disputes. A comparison between these tribunals and the proposed composition and procedures of the race relations tribunal in employment cases reveals basic similarities: as is the case with an industrial tribunal, the chairman of a race relations tribunal would have to be legally-qualified; he would have 'wing-men' drawn from both sides of industry; the tribunal would have the power to compel the attendance of witnesses; hearings would normally be in public and the parties could be legally represented.

Despite these common features, the Street Committee rejected the argument that employment cases should be referred to an industrial tribunal on the grounds that it might not be possible to convene them as quickly as a race relations tribunal. This objection could be met by strengthening the composition of the industrial tribunals. In any event, cases of racial discrimination are unlikely to take up much of the tribunals' time if the experience of Ontario is repeated in Britain. In 800 formal cases dealt with by the Ontario Human Rights Commission between 1962–6, only thirteen public boards of inquiry had to be instituted and in eleven of these the case was satisfactorily resolved at the hearing level. The major advantage which the industrial tribunals enjoy over the projected race relations tribunal is their considerable body of experience in the judicial handling of individual grievances in the employment field. Moreover, once allegations of racial discrimination were referred to these tribunals the way would be opened for them to deal in future with other 'human rights' problems in industry such as sex and age discrimination, victimization of trade unionists and so on. These other civil liberties are so closely related to racial discrimination[1] that it would be desirable for them all to be dealt with as part of the work of labour courts. The only advantage which can be seen in utilizing a separate race relations tribunal is that the expertise of race relations may be more useful in some cases than that of industrial conflict and a proliferation of tribunals dealing with issues of race relations may be undesirable.

Whatever form of tribunal is preferred, the advantage which such tribunals enjoy over the ordinary courts of law is that proceedings before them are relatively cheap, expeditious and free from technicality. The latter aim is served by freeing the tribunal from the formal rules of evidence applicable in the courts. This means that the tribunal can obtain information from any available source, provided the information is of some probative value and that all the parties are given an opportunity to comment on or contradict that information. This would enable the tribunal to consider evidence which might be inadmissible in an ordinary court.[2] The Street Report paid relatively little attention to the problems of proof at the hearing stage. Yet there is a very real danger that the effective enforcement of an anti-discrimination law might be defeated at the evidentiary stage. There is usually little difficulty in deciding whether or not there is 'reasonable cause' for the purposes of proceeding to conciliation. At the hearing stage, however, it may be impossible for the complainant to succeed if the tribunal obliges him to prove the reasons for the respondent's actions. At the same time, it would be unfair to cast the burden of disproving discrimination on the respondent since this might inhibit his legitimate free choice of labour. The solution appears to be that the tribunal should cast the initial burden of introducing evidence from which racial discrimination

1. See above, p. 23
2. See above, p. 102

might reasonably be inferred on the complainant. It would then be for the respondent to show that his actions complained of were for reasons other than racial discrimination. For example, if a rejected job applicant could show that he possessed the objective qualifications for the job in question, the employer could then be asked to justify his actions as non-discriminatory. The ultimate success of the law might depend on the skilful manipulation of the requirements of proof by the tribunal.

6. *Remedial orders.* The Street Report proposed that the tribunal should recommend to the Race Relations Board what form the order should take once discrimination was found. The reason for this round-about procedure is that only the Board is capable of making the kind of policy decisions which must enter into the shaping of the remedial order. In addition, the Board could continue its attempts at a settlement while discussing the form the order might take with the respondent.

Among the orders which could be made, if the Street proposals are adopted, would be: (a) a direction that the respondent shall cease and desist from the discriminatory conduct in question; (b) a requirement that the discriminator must post non-discriminatory policy notices at his place of business; (c) an order for the payment of damages (the amount having been assessed by the tribunal) in respect of pecuniary loss, including loss of employment, but not in respect of non-pecuniary losses such as humiliation and emotional distress or in the nature of punitive damages;[1] (d) a requirement that a body statutorily authorized to revoke the respondent's licence should convene a hearing to consider revocation of the licence; (e) an order against the employer to hire, re-instate, promote, admit to a training scheme, offer the next vacancy to the complainant or offer him the same facilities as other employees;[2] (f) an order against a trade union or employers' association to admit, or withdraw a decision to exclude, or to cease discrimination against a person. In all these cases the Board would be entitled to take steps to ensure that their orders were being obeyed.

7. *Role of the courts.* If one of the Board's orders was not complied with, or if the respondent violated the terms of a conciliation agreement, the law would have to impose a sanction. The precise form of this sanction may not be very important since few cases are likely to go

1. The exclusions are consistent with common law attitudes in respect of damages for breach of the contract of employment (see above, p. 107) but not, as regards aggravating features such as humiliation, in respect of tort actions (see the comment on Constantine's case, above, p. 106). It would obviously be undesirable to allow punitive damages since this would introduce a criminal sanction by the back door.

2. This proposal goes far beyond statutory precedents which authorize an order for *reinstatement*, since a job may have to be offered to someone with whom there has never been a contractual relationship: see above, p. 108

this far. In Ontario, only one criminal prosecution for breach of an order has taken place; in the U.S.A. very few instances are recorded, although this might be due in part to unsatisfactory follow-up procedures. The fact that four cases had to be referred to the Attorney-General in the first eighteen months of the Race Relations Act's operation[1] is a reflection on the ambiguity of the present law, the absence of subpoena powers and the complex nature of the machinery. The new procedures, proposed in the Street Report, would keep cases out of court by remedying these defects. For the few cases that do reach court, the alternatives are criminal prosecution (as in Ontario) or contempt proceedings in which the court would have powers similar to those now available to the High Court for non-compliance with an injunction it has decreed. The latter seems preferable because of the stricter standard of proof required in criminal proceedings and the greater possibility of a settlement (in the form of an undertaking to obey the order in future) in civil proceedings.

It would also be necessary to make available to the Board a power to seek interlocutory injunctions in the courts after there has been a finding of 'reasonable cause' by a local conciliation committee. In employment cases, the Board may wish the respondent to be restrained from filling the job until consideration of the complaint has been concluded. The grant of an injunction is always at the discretion of the court and there may be understandable reluctance to restrain an employer in this way, without some guarantee that the Board will make good his loss should the complaint prove to be unfounded. Apart from this, injunctions are most likely to be granted in circumstances where an employer complains that he is threatened by a strike if he obeys an order to employ coloured workers. As we have seen,[2] such conduct might entitle an employer at common law to damages and an injunction.

The other area of judicial intervention which might be expected is that the courts would have power to quash a decision made in circumstances in which the tribunal or the Board had no jurisdiction or in which bias had been shown or there was a failure to give a fair hearing, or in which the record showed that there had been an error of law. Any further appeal to the courts on question of fact or law might result in a loss of the advantages which flow from entrusting these matters to the Board and tribunal.

8. *Alternative remedies.* There are several circumstances in which a victim of discrimination may have a common law remedy[3] in addition

1. See above, p. 139
2. See above, p. 122
3. See above, Chapter 7, p. 109. For American practice, see p. 141

to the remedies provided by an anti-discrimination statute. The Street Report did not favour the abolition of these common law causes of action. Instead it proposed that the local conciliation committee could include in a conciliation agreement a term that the complainant would not pursue his claim for damages in the ordinary courts. In addition, the statute could include provisions to avoid the duplication of damages.

It might also be necessary to avoid the duplication of administrative remedies. For example, if industrial tribunals obtain jurisdiction to hear allegations of unfair dismissal there might be an overlap with the powers of the race relations machinery to deal with racial dismissals. This is a further argument in favour of centralizing all employment discrimination cases in the hands of a single, labour tribunal.

In conclusion, it must be remembered, as the Street Report stressed, that 'there is no necessary correlation between the quality of the drafting of a code concerning racial discrimination and the effectiveness of that code in operation'. Other measures are essential, such as whole-hearted support and financial backing from the Government, adequate enforcement machinery and an extensive educational programme. Moreover, the fact that it is feasible, from a legal standpoint, to devise a workable anti-discrimination statute does not mean that it is desirable to utilize legal controls in preference to voluntary procedures. The interaction between legal and voluntary controls must be considered in the next chapter.

Part Three

TOWARDS EQUAL EMPLOYMENT OPPORTUNITIES

9. The Role of Voluntary Procedures

In Part One the substantive rules[1] of industrial relations which affect persons differently because of their race were described. Broadly speaking, these are of two kinds. First, there are those which form part of the *internal* system of job regulation within particular enterprises: for example, shop floor understandings about quotas of coloured labour, promotion barriers, sharing of overtime work, ethnic work-units, and the separation of toilet and canteen facilities. These are described as internal, because they are settled autonomously within the enterprise.

On the other hand, there are a number of other rules of an *external* nature, in that they depend upon the participation and consent of persons and bodies outside the enterprise: for example, the policy of Ministry of Labour exchanges regarding discriminatory job referrals, collective agreements between unions and management (either restricting or protecting foreign labour), the intervention of union officials (normally) against discriminatory conduct within the enterprise, the non-discriminatory admissions policies of unions, vocational training schemes for immigrants, and legal rules.

These external rules are themselves of two kinds, depending on the type of procedure which is used to make, interpret and enforce the substantive rules. Those which are *legal* can, in the event of violation, be enforced by some compulsory mechanism provided by the state. They may take the form of criminal penalties, or civil remedies (such as an award of damages) or administrative enforcement (such as the procedure under the Race Relations Act). Those procedures which are *voluntary*, on the other hand, rest on moral or social sanctions, above all

---

1. 'Rules' is used as a generic term to describe all the means by which jobs are regulated, including custom, trade union practices, conventions, managerial decisions, collective agreements and laws

the threat of withdrawal of labour or dismissal. These voluntary sanctions are often far more effective and significant than the legal ones.

The key to an understanding of the changes which are taking place in regard to racial discrimination in industry lies in an appreciation of three levels of conflict over this issue: between the external rules and the internal ones, between legal and voluntary procedures, and between conflicting interests within the enterprise.

The internal rules, as we have seen, are the product of many causes. These include the economic needs of management to fill jobs local white workers do not want, managerial decisions to form ethnic work units because of language difficulties with Asian immigrants, and the racial prejudices of receptionists, gatekeepers and others who turn away coloured work-seekers. These rules share in common two features: they are principally derived from the attitudes and decisions of management, and they are rules which are deep-seated in the system of each enterprise. They result from such basic motives as the drive for maximum profitability, personal psychological tensions, fear of strangers, colour/status consciousness and so on. These rules, because of their deep roots, have not, nor are they likely *by themselves* to show any change in direction. And their present direction, we have seen, may be increasingly discriminatory.

The external rules, on the other hand, are showing all the symptoms of change. To appreciate this it must be understood that the principal feature of the traditional system of job regulation as it affected ethnic minorities is that the competition of the labour market was restricted by rules aimed at limiting the supply of labour and the terms on which competition could take place. In this sense, the limitations on foreign labour fall into roughly the same category as limitations on the number of apprentices, distinctions between men's and women's work, the requirement of union membership and so on. Opportunities to enter contracts of employment and the terms of work, were restricted by agreement between unions and management. We have noted those instances in which this was done on the basis of nationality, and less frequently, race or colour.

At the same time it is of considerable significance that these limitations on competition were almost exclusively achieved through the voluntary process. The sanctions were social. After the demise of slavery, legal sanctions to enforce the limitation of opportunities on grounds of race were virtually non-existent except in the shipping industry. The simple explanation for this phenomenon was that the problem did not exist elsewhere. There is nothing inherent in the nature of law to prevent it being used to achieve discrimination – as anyone familiar with the South African legal system would admit. In Britain, the law was not called upon to play any role (except marginally in the form of Commonwealth immigration control, 'conditions of entry' on aliens and the like) because the problem was sufficiently small to be dealt with by voluntary controls. This traditional system rested upon a set of values appropriate to the colonial era, with all its notions of national and racial superiority.

Since the Second World War, however, a new set of values has become predominant, inspired in part by the process of decolonization and the search for a new relationship with coloured peoples. The extent to which there is ambivalence in the implementation of the new values of racial equality is a measure of the doubt which still exists among British people about how to deal with the coloured population in their midst. Gradually, however, the notions of integration and equal opportunity are taking hold, becoming, for their part, a material force in changing the old system.

The changes are reflected in the new external rules which are taking shape: legislation which makes employment discrimination on racial grounds illegal, joint policy declarations by the T.U.C. and C.B.I. and, possibly most significant of all, the evolution of voluntary procedures to deal with racial discrimination in employment.

It is, indeed, the competing claims of the legal and voluntary procedures to implement the new set of values which forms the second level of conflict in regard to racial discrimination in industry. The T.U.C. and the C.B.I. would have preferred to exclude legal procedures entirely. The challenge of government intervention inspired them to develop the idea of new voluntary systems, and the legislative scheme which has emerged will 'provide the fullest possible opportunity for industry to use its own machinery for conciliation'.[1] The preference for voluntary procedures and the nature of the compromise which has been reached with those immigrant and political groups who wanted legal controls can only be understood in the light of the traditional system of industrial relations in Britain.

Allan Flanders has summed up the principal features of this system under three heads.[2] First, 'a priority is accorded to collective bargaining over other methods of external job regulation'. The distinctive feature of collective bargaining is that trade unions and employers regulate employment contracts and, incidentally, their own relations, some-

---

1. Home Secretary: 750 H.C. Deb., col. 747 (26 July 1967)
2. *Industrial Relations: What is Wrong with the System?* (London 1965) pp. 21–8

times using third-party assistance in the form of mediation, conciliation and arbitration. The other methods of external job regulation, such as trade union working rules, regulations of employers' associations and social convention have been far less important, historically, than the system of collective bargaining. In particular, state regulation has been used principally 'to cover those areas of employment where organization was inadequate to sustain voluntary collective bargaining'. Law has been treated as an inferior substitute, establishing minimum standards which can be improved upon by negotiated agreements and normally including built-in safeguards against their replacing such agreements.[1] Moreover, collective bargaining has had relatively little legal support (one of the cases where it has, is the procedure under the Terms and Conditions of Employment Act 1959, s. 8[2]). The reason for this is that it was realized that greater legal support would mean greater legal regulation over bargaining, as is the case in the U.S.A. In Britain, the preference for autonomy in collective bargaining is central to the system and rests upon a deep-seated reluctance to allow the state to intervene to protect any public interest that the parties are thought to be infringing.

This leads to Flanders' second point: 'The British system of industrial relations has traditionally accorded a priority to voluntary over compulsory procedural rules for collective bargaining.' This feature is admirably summed up in the Ministry of Labour's *Industrial Relations Handbook:*

It has been continuous policy for many years to encourage the two sides of industry to make agreements and to settle their differences for themselves, and no action . . . is normally taken by the Minister or his officials unless any negotiating machinery suitable for dealing with disputes has been fully used and has failed to effect a settlement. The overriding principle is that where there is a procedure drawn up by an industry for dealing with disputes, that procedure should be followed. Even where there is no agreed procedure of this kind it is desirable that the parties themselves should make an endeavour to reach a settlement.[3]

Flanders' third point is that 'the parties to collective bargaining in this country have generally preferred to build their relations more on their procedural than on their substantive rules'. This highlights the emphasis in Britain on procedural rules intended to regulate conflict, and the relative neglect of codified substantive rules about wages and

1. See e.g. Wages Council Act 1959, s. 3
2. Above, p. 114
3. 1961 ed., pp. 134-5

other conditions. 'A premium is being placed on industrial peace' comments Flanders 'and less regard is being paid to the terms on which it may be obtained.' The immediate relevance of this third feature of the system to the question of racial discrimination needs little underlining. It explains why rules against discrimination have not been expressly formulated and why certain discriminatory practices have been left undisturbed for so long. The system has been preoccupied with reaching a durable compromise, a state of industrial peace, rather than with securing the rights of minority ethnic groups. Incidentally, as well, one can observe that the notion of 'conciliation' which is found in the Race Relations Act may be miles apart from the type of 'conciliation' which is common in industrial practice. The latter means the intervention of third parties to bring the warring parties together and help them settle their differences by persuasion resulting in a compromise. The Race Relations Act procedure, on the other hand, is aimed at 'a settlement and assurance against further discrimination'. A particular result is aimed at and not simply industrial peace.

In the past, the system of industrial autonomy has been strengthened by the negotiation of national agreements in particular industries, and this has placed the parties in a stronger position to resist outside intervention. The basic values on which this autonomy was based were economic freedom ('free' collective bargaining, 'free' trade unions and so on) and industrial peace. Unlike the United States, the role of government was essentially as a peacemaker rather than a 'pacemaker'. The great advantages of this system were seen to lie in its flexibility, being guided by the spirit rather than the letter of industrial relations, and the responsibility it cast upon the two sides to compromise and stand by their agreements. These values have underlain the approach of the T.U.C. and C.B.I. to the question of racial discrimination. The advantages of flexibility, they believe, will be demonstrated in dealing with questions like quotas; and their 'responsibility' for industrial peace makes it essential that they superintend grievances of all kinds, including those about discrimination, which may later develop into disputes. Their approach is one which sees the need to subject individual complaints to autonomous grievance procedures which will achieve a rough justice for victims of discrimination, while maintaining the more important objective of industrial peace.

Peace, however, is not the only aim which the system is expected to serve. And the trade unions have always acknowledged and actively promoted the obligation of the state to prevent the worst forms of exploitation of labour. Protective labour legislation established minimum standards which indirectly led to an improvement in the standards of all workers. The unions led the movement for shorter hours for children and women because, in the case of children, combination was impossible, and because they realized that the competition of unprotected women and children which threatened to lengthen the working day of adult men, could best be regulated by the *legal* limitation of their hours. By setting the law in motion for women, the men's unions aimed at the virtual shortening of their own hours. In this they were not disappointed. Reporting in 1911, on the first half-century's experience of regulation of the conditions of women and children the leading historians state:

The best of the manufacturers . . . are found voluntarily reducing the working day to one, two or even three hours less than the maximum permitted by law. In the lower class tailoring and dressmaking, on the contrary, and in the industries to which the Act has not yet been applied, or in which it is insufficiently enforced, we find that the long hours that characterized the factory industry fifty or sixty years ago still prevail. . . .[1]

Paradoxically, the group which argued strongly against the limitation of women's hours was not labour, but the middle-class women's rights movement, which claimed that this special 'privilege' for women would result in employers preferring not to employ women, thus prejudicing their opportunities in employment. Today the roles appear to be reversed because middle-class organizations are in the forefront of the demands for legal intervention, and trade unions oppose it. This appearance is, however, misleading. The trade unions see in the problem of racial discrimination a wider question of conflict between workers and management about wages, conditions and security, and not simply one of fixing of certain objective minimum conditions of the kind found in the Nine Hours' Act. They perceive the need for flexible instruments to deal with attitudes, expectations and fears.

This traditional system is being subjected not only to growing government intervention against discrimination, but also to other, more central challenges by which autonomy is being subjected to national policies. Above all else, the government's response to economic difficulties in the form of a national incomes policy is causing a reassessment of the traditional boundaries of law and voluntary procedures. At the same time, as Flanders has noted, there is another striking development in the form of an upsurge of work-place bargaining. This has led to a declining role for joint consultation, a

1. B. L. Hutchins & A. Harrison, *A History of Factory Legislation* (London, 2nd rev. ed. 1911), pp. 198–9

weakening of industry-wide agreements and the transference of authority in unions from full-time officials to shop stewards at the workplace. The relevance of these developments for the question of racial discrimination ought to be fairly obvious. Attempts to legislate a wages policy may misleadingly be used both for and against those wishing to legislate against racial discrimination: for, by those who see in this a sign of growing legal intervention in collective bargaining; against, by those who oppose the wages policy and fail to distinguish the legislation against discrimination from other attempts at legal intervention. On the other hand, the growth of work-place bargaining presents a challenge to external controls over discrimination: how far is it possible to ensure that this healthy growth of democracy at the work-place is not won at the expense of ethnic minorities? This emphasizes the need for racial discrimination to be controlled by truly national and centralized policies, which will complement work-place bargaining and allow it greater freedom, provided that it is compatible with the national norm of non-discrimination. Sectional agreements in particular industries, negotiated on a piecemeal basis, are unlikely to be able to provide both the control over, and impetus to work-place bargaining that is required.

It remains to consider a third level of conflict which affects the control of racial discrimination in employment. 'Blame it on the unions', 'Blame it on industry' are catchphrases of those who fail to understand the real nature of the problem. They view each industrial enterprise as they would a team in which everyone pulls his weight towards a common objective. This vision of a 'partnership' becomes in relation to the question of racial discrimination, a black picture of conspiracy by workers and managers against defenceless ethnic minorities. This has little in common with the methods and findings of social science. Industrial organizations are made up of sectional groups with divergent interests and, in the words of Alan Fox, 'the degree of common purpose which can exist in industry is only of a very limited nature'.[1]

Once the existence of these conflicting interests is accepted, it becomes necessary to examine specific cases and attempt to analyse the real causes of what at first sight may appear to be racial grievances. So when 300 women workers walked out of a West Bromwich factory after a fifteen-year-old Jamaican girl had started work there in February 1967, a trade union official (well-known for his strong opposition to racial discrimination) found that this was the culmination of a long series of disputes with management and once their other grievances

---

1. *Industrial Sociology and Industrial Relations.* Royal Commission on Trade Unions and Employers' Associations, Research Paper 3 (H.M.S.O. 1966), p. 4

were examined by the management, the women returned to work on the understanding that they would work alongside coloured employees in future.[1] Sophisticated bargaining is required: a *quid pro quo* may be needed in some instances to induce workers to withdraw their objections to foreign labour in return for greater security for all workers in the enterprise. The recognition of these conflicting sectional interests also leads to a realization that group solidarity is not to be condemned out of hand. Individuals who reject this and appear to undermine it by refusing to accept its values are seen to be threatening the basis on which rests the advancement – through collective action – of their fellows. So, for example, if coloured workers who suffer discrimination go *first* to an outside body like the Race Relations Board without attempting to rely on group solidarity to resolve the individual injustice they have suffered, they will be seen by other workers as social deviants. Their position as individuals may for this reason not be improved. Instead, they may find themselves even more isolated and rejected than they were before lodging their complaints with an outside body.

All this implies a central role to the trade unions in controlling racial discrimination. It suggests the growth of centralized, national agreements on racial discrimination which will ensure:

(a) that all aggrieved persons have a right to present a complaint either through normal disputes procedures or, where these are inadequate, through special procedures;
(b) that all interested parties are given a hearing;
(c) that those who are forced to discriminate because of the pressure by others, are protected;
(d) that justice (in the sense of an assurance against future discrimination) is obtained.

The extent to which legislation has to be invoked will be a measure of the failure of unions and management to build and operate the appropriate voluntary procedures.

In the light of this, we must ask two questions: to what extent, if at all, is the American experience of the role of law in controlling job discrimination relevant; and what procedures of a voluntary kind are being evolved in Britain?

IS AMERICAN EXPERIENCE RELEVANT?[2]

The most convincing argument for legislation is its apparent success in

1. *The Times*, 23 February 1967
2. For a detailed description of how the American laws work, the reader may consult the studies mentioned in the bibliography

the United States and Canada. At the beginning of the Second World War discontent among Negroes at their exclusion from employment in government and defence industries led President Roosevelt to promulgate an Executive Order prohibiting discrimination in these industries. This in turn served as the foundation for similar orders by Presidents Truman, Eisenhower, Kennedy and Johnson. Thirty-nine states with about two-thirds of the population of the Union have enacted legislation which is based on it. In 1964 Congress enacted Title VII of the Civil Rights Act which for the first time outlaws employment discrimination throughout the U.S.A. In Canada, there has been a federal Fair Employment Practices Law since 1953 and eight of the provinces (including Ontario which started the process in 1951) have their own laws against employment discrimination.

The leading study of Fair Employment Practice (F.E.P.) laws sums up the American experience as follows:

In states and cities having established and enforceable laws, racial discrimination in employment is considerably less prevalent to-day than it was prior to the enactment of the laws. There are good grounds for believing that the existence of the laws and the efforts of the F.E.P. agencies in administering them have been significant factors in bringing about the change.[1]

The best evidence that these laws have brought about a significant reduction in employment discrimination is obtainable from reviews of cases handled by the Commissions set up to administer the laws. The New York State Commission for Human Rights conducts regular reviews of cases in which complaints of discrimination have been settled, in order to ascertain whether subsequent to the settlement there has been an overall improvement in the position of Negroes in relation to the particular firm. As early as 1951 the New York Commission (established in 1945 and the first of its kind) was able to report that in 85 per cent of the previously concluded valid complaint cases there had subsequently been a definite improvement in the employment pattern as compared with the conditions which existed at the time the original complaints had been filed. These changes were reflected in substantial increases in the number of members of different racial groups employed in professional, technical, skilled, semi-skilled and unskilled job categories.[2] Follow-up reviews conducted in subsequent

1. Paul H. Norgren and Samuel E. Hill, *Toward Fair Employment* (New York and London 1964), p. 115
2. N.Y. State Commission against Discrimination, *Annual Report* 1951, pp. 7–8. In the period 1945–64 8,379 complaints alleging employment discrimination on grounds of race, creed, colour and national origin, were filed: N.Y. State Commission for Human Rights, *Annual Report* 1964, p. 11

years have shown continuing improvement in racial employment patterns. Of thirteen banking concerns in which follow-up reviews were conducted in 1958, anything from two to ten years after the original complaint had been filed, seven showed marked increases and three modest increases in the number of Negroes employed and in their occupational status. Similar improvements were recorded in respect of insurance companies and department stores, a major breakthrough in view of the traditional resistance to Negro employment in white-collar and sales work.[1]

American researches have indicated tangible reductions in employment discrimination since the advent of the laws in other states and cities as well, although the extent of their progress has been considerably short of that in New York. The reason for greater success in New York than elsewhere is to be found in the superior organization, composition and general approach of its Commission. In particular the New York Commission has considerably greater funds than the other state and municipal commissions and consequently it employs more staff, encourages geographic specialization, and instead of contenting itself with the adjustment of individual complaints has consistently required employers to commit themselves to an over-all revision of their employment policies and practices. It has insisted on what has become known as the 'affirmative action' approach. As they stand, the Fair Employment Practice Laws merely require an employer to hire and promote the best qualified applicants regardless of race. In practice Negroes are likely to be less well qualified than whites because of inferior educational backgrounds. In many cases the educational standards set by employers are unnecessarily high, and as a result few Negroes are employed. To overcome this the New York Commission (now increasingly emulated in other states) tries to get employers to commit themselves to go beyond a literal observance of the statutes and to take affirmative steps to recruit and employ Negroes above the level of unskilled labour. This does not mean employing Negroes who are less well qualified than whites; it involves a reassessment of educational requirements and positive attempts to recruit Negro applicants.

Another advantage accruing to the New York Commission as a result of its substantial budget has been the ability to conduct follow-up reviews to ensure that employers are complying with orders that have been made. In Ontario, the Human Rights Commission has achieved a similar result by engaging university research teams to follow up its complaint settlement activities. Perhaps the most significant feature of

1. Norgren and Hill, op. cit., pp. 120 et seq.

the New York Commission's work has been investigations, often on its own initiative, of employment patterns in particular companies and even in entire industries. In other words, it has not limited itself to receiving and investigating individual complaints of discrimination. It has gone beyond this and sought to change overall employment patterns. The areas in which it has been least successful are in regard to federally-financed employment agencies (prior to the enactment of the 1964 Civil Rights Act) and in respect of discrimination by craft unions.

The overall impact of F.E.P. Commissions on Negro inequality has, however, been slight. The laws have opened new fields of employment for Negroes, but in the country as a whole Negroes have for the most part remained in their traditional low-level jobs. While the law has brought about significant changes in the climate of opinion among employers and unions, it has not shattered the basic patterns of inequality which were entrenched long before legislation was introduced. American experts tend to attribute this relative failure of the law to the fact that it came too late to remove entrenched discrimination and that the early laws were weak and inadequately administered.

The general lesson to be learnt from North America is that legislation can be effective in controlling job discrimination, but only if it is backed by adequate enforcement machinery, substantial budgets and a positive approach to their task by those entrusted with administering the law. This experience is useful in evaluating the *inner* structure and operation of the British law against discrimination. For example, such technical matters as how and when to conduct public hearings, the need for subpoena powers, budgetary requirements, and 'conciliation' techniques can be compared and, where appropriate, adaptations of the British machinery can be made.

What the American experience does *not* tell us, is the role that law ought to play in the total social and institutional framework of British industry. This is a point that is overlooked by those who propose a transplantation of American models into the British system. Their approach neglects the essential differences between the two national systems. In the first place, the American 'race' problem has its roots in slavery and reconstruction. By 1900, the Negro was almost completely segregated by law and custom: he rode in separate compartments, went to segregated schools, was buried in separate cemeteries and was relegated to 'Negro' work. Where unions existed, Negroes were either excluded from membership or, where they were too numerous to be excluded, they were organized into racially segregated locals. Unions were among the institutions used to restrict Negro workers from certain kinds of work. Before the 1930s, Negroes and whites rarely belonged to the same unions. Even in the absence of unions, however, Negroes would have been unable to compete equally with whites in the South because of racial prejudices among white employers and the relative lack of qualifications among the emancipated slaves. By 1941, Negroes were still barred from membership of many unions, although some had allowed the development of auxiliary and segregated locals. It was at this time, as we have seen, that pressure from Negro organizations led to the first positive anti-discrimination measures by the federal government, followed after the war by state legislation. In other words, public intervention against discrimination came about in a very different situation in the United States, to that in Britain. Legislation has had to be directed *against* union racial practices in the United States (with considerable success); in Britain, on the other hand, the primary role of legislation will be to stimulate and promote action by unions which already have declared egalitarian policies. Coloured workers are free to join unions, indeed many play an active part in them. This means that legislation must essentially be a 'fall-back' and a stimulant for voluntary action.

In the second place, the belief that legislation ought to be central to the control of discrimination in Britain as in America, is not based on any analysis of the historical development of the British system and of its main features. It ignores the fact that in the United States labour law in general has played an essentially different role from that in Britain.

The argument is sometimes confused by reference to American writings which demonstrate both theoretically and practically that law is *capable* of controlling discrimination and even of changing prejudices. One of the most frequently cited writers is Merton,[1] who has usefully broken down the types of persons who discriminate into three categories: the first is the unprejudiced discriminator (or 'fair-weather liberal'), the second is the prejudiced non-discriminator (or 'fair-weather illiberal') and the third is the prejudiced discriminator (or 'all-weather illiberal'). For those in the first category a legal sanction will control their discriminatory acts. For those in the second and third categories whose racial attitudes have been acquired through indoctrination buttressed by the sanction of social disapproval, a legal sanction against discrimination will stimulate the adoption of new values not only because of fear of the consequences which would otherwise

1. R. K. Merton, 'Discrimination and the American Creed' in *Discrimination and National Welfare* (New York 1949), pp. 103–10

follow, but also because the law against discrimination will come to represent an accepted norm of social conduct. As regards persons who are prejudiced due to personality disorders, the law can control their discriminatory acts (such persons are usually slavish respecters of power!) although it cannot strike at their prejudices. This latter group is not affected by tolerance propaganda at all. As Morroe Berger puts it:

The extremely prejudiced person has a high stake in his bias, which may function to keep his personality integrated; he does not easily succumb to verbalisms which attack his way of maintaining his equilibrium.[1]

Consequently education and voluntary persuasion will be of no value with this group; in their case legal sanctions are the *only* way of controlling discrimination. In sum, law is an effective means to control the outward behaviour of people; in addition, it can have an effect on prejudice both because it induces certain habits of conduct and because of the added weight which a moral principle gains once it is symbolized in legislation.

Now, this analysis is useful because it shows the role that law is capable of playing. But a source of misunderstanding is that what these writers are really discussing is the efficacy of *sanctions* in controlling discrimination. In the American context it was inevitable that these should be seen as *legal* sanctions, because of the weakness or absence of other social or moral sanctions against discrimination. In Britain, however, discrimination and prejudices may more readily be changed by sanctions other than law, for example, moral and social pressures. These are unlikely to be sufficient on their own and for this reason it is essential to have legislation as a fall-back. In sum, while the American experience shows that law is capable of controlling discrimination, it does not answer the question whether it is desirable to use it in Britain in the same way as in America. Our analysis of the traditional and changing role of law in British industrial relations indicates that a role of a *promotional* kind is desirable and possible in Britain.

THE EVOLUTION OF SPECIAL PROCEDURES

The case for legislation against racial discrimination in employment in Britain rests essentially on pragmatic grounds.

From the employers' angle the existence of legislation is a useful excuse for resisting the discriminatory demands of staff or customers.

1. *Equality by Statute* (New York 1952), p. 184, which contains the leading analysis of the case for legislation

It also ensures that he will not face unfair competition from trade rivals who practise discrimination, for it puts all employers on an equal footing by making it difficult for any of them to discriminate. From the unions' angle, officials will be in a stronger position to adopt anti-discriminatory policies. From the coloured workers' point of view, there will be a guarantee that in the event of a failure of the voluntary system they will not be defenceless.

The best evidence that legislation will promote voluntary action is the response of the T.U.C. and C.B.I. to proposals for state intervention. In 1966, the Government referred to these bodies the proposal of the Employment Panel of the N.C.C.I. that the Fair Wages Resolution clause in government contracts should be amended to include an undertaking by the contractor to refrain from discrimination.[1] Their response was to consult one another and draft a joint statement declaring a policy of non-discrimination, while at the same time opposing the proposed amendment.[2] The publication of the P.E.P. Report followed by the recommendation of the Race Relations Board that the legislation be extended to employment, led to further consultations as to how existing grievance procedures in industry could be modified to deal with complaints of racial discrimination.

These modifications were necessary because of the loopholes in the normal procedures. Of twenty-three million workers in Britain, about five million are not subject to any collective bargaining or wage-fixing machinery and it is precisely in those industries which are non-unionized that immigrant labour is often found. Secondly, the most frequent form of discrimination occurs in relation to engagement and at that stage the work-seeker will fall outside the normal procedures, which apply only to those already in employment. Thirdly, the discriminating party may be the union itself (e.g. in relation to promotion) with the result that the normal machinery will not be brought into operation.

Between January and July 1967, the industrial relations committee of the C.B.I. considered possible procedures which would fulfil the four requirements stated earlier.[3] The most desirable appeared to be a central joint council of the T.U.C. and C.B.I. to act as an appeal machine where arrangements in individual industries did not provide for independent arbitration as a final step in their procedure. The central body would also receive complaints and refer them to the individual industry machinery where this existed. The joint board would

1. Discussed below, p. 183
2. See Introduction above, p. 4
3. Above, p. 162

contain some independent members and probably have an independent chairman. The T.U.C. was broadly in sympathy with these proposals, and the C.B.I. recommended to employers' organizations that they should initiate discussions with their appropriate trade unions on the setting up of voluntary machinery. The major gap in the scheme was that no consideration was given to the many employers outside the employers' organizations. As hoped, the Government was influenced by these moves to agree that the legislation should make the fullest use of voluntary procedures.

The first employers' group to take the initiative was the Engineering Employers' Federation whose draft agreement on racial discrimination was accepted by the Confederation of Shipbuilding and Engineering Unions in July 1967. The full text of this agreement, likely to be the precedent for many others, is printed as Appendix III of this book.[1] It provides that questions of discrimination should, in the first instance, be dealt with by the Provisions for Avoiding Disputes. In the case of manual workers, the current agreement with the manual workers' unions provides four levels for settling a dispute: (1) between the management and the workman directly concerned at the work-place; (2) failing settlement, between deputations of workmen who may be accompanied by their organizer (in which event a representative of the employers' association shall also be present) and the employers 'without unreasonable delay'; (3) failing settlement, at a local conference between the local employers' association and representatives of the unions 'within seven working days'; (4) failing settlement, at a central conference which may make a joint recommendation to the constituent bodies – this conference must be held on the second Friday of each month at which questions referred to it prior to fourteen days of that date can be considered. Until this procedure has been carried through there may no stoppage of work.[2] In the case of staff employees, a typical procedure agreement is that with the Association of Engineering and Shipbuilding Draughtsmen (dated 29 February 1956). This is identical with the procedure applicable to manual workers, except that central conferences are to be held 'when necessary but not more frequently than monthly'. The fourteen-day rule applies in this case as well.

The main features of these provisions are that they depend upon the support of the union concerned, that the sanction of stoppage of labour

1. Below, p. 226
2. Agreement between the Engineering Employers' Federation and the Trade Unions dated 2 June 1922 as amended 10 August 1955. For a full discussion, see Arthur Marsh, *Industrial Relations in Engineering* (London 1965)

may be invoked only after the procedure has been exhausted, and that the central conference is empowered only to make recommendations. Moreover, there is no provision for any form of independent arbitration or of independent participation in the local or central conferences.

In those cases where the procedure is not applicable, for example where there is no dispute between the employer and his work-people, but a person has a complaint of discrimination, the 1967 agreement lays down a special procedure. The employers' association in each area is required to set up a committee or, if necessary, committees comprising an equal number of representatives of the Association and local union officials. Each committee must have a secretary or joint secretaries to whom complaints can be made. If, after investigation, the secretaries cannot dispose of the question, the complainant may take his case to the committee. If the committee finds that discrimination has been established it must take all practicable steps to ensure that the discriminatory practice ceases forthwith. An annual report is to be submitted to the Federation and Confederation.

Several aspects of this novel procedure ought to be noted. First, it covers 4,764 federated engineering establishments which employ some 2,150,000 people. While the parties are prepared to make it available to non-federated firms (e.g. Fords) whether or not it is thus extended will depend upon those firms. Secondly, it does not provide for any form of independent arbitration or of outside participation in the machinery. Thirdly, it is to be made known to work-seekers through Ministry employment exchanges. Even assuming this is uniformly done, there is no means laid down for making its provisions known to work-seekers who do not use the exchanges, and many complaints may, for this reason, never be lodged. Fourthly, unlike the Provisions for Avoiding Disputes, there is no standstill on work stoppages. Finally, no sanction is expressly provided and reliance will accordingly be placed on the influence, prestige and ability of the committees to secure the ending of the discriminatory practice. (In this respect it is worth noting that the Points for Guidance accepted by the parties to the Agreement require the investigation to be carried out by that Joint Secretary against whose constituent – i.e. employer or work-people – an allegation of discrimination has been made. The complainant may be accompanied, during the initial investigation or at meetings of the joint committee, by a friend who is employed in and familiar with the engineering industry.)

The major defects of this special procedure are that justice may not be seen to be done, because of the absence of independent arbitration or even of an appeals procedure, and that there is no protection for those who are forced against their will to discriminate.

The principal remedy for these defects lies in the use of 'fall-back' provisions in the new Race Relations legislation.[1] Another way in which collective bargaining could be strengthened to deal with racial discrimination is by an amendment to section 8 of the Terms and Conditions of Employment Act 1959, to enable an individual worker to complain that 'recognized terms and conditions' of employment are not being observed by an employer, where for some unjustified reason the union or employers' association refuses or neglects to make a complaint on the worker's behalf.[2] In this way a coloured worker who fails to persuade his union to take action to ensure that he is employed on standard conditions will himself be able to take action against the discriminatory employer.

In summary it can be said that the immediate result of legislation is likely to be an increase in the use of voluntary grievance procedures to deal with allegations of discrimination. The acceptability of these procedures will be enhanced if a series of related measures are taken, including: (1) the termination of formal and informal agreements at national and local level which discriminate against non-British workers;[3] (2) the development of positive integrative techniques by employers such as the dispersal of immigrant workers throughout the labour force, use of special training programmes in skills and language for immigrant employees, willingness to recruit and promote coloured workers in the teeth of opposition from local white labour, respect for the customs and religions of ethnic minorities and public commitment to a policy of non-discrimination; (3) an active policy of integration by trade unions such as recruitment drives among immigrant workers, appointment of full-time officers aware of the special needs and problems of members of ethnic minorities, the use of educational material and training courses in the immigrants' own languages, and education of local workers on the subject of race relations.

VOLUNTARY GROUPS OUTSIDE INDUSTRY

In recent years there has been a rapid increase in the number of voluntary liaison bodies concerned with community relations. In 1964 there were fifteen such committees, groupings of representatives from the local authority, the local immigrant communities and a wide range of

1. See above, p. 146
2. See above, p. 114
3. See above, p. 50 and Appendix II, below, p. 218

other local interests. During 1964 and 1965, with the help of the National Committee for Commonwealth Immigrants and its predecessor, the number rose to thirty-two. By October 1967, fifty-six committees were in being.

In order to obtain a picture of how these organizations see their own role in regard to complaints of racial discrimination in employment, a questionnaire was sent, in November 1967, to thirty-two committees which came into existence before the end of 1965. In some instances the information supplied was followed up with interviews and correspondence with local liaison officers.

Of the twenty-one committees which replied, thirteen have a special committee to deal with employment matters; nearly all of these include representatives from the local Trades Council and individual unions. The local Chamber of Commerce is represented on about half, and a handful have representatives from the Institute of Personnel Management and from individual employers.

Only two of these committees have *never* received complaints of racial discrimination in employment, and in both instances these were recently-formed bodies which lacked the staff, funds and local support to work in the employment field. The scale on which the others receive complaints is indicated by the statistics furnished by thirteen committees which had available records. In the first ten months of 1967 these committees received a total of 116 complaints, but nearly three-quarters of these were received by four committees: the Oxford Committee for Racial Integration (25), the Manchester Council for Community Relations (18), Hackney Citizens Liaison Council (18) and the Nottingham Commonwealth Citizens' Consultative Committee (15).

The most usual course appears to be for the committee itself to take up the complaint directly with the employer; less than half the committees who replied make it a practice to refer the matter to the appropriate trade union (where one exists) or to the Ministry of Labour. Nearly all insist on the complaint being verified before they proceed to obtain a settlement. The degree of verification required varies. Usually an oral interview with the complainant followed by an interview or correspondence with the respondent is considered sufficient. It is very rare for a situation test (e.g. similarly qualified white and coloured persons applying for the same job) to be conducted.

In general, liaison officers were unable to furnish statistics or to guess percentage of complaints received since 1965 which had been verified to the satisfaction of their committee. Some believed the number to be below 20 per cent of the complaints received, while others thought the percentage might be as high as between 60 – 79 per cent. They were even more hesitant about estimating the percentage of verified complaints which had been settled to the satisfaction of their committee. About half, was a common guess. All the organizations seek to do the 'best possible' for the complainant, yet there was little clarity or agreement about what constituted a 'satisfactory settlement'. Only two of the committees who replied thought this should include an agreement to employ (either generally or in particular jobs) a certain number or proportion of coloured persons. Some wanted an assurance against future discrimination, and some of these also wanted some redress for the particular complainant (e.g. employment or promotion).

The statistics and percentages supplied must be regarded as unreliable in themselves. Yet the replies do indicate that the role which these committees see for themselves in regard to specific complaints of racial discrimination is an extremely limited one; indeed they have, in general, received relatively few complaints. This may be attributed to several causes such as lack of awareness of discrimination (particularly in areas of high concentration of Pakistani and Indian settlement), ignorance of the committee's existence, and lack of confidence on the part of immigrants about the committees' ability to resolve their grievances.

Most of the committees do not see it as their role to discover discrimination or to present an image of an active anti-colour bar organization to the immigrant communities. On the contrary, the very 'respectable' composition of the committee and its desire to win and retain the ear and support of the local authority and other official bodies, are likely to compel the committee to avoid such an image at all costs. This, in turn, is bound to disenchant the more militant immigrant organizations who seek, instead, to redress their complaints through alternative channels or do nothing about them.

The older committees, which have done valuable work in the past in resolving *immigrant* problems, now find themselves largely unsuited to handling *racial* ones. An example, in the author's personal view, is the Nottingham Commonwealth Citizens' Consultative Committee, which had its origins in a decision in May 1954 of the Council of Social Service and the Council of Churches to 'set up a coordinating committee to attend to the welfare of coloured people'. As part of this welfare work, the committee conducted training schemes (e.g. for women machinists and domestic staff), English language classes, produced a booklet containing information about trade unions and social services, and conducted meetings on 'Working in an English factory'. There were frequent discussions with employers and the local authority about the employment of immigrants, and weekly meetings were held at which a panel of experts answered immigrants' questions about matters such as unemployment benefits, taxation and sick pay, and helped them to find jobs. At its peak in 1958 and 1959, 258 immigrants were interviewed in a six-month period. By the end of 1962 the number of newcomers to England had dwindled and it was decided that the work of the panels could be more effectively performed by the Ministry of Labour employment exchange. The weekly panels and the work of the employment sub-committee was, it seems fair to say, a significant contribution to the relative ease with which immigrants were absorbed into Nottingham industry. Yet it has not had much success in dealing with specific complaints of racial discrimination. In its early years the committee eschewed public debate about the colour bar; for instance, a move by a Trades Council representative for an open forum on the colour bar in 1955 met with a rebuff from the majority of the committee on the grounds that this might lend 'an unhealthy significance to the problem which could best be solved by quiet and constructive steps'. At present its work in this field suffers from lack of cooperation from some of the immigrant bodies alleging discrimination and the absence of powers to deal with hostile employers. Although, as a matter of practice, it handles complaints through the appropriate unions and employers' organizations, it lacks sufficient staff and funds to pursue cases to the hilt.

An interesting comparison may be made with the Oxford Committee for Racial Integration, formed in January 1965, which undertakes annual surveys of what happens to immigrant school-leavers, gives (or threatens) press publicity to complaints where it considers necessary, pursues anti-colour bar campaigns and attracts a far larger number of complaints than any other voluntary liaison committee, despite the fact that Oxford is a one-industry (car) town with an immigrant population of only about 4,000. Its active conception of itself as an anti-colour bar body, whose primary aim is 'to uphold the civil rights of immigrants', appears to be directly related to its composition. Over half its executive consists of immigrants, its chairman, vice-chairman and treasurer are immigrants and it conducts recruiting drives for new immigrant members. It does not have on its executive representatives of statutory bodies who are not really in agreement with its aims, and it has cultivated good relationships with individual trade unionists and the major employers without inviting their official participation. Its reputation among immigrants has grown with the knowledge that it takes action on every complaint of discrimination. Nevertheless the Committee would be the first to admit that its work in the field of individual complaints has been incomplete and imperfect. Among its major difficulties are reliance on voluntary workers, intransigent employers, absence of unionization in some firms, and the unwillingness of some complainants (through fear of consequences and other causes) to have their cases pursued.

If, by and large, the voluntary committees are unsuited to the handling of specific complaints of discrimination this does not mean that they have failed in regard to their role of educating public opinion. In the future they should be able to concentrate more effectively on this role, being released from the time-consuming and relatively fruitless task of individual casework. At the time of writing, none of the committees had thought out what its role would be once an enforceable Race Relations Act covering job discrimination was on the statute book. Committees like O.C.R.I. are likely to look for cases of discrimination and report them officially. Others may confine themselves to handling employment cases where there appears to be no discrimination, wherever possible referring these to the appropriate trade union. Other general activities in which committees might engage are: (1) the organization of private and public discussions between unions, managements and ethnic minorities on the problems of integration; (2) the holding of meetings at factories to educate British workers about the cultures and backgrounds of minority groups; (3) encouraging members of minority groups to join and participate in their trade unions; (4) sponsoring local research; (5) liaising with employers, unions and official bodies about general issues. To carry out these tasks successfully the committees will need specialized staff with knowledge of industrial relations, and adequate funds.[1]

The sponsor-role of the liaison committees stands in contrast to the more militant activities of some immigrant-based organizations. Groups such as the Campaign Against Racial Discrimination, the Indian Workers' Association and the West Indian Standing Conference have prompted individuals to test employment discrimination and to make complaints to the local conciliation committees of the Race Relations Board. C.A.R.D., for example, received complaints of job discrimination at the rate of five to ten a week during 1966–7. The Race Relations Board takes the view that such independent groups concerned with the interests of minorities are essential if the individual complaint procedure provided by the Race Relations Act is to work satisfactorily. A proposal by the Street Committee to allow local conciliation committees,

1. Since 1967 the National Committee for Commonwealth Immigrants has had a full-time industrial relations officer.

at their discretion, to investigate allegations from these groups without an individual complaint, would facilitate their role in testing and reporting discrimination.

These bodies have failed to settle a significant number of complaints of job discrimination. In general, they have found that where a trade union exists and is active on behalf of its members, jobs and promotion can be secured for individuals who allege discrimination. On the other hand where a union exists but is inactive or allies itself with management discrimination, no settlement can be reached. Similarly, where no union exists the immigrant-based groups have neither the status nor the power to negotiate with the management. From the trade union angle the view is sometimes expressed that ethnic organizations prevent the unions from properly representing members of minority groups. Such evidence as there is[1] suggests that ethnic organizations have encouraged members of minority groups to join their appropriate trade unions but that their membership, owing to community pressures, may be more vacillating than is the case with English workers. Moreover, the activities of an ethnic organization may emphasize the distinctiveness or separateness of a group of workers. The decision taken at a C.A.R.D. conference in 1967 to organize factory groups of C.A.R.D. members has provoked a trade union reaction that these members should rather help to form trade unions where none exist or persevere in their efforts to persuade the majority where union attitudes are hostile.

The relative failure of the organizations of recent coloured immigrants is significantly different from the experience of an organization of another minority group, the Jews. The Trades Advisory Council (T.A.C.) of the Board of Deputies of British Jews has been investigating and resolving by voluntary means complaints of economic discrimination against Jews for over twenty-seven years. Its aim (as stated in one of its Annual Reports) 'is the avoidance of friction and misunderstanding in the economic field which endangers the maintenance of harmonious relations between Jew and non-Jew in trade and industry'. It took shape in its present form in 1940 and by 1947 its membership exceeded 8,000 or about one-third of Britain's Jewish traders and businessmen. By 1967 its membership had declined to about 2,000 owing to the retirement of many of its founders, the amalgamation of small member firms into larger units and the absence of a sustained recruitment drive. It handled about thirty-one allegations of discrimina-

1. See, in particular, P. Marsh, *Anatomy of a Strike* (London 1967), pp. 83–5, and above, p. 79. As regards occupational organizations of ethnic groups, see above, p. 85

tion in 1965–6 and twenty-seven in 1966–7. Typical of these were the alleged refusal of a large firm to employ a Jewish legal assistant on the ground that the firm had no other Jewish employees at executive level, and the refusal of an arts and crafts school to accept a Jewish apprentice on the ground that this might cause friction with other non-Jewish apprentices.

The T.A.C. has had little difficulty in persuading firms that discrimination against Jews is unjustified and does not pay. The fact that it has managed to succeed in this without any obvious sanction is probably due to the widespread belief that Jews 'dominate' in trade and industry and that it is therefore economically unwise to be found discriminating against them. By contrast, the recent coloured immigrants lack the apparent economic power to induce firms to cease from discrimination against them. It may also be significant that while recent immigrant groups have concentrated their attention on the question of discrimination by the host society, the T.A.C. has also been concerned with ensuring the 'good name' of Anglo-Jewry by shielding the host society from alleged malpractices by Jews. Accordingly, in 1965–6 the T.A.C. dealt with no less than forty-seven allegations of unethical conduct by Jewish traders, ten disputes between Jewish traders and eight between Jewish and non-Jewish traders.

The decisive factor in determining whether or not racial discrimination is brought under satisfactory control in the future is likely to be the attitudes and organization of the people most directly affected. What is noticeably absent is cohesive and durable political organization among coloured people. Bayard Rustin, American civil rights leader, admirably summed this up when he said: 'Until the coloured people in Britain are brought into the centre of [the] deliberations and are, in fact, themselves in movement you will not arouse the great masses of people here. . . . No social change can take place basically without their movement.'[1]

---

1. *Racial Equality in Employment.* A report of a conference held on 23–5 February 1967 (N.C.C.I.), p. 45

10. The Role of Government

The Government can give a lead in creating equal employment opportunities by making the public services and nationalized industries model employers, by insisting that those who contract with the Government or seek licences or subsidies to carry on business activities observe fair labour standards, and by utilizing the Ministry of Labour employment exchanges to encourage non-discrimination by private employers.

MODEL EMPLOYERS?

A number of coloured persons are employed in the Civil Service. No statistics are kept in regard to their recruitment and promotion but it is clear that no racial or colour barriers stand in their way. At the same time the Nationality Rule (for permanent appointments) may operate to bar some immigrants.[1] This Rule has nothing at all to do with race or colour, but it requires candidates for the Civil Service to be British or Irish (i.e. British subjects, British protected persons or Irish citizens). In addition, the candidate must satisfy one of the following conditions:

(1) If he was British or Irish *at birth* then either (a) at least one of his parents must be British or Irish, or (b) he must have resided in a Commonwealth country or the Irish Republic or have been employed elsewhere in the service of the Crown for at least five years out of the last eight years preceding the date of his appointment;

(2) If he was not British or Irish at birth, he must have resided in a Commonwealth country or in the Irish Republic or have been employed elsewhere in the service of the Crown for at least five

1. This Rule is made by the Civil Service Commissioners under the Civil Service Order in Council of 1956 with the approval of the Treasury and Foreign Secretary. The Act of Settlement 1700 (23 Wm. 3 c. 2) prevents aliens from holding office under the Crown and the Aliens Employment Act 1955 (4 Eliz. 2, c. 18, s. 1) prohibits employment of aliens in the civil service without certificate. See above, p. 33

years out of the last eight years preceding the date of his appointment;

(3) If he does not qualify under (1) or (2) he must satisfy the Commissioners that he is so closely connected with a Commonwealth country either by ancestry, upbringing or residence, or by reason of national service that an exception can properly be made in his favour.

More stringent requirements are imposed in respect of appointments in the Ministry of Aviation, the Cabinet Office, the Ministry of Defence (other than the Meteorological Office) or the Ministry of Public Building and Works. A candidate for such appointments must (1) at all times since birth have been either a British subject or an Irish citizen, and (2) have been born in a country which is (or then was) within the Commonwealth or the Irish Republic, and (3) each of his parents must have been born in a country which is (or then was) within the Commonwealth or the Irish Republic and must be (or have been at death) a British subject or Irish citizen and be or have been one or the other at all times from birth. The Minister responsible for the Department may waive these exceptional requirements if he so wishes. There are special and more stringent requirements for appointments to the Diplomatic Service, the Foreign Office and the Commonwealth Relations Office.

The Civil Service Commissioners interpret the Rule liberally, in particular construing 'British' as covering citizens of all Commonwealth countries even if they hold only the nationality of their own countries and are not citizens of the United Kingdom and colonies. This means that all Commonwealth citizens irrespective of race or colour who satisfy the detailed requirements of the Rule may compete for posts for which they are otherwise eligible. As regards promotion the principle of advancement according to merit with due regard to seniority appears to be maintained.

Is the Nationality Rule justified? That it sometimes works curious results is illustrated by the recent case of a young woman, born in the United Kingdom, who was rejected for the Women's Royal Air Force on the ground that her father, a naturalized United Kingdom citizen, was born in Poland. What made the case even more bizarre was that her father fought with the British Eighth Army during the Second World War.[1] A person's nationality is obviously a 'bona fide occupational requirement' (to borrow the language of F.E.P. statutes) in

1. *Daily Express*, 9 August 1966. Other examples are given in the Race Relations Board's *Report for 1966–7*, App. VI, p. 31

regard to posts in the public service because it is an indication of his close connexion with the country he is to serve. It could be argued, however, that the requirements for recruitment to the service Departments, Cabinet Office and Ministry of Public Building and Works are unduly stringent, apparently resting on the assumption that the more durable a person's connexion with Britain (through parentage) the less likely he is to be a 'security risk'. To the casual observer it would seem that the intelligence services of foreign powers are just as likely to be successful in recruiting native-born British subjects as they might be in subverting one whose parents were born abroad. Rather than treat ancestry as the criterion of 'loyalty' the Civil Service Commissioners might be better advised to adhere to a security rule along the lines suggested in the I.L.O. Convention in Respect of Discrimination in Employment.[1]

The Armed Forces impose restrictions, required by statute, on the recruitment of aliens[2] but there is no official colour bar in the services. However, it has been alleged that the Guards and some Highland regiments and cavalry units remain closed to coloured recruits.[3] In 1961, a War Office spokesman said that the Army was working on the basis of 2 per cent coloured men among total recruitments, but this was later explained on the footing that there is no legal ceiling and the figure of 2 per cent represented a yardstick which could be changed at any time.[4] It must be added that in 1961 African and other overseas candidates at Sandhurst and Aldershot formed 13 per cent of the total strength of officer cadets.

The first coloured policeman in Britain was sworn in as a member of the Coventry police force in March 1966. He had previously been a probationary sub-inspector in the Tanganyika police and arrived in Britain in November 1965. A second coloured policeman, a Trinidadian, was appointed in Leamington Spa later in 1966. The Metropolitan Force has taken longer to accept a policy of recruiting coloured police. In 1963 a spokesman of the Force said that Londoners were 'not yet

1. See above, Chapter 2, p. 26. The Street Report on Anti-Discrimination Legislation, (above, p. 6) proposed that any new Race Relations legislation should bind the Crown but in the case of Crown employment a Minister should be able to create exceptions (e.g. in respect of birthplace or nationality) by statutory instrument. This would, in effect, leave the Nationality Rule as it is
2. The relevant statutes are cited in Chapter 2, p. 33. The number of aliens serving at any time in the Army may not exceed one fiftieth of the aggregate number of persons in the Army at that time
3. *Daily Mirror*, 6 March 1964; *Nottingham Evening Post*, 1 December 1966
4. *The Times*, 19 July 1961. More recently, a news team (*The Times*, 5 May 1967) has found that the Army operates a colour quota of about four per cent for most units. The Royal Air Force admit to no such quota

prepared' for coloured policemen.[1] But more recently a positive policy has resulted in the acceptance of the first coloured recruits in the Metropolis. Apart from this the results of applications by coloured men for police work have been disappointing. Of thirty-six applicants to join the Metropolitan Force in 1966, five were summoned for interview, four failed to attend and the fifth was rejected as being below the general standard required. Of the thirty-one not called for interview, seventeen were recent arrivals in Britain, seven were of poor education, five were rejected on medical grounds, one was below minimum height and one was above the maximum age limit.[2] There have been appointments of coloured special policemen in some areas, of coloured police liaison officers in Bradford, and of coloured traffic wardens. The Home Secretary (then Mr R. Jenkins) made it clear that he was anxious to speed up the recruitment of suitably qualified coloured policemen but the major difficulty in securing a national policy of this kind is that recruitment is a matter for each of the large number of local police authorities.

As regards the National Health Service, Commonwealth immigrants make up about 40 per cent of the staff in the hospital services. But it has been pointed out that the percentage of these employed in teaching hospitals is small. For example, a report to the Oxford Area Nurse Committee in 1961 stated that only 3 per cent of the student nurses in teaching hospitals in the Oxford Area were Non-European compared with a comparative figure of 21 per cent in non-teaching hospitals in that area. On a national scale the alleged figure of only 1 or 2 per cent of Commonwealth immigrants in teaching hospitals requires urgent investigation to ensure that the cause is not racial discrimination.[3] Following complaints that candidates for hospital posts are required to answer questions about their religion, the Minister of Health has informed hospital authorities that there should be no religious discrimination in the appointment or promotion of suitably qualified nursing or other staff and application forms should not therefore include a question on this subject.

Where local authorities have immediate control of employment policies patterns are not uniform. At one extreme there are attitudes like that of a rural council which in 1965 decided not to accept applications from firms interested in moving from London to their area as

1. *Evening Standard*, 8 November 1963; and Ben Whitaker, 'Why Have We No Coloured Policemen?' *Spectator*, 30 April 1965
2. 740 H.C. Deb. Written Answers, 278–9 (7 February 1967)
3. The allegation was made by Mr R. Freeson, M.P., Standing Committee B, H.C. Off. Rep., col. 349 (29 June 1965) and repeated by him in 738 H.C. Deb., col. 910 (16 December 1966)

part of an 'overspill' scheme if those firms employed large numbers of coloured workers.[1] At the other end of the scale is the tolerance shown by a majority in the Manchester Council which in October 1966 agreed to the wearing of suitable coloured turbans by Sikh busmen.[2] Local education authorities generally do not practise discrimination, but they do find that many immigrant applicants for teaching posts cannot be appointed because their English is inadequate. The Plowden Committee has recommended special remedial courses for immigrant teachers[3] and if this is implemented it should go some way towards meeting the point made by the National Union of Teachers that Commonwealth graduates, at present prevented from teaching in Britain by lack of the necessary qualifications, are ideally suited to act as liaison officers between the immigrants and the host society.[4]

The thorniest problems confronting local authorities have been in relation to municipal road passenger services. Some corporations have maintained a policy of not recruiting coloured workers, but many have taken in a considerable number and have successfully integrated them. This is particularly the case with London Transport which brought over a large number from the West Indies, trained them, started them in the lowest grades, like all other new recruits, and promoted them in the ordinary way. Occasionally white busmen have opposed these steps, but by and large progress has been satisfactory.

British Rail has integrated a considerable number of coloured recruits. Yet it is still said that no coloured employee has achieved a senior job. There is a handful of coloured accountants, quantity surveyors, motormen and guards and officially there is no colour bar.[5] The major reason for the absence of coloured men and women in senior posts is that most of them have not worked long enough to qualify for these positions. At the same time, incidents like the 'colour bar' row at Euston station in July 1966 about the promotion of a West Indian railwayman of ten years' standing emphasize that there is still considerable resistance to the promotion of coloured employees.[6]

No legal difficulty stands in the way of the Government in laying

---

1. *The Times*, 24 and 25 February 1965
2. See above, Chapter 5, p. 81
3. Central Advisory Council for Education (England), *Children and their Primary Schools*, (H.M.S.O. 1966), s. 199, p. 73
4. *The N.U.T.'s View on the Education of Immigrants* (January 1967)
5. There is a collective agreement with the National Union of Railwaymen restricting the employment and promotion of foreign nationals: Appendix II, p. 222
6. Above, Chapter 5, p. 75

down a policy of non-discrimination for the nationalized industries. Yet the reluctance of the Government to exercise its powers of general direction is indicated by the refusal (in June 1965) to direct the Bank of England to remove its requirement that the Bank's employees must be British by birth and parentage.[1] The overall impression of government performance is that the implementation of declared policies of equal opportunity has barely started.

GOVERNMENT CONTRACTORS

The Employment Panel of the National Committee for Commonwealth Immigrants proposed on 18 February 1966 that a provision should be included in the contract of everyone supplying goods or services to the Government, reading as follows:

The contractor shall not practise or condone discrimination on the ground of colour, race, religion, or ethnic or national origins, in engaging, training, promoting or discharging any persons in his employment or in fixing any terms or conditions of employment.

The obligation on civil servants to incorporate this clause in future contracts was to be achieved by an amendment to the Fair Wages Resolution of the House of Commons (dated 14 October 1946). This Resolution traces its history back to 1891 when a Resolution of the House stated:

It is the duty of the Government in all Government contracts to make provision against the evils recently disclosed before the Sweating Committee, to insert such conditions as may prevent the abuse arising from sub-letting, and to make every effort to secure the payment of such wages as are generally accepted as current in each trade for competent workmen.[2]

Mr Sidney Buxton, M.P., moving the Resolution, pointed out the tremendous power the Government had over its contractors stemming from the popularity of these contracts, which gave the contractor a guarantee against bad debts, and resulted in quick returns and useful advertisement. A consequence of their popularity was great competition and this meant that tenders were cut down at the expense of the labour market. This placed the fair employer at a great disadvantage in

1. Is origin and ancestry a 'bona fide occupational qualification' for the business of central banking?
2. The texts of this and the subsequent Resolutions are reprinted in the Ministry of Labour's *Industrial Relations Handbook* (H.M.S.O. 1961), p. 214

comparison with the employer who paid low wages. Buxton's reasons were compelling and the House authorized the use of this technique to encourage the payment of fair wages.

The first Resolution was followed by another in 1909 which added the requirement that the contractor was to observe hours of labour 'not less favourable than those commonly recognized by employers and trade societies (or in the absence of such recognized wages and hours, those which in practice prevail among good employers)'. This extension from a 'fair wages' to a 'fair labour standards' Resolution was, as Professor Kahn-Freund has pointed out,[1] all the more remarkable because it went beyond what Parliament was prepared, or even invited, to do by legislation at that time. This lesson has not been lost on the present anti-discrimination lobby.

The other important feature of the Resolutions was that they did not empower the Government to fix wages and conditions. Instead they encouraged obedience to standards established by collective agreements. The 1946 Resolution, which emerged from discussions between the British Employers' Federation, the T.U.C. and the Government, elaborates on the requirements of the earlier Resolutions and adds that the contractor must recognize the freedom of his work-people to be members of trade unions.

What sanction can be imposed on a contractor who fails to observe the terms of the Resolution? Once incorporated in his contract, the Resolution becomes a contractual term and the procedure which it lays down will be followed in regard to disputes arising under it which cannot be settled by negotiation. In practice complaints regarding non-compliance are made to the contracting Department or to the Minister of Labour. In either event, the contractor is informed of the complaint and is reminded of his obligations under the Resolution. The Minister may try to bring about an amicable settlement by way of conciliation. Failing this, the matter is usually referred to the Industrial Court for decision. The onus of proving a breach rests on the complainant (usually a trade union). The Industrial Court, following its ordinary procedure as laid down by the Industrial Courts Act 1919, decides whether and to what extent the contractor has breached his obligations. Its decision has no further legal effect but in general the Court has sufficient moral prestige to secure obedience in fact. The real sanction, however, is that failure to comply would, no doubt, result in loss of future government contracts. An ancillary sanction is that the Resolu-

1. 'Legislation through Adjudication. The Legal Aspect of Fair Wages Clauses and Recognized Conditions' (1948) 11 *M.L.R.* 269, esp. 276–7

tion requires the contractor to display a copy of the Resolution for the information of his work-people in his factory. It is to be noted, however, that the Resolution does not permit inspection by departmental officers to ensure compliance.

Will these sanctions prove effective if the non-discrimination clause is included in government contracts? With the expansion in scope of the Race Relations Act it would be appropriate for local committees to investigate and the Board to hear questions arising in respect of alleged breaches of the non-discrimination clause. In that event, once the complaint was referred to the Board the ordinary procedures laid down by the amended Race Relations Act would be followed.[1]

The principle of the Resolution has been incorporated in a number of statutes which provide assistance to industries or public authorities by way of grant, loan, subsidy or licence. There is a good case for amending these 'fair wages' provisions where they appear in statutes to include a prohibition on discrimination. At present these Acts provide various sanctions for non-observance. The most severe is loss of licence or other privilege. The majority enable the employee to enforce the relevant awards of the Industrial Court (after referrals by the Minister as above) as an implied term of their contracts of employment.[2] Both of these sanctions could work fruitfully in relation to discrimination. The fear of being put out of business is likely to be a powerful deterrent to potential discriminators; making non-discrimination an implied term of the individual's contract of employment could be linked with the proposals made in Chapter 9.[3] The criminal sanctions applied by some statutes, however, would not be appropriate in the area of discrimination.

The promise of success for non-discrimination clauses in government contracts lies not only in the important part which the Fair Wages Resolution has played in the past in establishing fair labour conditions in Britain, but also in transatlantic experience. Since 1941 executive orders issued by successive presidents have obliged government contractors and sub-contractors in the U.S.A. not to discriminate against any employee or applicant for employment on racial grounds. Responsibility for administering the orders was placed in presidential committees

1. The Street Report (above, p. 6) suggested that the supervision of the proposed anti-discrimination clause should be made the special responsibility of a division of the Race Relations Board. The conciliation and fact-finding processes would be carried out in the ordinary way but it would be for the Ministry under contract to decide whether to suspend or cancel the contract or to black-list the contractor

2. Proposals have been made to the Royal Commission on Trade Unions, etc. to add a similar sanction to the Fair Wages Resolution

3. See above, p. 171

until October 1965, when President Johnson assigned jurisdiction over government contractors to the Labour Department.

Before President Kennedy set up his Equal Employment Opportunities Committee in 1961 the verdict amongst most commentators was that the executive orders had *failed* to bring about any significant improvement in the employment status of Negroes in federal contract establishments. The reasons put forward by a leading authority[1] were (1) the Committee could not deal directly with non-complying employers; (2) procedure was focused on individual complaints rather than towards eliminating overall discriminatory practices; (3) the approach to contractors was based exclusively on voluntary methods to secure compliance and the power not to renew contracts, on grounds of non-compliance, was never invoked; (4) the Committee made no efforts to deal with labour unions which barred Negroes from membership.

President Kennedy's executive orders, and the current Order 11246, issued by President Johnson, have to a large extent remedied these defects. In particular, individual complaints are used as a basis for general compliance reviews in the firms concerned; compliance reviews are initiated in some circumstances without complaints having been received; reports concerning employment practices have to be filed by employers who also have to allow access to their records by government inspectors; there are periodic reviews of all firms; and contractors have to commit themselves to 'affirmative action'. If conciliation fails to elicit compliance the Secretary of Labour may invoke a large number of sanctions including publication of the names of violators, cancellation of existing contracts and barring non-compliers from future contracts. The result of these improvements has been startling. In the first two and a half years of its operation (up to October 1963) the Kennedy Committee had received more than twice as many complaints as its predecessor under the Eisenhower Administration received in a seven-year period. Whereas the Eisenhower Committee found and removed discrimination in about 200 cases (i.e. around thirty a year) the Kennedy Committee settled 937 cases (around 360 a year). The Johnson Committee (and subsequently the Labour Department) appear to have continued this new trend.

From this experience there are many lessons to be drawn in regard to the eradication of discrimination by government contractors in

1. P. H. Norgren, 'Government Contracts and Fair Employment Practices' (1964) 29 *Law and Contemporary Problems* 225

Britain. Perhaps the most pertinent is that a specialized body (the Race Relations Board) equipped with wide and general powers of investigation is essential if the non-discrimination clause is to be made successful.

So far the most useful reaction to the N.C.C.I.'s proposal has come from local authorities. The London borough of Camden gave the lead in May 1966 by amending its standing orders so as to demand a written promise from firms supplying goods or services to the Council that they will not discriminate. The orders now read:

Before entering into a contract for the execution of works or the supply of goods or materials, the Council shall obtain from the contractor an assurance in writing that when engaging, promoting, or discharging employees, or in conditions of employment no discrimination is made against any person because of colour, race, ethnic or national origins, religion or sex.

Camden's Committee for Community Relations, which suggested the amendment, has formed a Human Rights Group which will be able to receive, investigate and report to the Camden Council on any complaints. Early in 1967 the town council at Reading set up a sub-committee to investigate the suggestion that it should follow Camden's example, and there are indications that other local authorities are doing the same.[1]

MINISTRY OF LABOUR EXCHANGES

There are hopeful signs that several extraneous events will improve the ability of Ministry employment exchanges to influence employers towards non-discriminatory recruitment policies. One of these could be the enactment of the Employment Agencies Bill, barring discrimination by fee-charging agencies, which would remove the fear of unfair competition from agencies prepared to comply with employers' discriminatory requests. Another possible development is that employers may be obliged to notify all vacancies to the exchanges (as they were until 1956). This would result in a wider range of prospective employment for coloured work-seekers.

Although the Ministry's 1966 directive to employment officers[2] offers greater prospects than ever before that attempts will be made to persuade employers against discriminating, it has to be recognized that there are limits to the ability of the employment services to change the situation.

1. Since this was written, the local councils at Reading and Hackney have adopted such resolutions
2. See above, Chapter 5, p. 71

It seems likely, notwithstanding compulsory notification of vacancies by employers, that use of the exchanges to *find* work will remain voluntary. At present only about one out of five of total engagements in manufacturing industries is made through an employment exchange and in a 'free' labour market the most usual way in which coloured workers, like all others, get work is likely to remain the direct approach to potential employers.

11. Perspectives

Britain's performance in eradicating discrimination must be viewed against the background of international pressures to establish a basic standard of human rights.

The rights to work, to free choice of employment, to just and favourable working conditions, to protection against unemployment, to equal pay for equal work, to social security and to form and join trade unions are among the rights to which the Universal Declaration of Human Rights proclaims everyone as being entitled 'without distinction of any kind such as race, colour, sex, language, religion, political or other opinion, national or social origins. . . .' The prominence given to racial equality in this and all other international pronouncements on human rights stems from the deep scars left in Europe by the Nazi persecution of the Jews and the peoples of the occupied countries. Since the end of the war a whole new set of social forces has been unleashed against existing racial orders. National revolutions in the Afro-Asian world, mounting resistance against apartheid, and the Negro civil rights movement have rocked the balance of world power. These world developments, reflected in a growing number of declarations, treaties and conventions, are bound to play an important part in persuading Britain to live up to her avowed principles.

Britain has ratified various international instruments which impose on her the obligation to eliminate racial discrimination. In particular a number of conventions and recommendations of the International Labour Organization which the United Kingdom Government has ratified remain to be translated into practice. For example, in ratifying the Convention Concerning Employment Policy 1964 (No. 122), the U.K. undertook

to declare and pursue as a major goal active policy to promote full, productive and freely chosen employment . . . irrespective of race, colour, sex, religion, political opinion, national extraction or social origin.[1]

1. Art. 1 (1) and 1 (2) (c). Cmnd 2790, 1965

In ratifying the Migration for Employment Convention (Revised) 1949 (No. 97) the U.K. undertook

to apply, without discrimination in respect of nationality, race, religion or sex, to immigrants lawfully within its territory, treatment no less favourable than that which it applies to its own nationals [in respect of matters such as remuneration, membership of trade unions, enjoyment of the benefits of collective bargaining, accommodation and social security].

A particular obligation under this Convention is that every migrant must receive before departure for Britain a document informing him of general conditions of life and work there, and either before departure or on arrival he must be given a copy of his contract of employment.[1] In accepting the Termination of Employment Recommendation 1963 (No. 119) the U.K. agreed that race, colour, sex, marital status, religion, political opinion, national extraction or social origin should not constitute valid reasons for termination of employment. Apart from these, there are other I.L.O. Conventions and Recommendations ratified by the U.K. which expressly forbid the taking of discriminatory measures and provide for their abolition, for example, the Freedom of Association and Protection of the Right to Organize Convention 1948 (No. 87) art. 2, and the Employment Service Recommendation 1948 (No. 83) para. 12.

These instruments share the common feature that they impose on the United Kingdom no specific obligation to *legislate* against racial discrimination. It was because of a mistaken supposition that the I.L.O. Convention Concerning Discrimination in Respect of Employment and Occupation 1958 (No. 111) demanded legislative intervention that the Government refused to ratify it or to accept its supplementary Recommendation. These are the most comprehensive international statements on equality of opportunity and treatment in the field of employment, but the Government has said that their provisions 'would conflict with the long-established practice in the United Kingdom whereby conditions of employment are negotiated between employers' and workers' organizations free from Government intervention'.[2] In reply to this the I.L.O.'s Committee of Experts has pointed out that the Convention and Recommendation do not specifically require legislation. In fact, at the time of their adoption, the 1958 International Labour Conference

1. To some extent the latter requirement is met by the legal obligation on employers to supply a copy of his contract of employment to each employee in terms of the Contracts of Employment Act 1963 (above, p. 113)
2. Cmnd 783, 1959, p. 3

expressly took note of a remark by the U.K. Government member that the wording of the Convention meant that a government which calculated that legislation would be ineffective would not be expected to legislate.[1] The Committee of Experts has admitted that legislation may not always be appropriate since 'it may well be that in some fields it will be more practicable . . . to take measures of another kind'.[2] Consequently the justification for non-ratification given by the U.K. Government is contrary both to the sense in which the Government's own representative interpreted the Convention in 1958, and to the opinion of the Committee of Experts. The more substantial reason for failure to ratify is that given by a Government spokesman in 1966. It was then said that 'the present position in the U.K. is not fully in accordance with all the detailed requirements of [the] instrument. . . .'[3] In particular the removal of sex discrimination would be necessary before the Convention could be adopted in its entirety. There is, however, no reason why the Government should not ratify the Convention piecemeal, that is, at first in respect of racial discrimination and later in regard to other forms of discrimination.

Those who regard legislation as essential for the achievement of equality of opportunity in Britain will regard the 1958 Convention as defective in not imposing an obligation on states to prohibit discrimination. Moreover they can point to a further weakness of the Convention in failing to provide any special machinery for dealing with specific complaints of non-observance. Of course, standard I.L.O. procedures such as the examination of annual reports from states who are parties to the Convention and of periodic reports requested from states which are not parties can be (and have been) utilized. But in themselves these methods provide little immediate benefit to victims of job discrimination.

It is in the light of such criticisms of the 1958 and other I.L.O. Conventions that one has to view two recent international developments. The first is the recognition by the U.K. Government (for an initial period of three years from 1965) of the competence of the European Commission on Human Rights to receive individual petitions. The Commission hears complaints of non-observance of the European Convention for the Protection of Human Rights and Fundamental Freedoms (1950–2) which enumerates a number of human rights

1. *Record of Proceedings International Labour Conference*, 42nd session, 1958, para. 24, p. 712 (Geneva I.L.O. 1959)
2. I.L.O. Committee of Experts op. cit. Report III, para. 60, p. 198
3. 725 H.C. Deb., cols. 178–9. The Convention has become one of the most widely ratified of I.L.O. Conventions. By June 1967, fifty-eight states had ratified it

secured 'without discrimination on any ground such as sex, race, colour, language, religion, political or other opinion, national or social origin, association with a national minority, property, birth or other status'. A defect of the Convention is that it does not provide a general guarantee of non-discrimination but one only in respect of the specific rights set out in the Convention. Since free choice of employment, just conditions of work and the like are not among the enumerated rights there can be no redress in respect of social and economic forms of racial discrimination. The major reason for this omission appears to have been the fear that defining racial and national discrimination would give rise to 'insoluble problems'.[1] The European Social Charter, which came into force on 26 February 1965, does guarantee the right to work and to collective bargaining together with other social rights. Its preamble declares that these rights shall be secured without any form of discrimination, but it provides no right of individual complaint. The Charter was ratified by the United Kingdom on 11 July 1962.

A second and more recent development is the signing by the United Kingdom Government of the International Convention on the Elimination of All Forms of Racial Discrimination, adopted by the U.N. General Assembly on 21 December 1965.[2] The parties to the Convention must undertake 'to pursue by all appropriate means . . . a policy eliminating racial discrimination'. Most significant is the undertaking in Article 2 (1) (*d*) to 'prohibit and bring to an end, by all appropriate means, including legislation as required by circumstances, racial discrimination. . . .' This goes beyond any existing international instrument because in effect it requires the parties to legislate against discrimination unless there is no discrimination within their borders. During discussions on the draft Convention the U.K. representative proposed that the words 'to prohibit' be deleted and be replaced by an undertaking 'to adopt all necessary measures, including legislation if appropriate' to end discrimination. But this was rejected by other states because it would have created too many loopholes. Among the rights in respect of which the parties undertake to protect persons against racial discrimination are 'the rights to work, to free choice of employment, to

1. Consultative Assembly of the Council of Europe. Report on the Second Protocol to the Convention on Human Rights. Doc. 1057. 17 November 1959, p. 12. British experience now indicates the error of this view. In addition it was feared that such a provision would place all member countries under the obligation to put into their legislation effective guarantees against matters such as 'the employment of workers in private enterprises': ibid.

2. As at December 1967 the Government had not ratified the Convention, but it was reported to be giving the matter 'immediate consideration'. The Convention will come into force thirty days after deposit of the twenty-seventh instrument of ratification or accession

just and favourable conditions of work, to protection against unemployment, to equal pay for equal work, to just and favourable remuneration, and to form and join trade unions'. The 1965 Convention accordingly shows a progression from the promotional standards of I.L.O. Conventions to a new mandatory obligation to prohibit discrimination.

Another important feature of the 1965 Convention lies in the remedies for which it provides. In the first place, article 6 declares that the victim of discrimination is entitled to seek in municipal tribunals 'just and adequate reparation or satisfaction for any damage suffered as a result of such discrimination'. This was agreed to despite the objection of the U.K. representative who said that no court in Britain could put a price on an act of discrimination.[1] Secondly, the Convention gives state parties the optional right to establish a special national authority to hear complaints of discrimination. Thirdly, it gives state parties the optional right to recognize the competence of the newly constituted U.N. Committee on the Elimination of Racial Discrimination (composed of eighteen persons elected by member states) to receive communications from individuals or groups within its jurisdiction alleging non-observance of the Convention. If the state has recognized the competence of a Committee, it will be called upon to submit a written reply to the individual complaint. The Committee must then consider the matter and, if necessary, make suggestions to the offending state. Apart from considering individual communications in this way the Committee is empowered to handle and conciliate inter-state disputes concerning the application of the Convention and it must report annually to the General Assembly.

Britain's immigrant groups may also benefit in the future from bilateral agreements with countries of emigration guaranteeing equality of treatment for migrant workers. At the private level this development has been presaged by an agreement between the Employment Agents' Federation of Great Britain (a private body) and the Norwegian Government regarding the recruitment and treatment in Britain of Norwegian *au pair* girls. This 'Mini Charter', as it has been called, provides that these young women must be recruited in future through the Norwegian labour exchange by an authorized British employment agency, and no girl under eighteen is to be recruited. Each British 'hostess' is to be required to enter into a contract with the Norwegian *au pair* in a standard form laying down such matters as the maximum number of hours' domestic work which the girl is to be required to do

1. UN Doc. A/C3/SR. 1309. In Constantine's case the 'price' was 5 gns. See the discussion above, p. 106

daily (five hours), the minimum period of notice in writing (one week), holidays and such like.[1] Of nearly 25,000 foreign young women in domestic service in Britain only about 400 come from Norway so this agreement can be described as no more than a beginning. But already negotiations are in process with the Finnish Government for a similar agreement and an international convention relating to *au pair* girls may emanate from the Council of Europe.

At the governmental level Britain could learn from the experience of other European countries which enter into bilateral treaties with countries of emigration protecting migrant workers. For example France and Tunisia signed a treaty on 9 August 1963, for an initial ten-year period requiring (1) the issue of a contract of employment conforming to models laid down in French legislation to each Tunisian worker recruited in terms of the treaty; (2) that while in France Tunisian workers will receive the same treatment as French workers as regards conditions of work, payment, holidays with pay, unemployment benefits, housing and welfare; (3) the French Government to ensure that they are properly treated as regards transport, canteens and social assistance; (4) employers to ensure that Tunisian workers are admitted on the same terms as other workers to vocational training centres (10 per cent of the places in Government Accelerated Vocational Training programmes are reserved for immigrant workers); and (5) that if the Tunisian worker becomes unemployed through no fault of his own, the French Ministry of Labour must endeavour to find him comparable employment, and until it does so the French Immigration Office must find him board and lodging and see that he is paid unemployment benefits.[2] These theoretical rights are not always observed in practice, particularly in regard to vocational training and the housing needs of the immigrants, but the formal commitment by way of treaty to minimum standards of treatment for migrant workers goes beyond anything yet undertaken by the United Kingdom Government in relation to Commonwealth countries.

This type of treaty will become particularly relevant if the Ministry of Labour presses ahead with plans announced in 1966 for the entry of Commonwealth immigrants for seasonal employment for specified periods not exceeding eight months. This scheme would be additional to the entry of Commonwealth citizens under the voucher system and arrangements would be made in advance with the appropriate employers.

1. *The Times*, 7 March 1967
2. Decree No. 63–1055 dated 15 October 1963. *Journal Officiel de la République Française* (Lois et Décrets) No. 249, pp. 9470–1. There are similar treaties with, for example, Morocco and Portugal

Without adequate safeguards such a scheme might place Commonwealth immigrants at a disadvantage compared with aliens who, when recruited for fixed periods of employment, are usually allowed to extend their work permits and after four years the restrictions on the type of employment they might take are normally removed. Commonwealth immigrants admitted for seasonal employment, on the other hand, would be required to leave when their fixed period of employment had ended. The T.U.C.'s attitude to the proposal has been that it would be undesirable to create a new floating element in the labour force; instead workers should be recruited who would have the prospect of secure employment if they took the risk of settling and bringing their families to Britain. One way in which this might be achieved is by spelling out proper guarantees for migrant workers in treaties with the countries of emigration. On the one hand, the migrant worker might be required to undertake that he will work in Britain for a minimum period of, say, one year in the occupation for which he will be trained; on the other hand, the U.K. Government could undertake to allow the migrant to remain in this country after a certain minimum period of residence, say, two years. Other minimum standards of treatment would also be provided for in the treaty.[1]

Internationally, then, conditions are becoming increasingly favourable for Britain to take steps to eliminate racial discrimination in employment. What are the domestic prospects for legal and social change? To answer this it is necessary to restate briefly some of the basic themes of this book:

1. The labour shortages of the 1950s were met in the expanding regions by the employment of coloured immigrants from the Commonwealth rather than by the attraction through higher wages of internal migrants or by automation. Since these were, in general, areas in which the demand for unskilled and semi-skilled labour exceeded the supply, resistance from local labour was at a minimum. Like the Irish before them, many of the immigrants were of poor schooling, lacked industrial experience and skills measuring up to British standards and, in addition, had language difficulties. Their concentration in particular enterprises and departments has given some disputes between them and their employers and between them and their unions the appearance, but not the real substance, of racial conflict.

2. As this first generation has attempted to move up the occupational scale and into supervisory and white-collar work another factor, racial discrimination, has become apparent. The coloured second generation,

1. The impact of possible British entry of the E.E.C. was discussed above, p. 35

with far greater aspirations than their fathers, now feel themselves threatened by this discrimination which is the product of employers' and workers' economic fears, beliefs about status, mild xenophobia and sense of social conformity. In the economy of the future skilled white-collar work will be the typical form of employment; yet discrimination makes it increasingly likely that one section of workers, identified by colour, will be deprived of this very avenue to satisfy their abilities. The spread of automation, so far from relieving this section, along with others, of the burden of manual labour, may result in a growing reserve of unemployed coloured workers. This new inequality might lull white workers into a false sense of security; in reality it will erode their own social, economic and moral standards.

3. The solution offered by politicians has generally taken the form of immigration control, a ploy which becomes increasingly irrelevant as the disparities in socio-economic status and job opportunities between the white community and settled coloured minorities grow. The framing of adequate measures is also hampered by the misleading use of concepts such as 'integration' and 'discrimination'. For sociologists engaged in factual description both have fairly precise meanings indicating, in the one case, a phase in the absorption of minorities and, in the other, a basis for generalizing about social distance. As used by politicians 'integration' is capable of concealing forms of pluralism which ought to have no part in the life of a modern industrial enterprise. Moreover, the legal approach to what is described as 'discrimination' is based on certain ethical and political assumptions which exclude all forms of discrimination save those on racial pretexts (ignoring such related phenomena as religious and sex discrimination). Even more important than this is the fact that the lawyer's case-by-case orientation is, by its very nature, incapable of changing overall economic and occupational patterns, although it can create a climate of opinion in which social change may occur. Unfortunately the terminology of 'discrimination' used by lawyers creates the illusion that they are capable by themselves of altering the broad patterns of discrimination which the sociologists have described.

4. The limits on competition in the jobs market have in the past been determined largely by voluntary means. The system of regulation of jobs within enterprises is unlikely by itself to show any change in direction and may tend to become increasingly discriminatory. On the other hand, external voluntary procedures, themselves prompted by the threat of legislation, are beginning to be used to declare national policies and to provide a rough justice for individual victims of discrimination.

But other, older, rules of a discriminatory nature have been left undisturbed largely because of the emphasis in labour relations on procedural rules instead of the substantive aim of racial equality.

5. Other voluntary means of controlling discrimination have proved to be unsuccessful. The Civil Service stands in an ambiguous position because of its Nationality Rule, while the Ministry of Labour is under conflicting pressures to satisfy employers' requirements and at the same time to pursue national policies of equal opportunity. Without being given a more active role in the direction of labour generally the Ministry is unlikely to escape from this dilemma. Voluntary liaison committees have failed to make an impact on patterns of job discrimination partly because of their concern with individual casework rather than broad social problems. The ethnic minorities themselves lack the cohesive economic and political organization required to make a real impact on the situation.

6. The common law provides no direct protection to victims of discrimination because of the absence of constitutional guarantees, the judicial treatment of racial incidents as relating primarily to the maintenance of public order rather than as wrongs to particular individuals, reluctance to expand the heads of public policy, difficulties of proof and the absence of suitable remedies to redress discrimination. Indirectly, labour law provides a few remedies but these are inapplicable in the major areas of social concern. If the Report of the Donovan Commission proposes some general revision of the legal structure of labour relations, and these proposals are implemented, it is possible that some basic legal guarantees of importance to members of ethnic minorities will be provided, for example procedures to deal with unfair dismissals and the strengthening of the system of conciliation and arbitration in disputes about the employment and non-employment of persons. On the other hand, some projected developments, such as the legal enforcement of collective labour agreements, might lead, in the present state of race relations, to the legal codification of certain discriminatory practices unless adequate safeguards are devised. The major legal development, however, is the Race Relations Act which, in 1965, introduced the valuable technique of conciliation in matters of race relations. A well-drafted extension of the Act to cover employment discrimination can provide the basis for affirmative action by the Race Relations Board against racial discrimination.

7. American experience indicates that the law plays a useful role as an unequivocal declaration of public policy; in time it can increase the job opportunities open to members of minority groups and it can change

the practices and attitudes of employers and workers. But it has failed to change entrenched patterns of inequality. In Britain the value of the law lies principally in the protection it affords to employers against the fancied reactions of customers, employees and trade competitors, the backing it gives to union officials in educating their rank-and-file, and the sense of justice which it gives to members of minority groups so easing the process of absorption. In Britain, subject to the economic and political limits described above, the law may achieve more than in America because of its relatively early introduction into a mobile situation.

8. The evolution of voluntary procedures is desirable because of the importance of group solidarity and corporate autonomy in British industrial relations. Reliance by members of ethnic minorities on what members of the majority group perceive as 'outside' institutions tends to weaken this solidarity and autonomy and this, in turn, is seen by the majority as a threat to the common advancement of them all. The consequent resentment and hostility between ethnic groups, and the emphasis on their own distinctiveness by members of the minority, retards the process of absorption. To avoid this 'backlash' it is proper to rely principally on voluntary controls, with legislation providing a basic minimum standard below which no individual may fall. Existing procedures, however, are defective in several important respects and until they are improved legislation will be neeeded as the main means of control.

These conclusions are based on the author's evaluation of published and unpublished materials, interviews with employers, trade union officials, leaders of minority groups, government officials and others, his personal experience in handling the employment problems of immigrants and an analysis of the legal situation. The limits of this kind of study by an individual are obvious, but the book will have succeeded in its aim if it prompts students of race and industrial relations to further research and practitioners of industrial relations to action. In particular, once the immediate arguments about legislation are over, a new period for race relations will open. A deeper and more realistic analysis will become possible once bodies such as the Race Relations Board and voluntary industrial committeees have had a chance to bring about deliberate changes in the situation. Then the precise role of groups such as trade unions and ethnic organizations will become clearer. While most existing research concentrates on attitudes and behaviour of individuals towards members of ethnic minorities, the new period will offer the chance to study institutions, social codes and the established opportunity structure. In this work the social scientist, the lawyer and the practitioner of industrial relations should be able to cooperate in an examination of how the legal and social controls operate in action.

There are no quick solutions for the problems of racial inequality of opportunity. But it may be worth while to summarize a few of the proposals which emerge from various parts of this book:

1. A minimum standard of human rights in the field of employment should be established by legislation. This must include discrimination on grounds of religion, sex, social origin and political opinion as well as colour, race, ethnic or national origins, and might also deal with matters such as victimization on grounds of legitimate trade union activities. Such legislation may have to be enacted piecemeal, depending on social and economic conditions, but ought to be a declared policy goal.

2. This standard could be enforced either by an extension, in the field of employment, of the present Race Relations Board into a 'Human Rights Commission', or by the allocation of all questions of human rights in employment to a system of labour courts.

3. The primary aims of the legislation would be to provide a foundation for voluntary action to secure its goals, and to provide a safety net through which no individual could fall.

4. The repeal of legislation discriminating against aliens in industry (i.e. sections 3, 4 and 5 of the Aliens Restriction (Amendment) Act 1919); and the repeal, or modification, of those sections of the Merchant Shipping Act 1894 which discriminate against Asian and African crews.

5. The abandonment of the practice of restricting the types of employment into which aliens may go once they have lawfully entered the country for purposes of employment.

6. The amendment of section 8 of the Terms and Conditions of Employment Act 1959 to enable individual workers to complain that 'recognized terms and conditions' of employment are not being observed.

7. The development of an effective legal remedy against unfair dismissals.

8. The use of their powers under factories' and other legislation by local authorities to prevent the segregation of facilities on the premises.

9. The abandonment of those provisions in formal and informal collective labour agreements which discriminate against non-British workers, whether on grounds of nationality or otherwise.

10. The rapid development of voluntary grievance procedures to deal with individual complaints of racial discrimination, with provision for independent arbitration and participation in the conciliation process by members of ethnic minorities.

11. Recruitment drives by employers among sections of the population

who may not otherwise apply for vacancies because of past experiences of discrimination; ability tests for job applicants which take account of differences in cultural background; and active steps to disperse concentrations of minority ethnic groups in particular enterprises.

12. The voluntary introduction of trade testing to replace nepotism and other subjective criteria for entry into restricted trades; the expansion of industrial training and re-training for all employees, and where special disabilities are found (e.g. in the case of recent immigrants) such persons should receive priority in training.

13. The reintroduction of compulsory notification of vacancies to Ministry of Labour exchanges; the control (or abolition) of fee-charging private employment exchanges; and the discouragement of pre-employment inquiries which may cloak a colour bar.

14. Continuing action by the Youth Employment Service to encourage school-leavers to take up further education, stressing the importance of spoken English to those who come from abroad.

15. Training programmes for trade union officers and members in the difficulties, customs and backgrounds of ethnic minorities; and the education of ethnic minorities in the practices of industry.

16. An independent inquiry into the scope and objectives of the Civil Service Nationality Rule; government pressure on nationalized industries to set an example in inter-group relations; and the amendment of the Fair Wages Resolution of the House of Commons to direct the inclusion of a non-discrimination clause in government contracts.

These are by no means all the suggestions which have been made in this book. Nor is it supposed that they will necessarily lead to an immediate abatement of racial discrimination; on the contrary, some of them, such as proposals for improved training, may lead members of ethnic minorities into situations in which discrimination is likely to occur. The proposals do, however, share one common feature and this is that they do not offer *racial* solutions to what are industrial and social problems. Indeed, many of these reforms would be of far wider application and benefit than in the area of race relations. The main guideline of action against racial discrimination should be to take effective measures against underlying social evils, making special allowances, where necessary, for the disabilities of ethnic minorities. We do not need to hot-up a mythical 'race-war'; rather we should seek to resolve the underlying conflicts which erupt when immigration, colour and class interact. Full employment and a guaranteed standard of human rights – these are the twin conditions for the achievement of equal opportunities.

Appendix I. Selected Examples of Allegations of Racial Incidents in Employment in Britain, 1 January 1961 to 31 December 1965

What types of allegation are voluntary and statutory bodies charged with administering anti-discrimination procedures likely to encounter? To provide a rough guide, this selection has been culled from the provincial and national press, television scripts and other publications which appeared during a five-year period. Use has also been made of the files of the National Council for Civil Liberties. Some further examples are to be found in the text. Examples of opposition by white workers to the employment of coloured workers before 1960 are given in the Appendix to J. A. G. Griffiths *et al.*, *Coloured Immigrants in Britain* (London 1960).

These examples are in no way intended to 'prove' the extent of discrimination (that task was admirably and scientifically undertaken by the P.E.P. Report); indeed, each of them depends on the reporter's view of the situation. But they do indicate the wide variety of allegations requiring investigation.

I. ENGAGEMENT FOR EMPLOYMENT
    (a) *Recruitment policy*
        (i) Advertisements and pre-employment inquiries
[1]   Building workers in certain firms in North-Eastern England alleged that they were obliged to answer questions about their nationality, religion, age and other matters before being considered for a job. They said: 'questions about nationality bring in a colour bar. A coloured man was literally run off one site.' (*Evening Gazette*, Yorks, 25 March 1965)
[2]   An advertisement was sent to the *South London Press* asking for kitchen staff at a local teachers' training college and adding 'No Coloured'. The words were apparently written by an employee of the college without authority. The Chairman of the Board of Governors of the college refused to say whether disciplinary action would be taken against the employee. (*South London Press*, 22 January 1965)
[3]   An advertisement asked specially for coloured workers to apply for work in the brass gravity diecasting shop of a West Bromwich firm. Two hundred and fifty white men and women workers stopped work at the firm in protest against the advertisement which, they alleged, implied that coloured workers were better time-keepers than whites. They said this was a 'colour bar in reverse'. Fifteen coloured workers

remained at work during the stoppage. The management said no slur had been intended and that the advertisement had been so worded because white workers did not seem interested in applying. (*Daily Telegraph*, 29 June 1965; *Birmingham Post*, 29 June 1965; *Birmingham Evening Mail*, 28 and 29 June 1965)

[4] There were seventy cards advertising jobs recently in one of the five employment agency windows near Paddington station. Sixty-nine had typed at the bottom: 'Regret no overseas applicants for this post'. There was one exception. 'Would possibly consider' said a Middlesex firm looking for a cost clerk 'first-class overseas applicant for this post'.

The secretary of the agency said: 'We still have difficulty in placing the very good coloured applicants who have been in England for many years. People who have been to university have to take ordinary run-of-the-mill jobs. One has to try to put them off as kindly as possible. Unless they have had three – four years' experience employers won't take them. The Labour Exchanges won't help them either, so how are they to get experience?' (Peter Dunn, 'The Black-List of Jobs', *Observer*, 3 May 1964)

(ii) Refusal to employ members of specified minority groups

[5] In its quarterly report the Bradford and District Employment Committee said a number of textile employers showed reluctance to engage coloured workers. Their stated reasons were that some coloured women had not proved sufficiently adaptable and had left after a few weeks; others were not sufficiently experienced. (*Yorkshire Post*, 2 March 1961)

[6] It was alleged at Parkstone Sea Training School, Dorset, that it was difficult to place coloured trainees in the Merchant Navy at Southampton, where two steamship companies (one of them on the South African run) between them employing 80 per cent of all seamen would not take coloureds. (*Poole & Dorset Herald*, 4 October 1961)

[7] A twenty-nine-year-old Jamaican-born British subject, who had been a coal-miner for seven years and seemed to fulfil all the requirements for a trainee fireman in the merchant navy applied for employment, but was rejected. The case was taken up by Mr Harold Walker, M.P., who was informed that there were a number of West Indian crews employed in vessels which open Articles of Agreement in the U.K. 'It is because their numbers are already adequate to meet the requisitions placed on the [Merchant Navy] Establishment that we must continue to decline to accept [the] application.' Mr Walker was told 'At the present time there are sufficient engine-room ratings of differing nationalities registered with the Establishment and available for work. . . . I ought perhaps to add that, if it should become necessary to recruit more West Indian seafarers, we would probably be asked by the union to admit experienced seafarers first, and we would normally agree to this as being fair and equitable.' (Information supplied by Mr H. Walker, M.P., 21 December 1965)

[8] A Jamaican woman who claimed to have had a good education and to be qualified to work as a statistical clerk answered an advertisement for female workers by a plastics firm. She telephoned and was told that vacancies still existed and she could be interviewed at 11.30 a.m.

Arriving at noon, she was told all vacancies had been filled. She again telephoned and was told there were still vacancies and she could return in the afternoon. She asked whether the firm employed coloureds and was told: 'No we don't [at this factory] but we do take them at [our other factory].' The manager later said the policy of the firm was to treat everyone alike although it did not have any coloured people working at one of its two factories 'at present'. He said he would find the Jamaican woman a job 'if she was suitable'. (*Bolton Journal & Guardian,* 4 June 1965)

(iii) Quota systems

[9] A personnel manager in a West London firm said: 'Twice we have reduced or stopped taking coloured people on, temporarily in order to maintain a balance, say of 20 per cent or 30 per cent coloured. If you get to 40 per cent in a factory you are in a position wherein you cannot possibly stop it becoming a permanently coloured factory. Officially there is no colour bar in unions. But you get pressure from the shop floor. . . . They do a bargain – the same as with wages. They say "get the proportion of coloureds down to 10 per cent" but really expect to get 20 per cent. If you took on coloureds and white people were unemployed, you would get pressure building up. We would want to employ white people anyway. They are much easier.'(*The Times,* 27 January 1965)

(iv) Informal agreements relating to recruitment[1]. (For provisions in collective agreements, see Appendix II.)

[10] A branch of the Amalgamated Society of Wire Drawers and Kindred Workers demanded that an Arab worker be dismissed by a Sheffield firm in accordance with an *agreement between them.* Men from Jamaica, Pakistan and India had worked at the firm and it was therefore alleged that his dismissal was due to national origin rather than colour. (*Star,* 10 April 1962)

[11] At a West Riding textile firm some weavers and overlookers stopped work in protest against the taking on of more Pakistanis and the setting on of one to learn to weave in contravention of a local agreement giving preference to local labour. The union refused support. (*Yorkshire Post,* 15 and 16 June 1962)

[12] Sixty-four workers in a machine shop at Keighley went on strike because two Pakistanis were taken on. After discussions between the local branch of a trade union and the management's representatives it was agreed that coloured labour would not be employed on skilled work and no coloured would be started in the shop without management – union discussions. The men thereupon decided to return to work. (*Bradford Telegraph & Argus,* 27 July 1961)

(v) School-leavers seeking employment

[13] [Television documentary]

Commentary: These girls wanted to be secretaries. There's a desperate shortage of secretaries.

1st Girl: Well, I tried ten jobs and I was only successful with four.

---

1. Another example is case 42 below

Interviewer: What did the six who turned you away say?

1st Girl: Well, they're very sorry but the staff won't like it. And so they'll have to say no.

Interviewer: The staff wouldn't like what?

1st Girl: Me being a coloured person – they wouldn't like a coloured person to join them.

Interviewer: Is that the only reason they gave?

1st Girl: Yes. . . .

Interviewer: How do you know that you didn't get some of those jobs because you're coloured, because you're black?

1st Girl: Because when I phoned up they said – Oh yes, come along and get the interview. When I reached there most of them say to me – Was it you that rang up? And I say yes. And they look at me all funny and I say – something wrong? And they say – Are you sure? And I say, yes. And they say, Well we're very sorry, but we were deceived and we thought you was an English person. You've got a very English voice. So I said, well yes. Well if you get a job you're just lucky, it's just luck. . . .

(Post Production Script 'Coloured School Leavers' transmitted on I.T.V. in the programme *This Week* 4 November 1965)

[14] The British-born coloured son of an Indian doctor in Birmingham alleged that he was turned down by a large firm in Birmingham when he applied for a vacancy for graduate apprentices. The letter of rejection said the company gave preference to 'local products'. Later a company spokesman apologized and said 'We had not realized [he] was a local man. . . . No colour bar of any sort is operated in this company.' (*Sunday Times*, 1 July 1962)

(vi) University graduates seeking employment

[15] The University Appointments Boards report that employers are sensitive to the possibility of friction between immigrants and other staff, particularly if the job involves responsibility, the management of other employees, or representative work with the public. There are less likely to be objections to employing them on research work. Approaches by the Appointments Boards to industry for junior executive jobs and management traineeships for young coloured graduates are generally unsuccessful, again largely for fear of friction with other employees. However, in view of the shortage in their respective professions, doctors and teachers experience less difficulty in gaining posts for which they are qualified providing their own spoken and written English is of the required standard. (Christopher Brocklebank-Fowler *et al.*, *Commonwealth Immigration*, Bow Group 1965, p. 28)

(vii) Management fears of customer reaction

[16] A survey of employment of coloured workers in stores in Nottingham revealed that none were employed at the counter in the city centre. Store managers were said to have reservations about the reaction of customers. (*Nottingham Evening News*, 22 February 1962)

[17] Coloured workers are normally employed 'behind the scenes' in stores and a spokesman of one of the largest stores in West London explained: 'Anyone in direct contact with all customers must be acceptable to all

customers.' Banks and insurance companies also said that 'customer reaction' to coloured employees would have to be tested. (*Observer*, 3 May 1964)

[18] An investigation conducted in late 1965 by the trade magazine *Hotel and Restaurant Management* reported there was no colour bar in the hotel and catering industry, but the inquiry team found very few coloured immigrants employed in anything but service jobs and only two had white workers under them. The industry could not function without coloured immigrants and was facing a crisis as a result of the new restrictions on immigration. The supposed prejudice of customers was largely a myth, though there seemed to be some caution among more expensive caterers in deference to what they assumed to be the feelings of their customers.

(b) *Employment Exchanges*

(i) Ministry of Labour Exchanges

[19] A firm made an inquiry at a London Employment Exchange regarding the employment of a machine operator for a duplicating machine. An employment officer asked the firm: 'I suppose you would not be wanting a C.W.?' When asked what was meant by a 'C.W.' the officer said it stood for 'Coloured Worker'. On being informed that the firm did not practise discrimination, the officer replied that she would note that 'you would not object to a better-class coloured worker'. The matter was taken up by the National Council for Civil Liberties. The Manager of the Employment Exchange informed the Council that it was necessary to ascertain every employer's exact requirements when notifying a vacancy, including willingness to employ Irish, Cypriots, West Indians and natives of other countries, in order to make successful submissions. He said 'The abbreviation "C.W." is occasionally used by the order clerk to avoid embarrassment to coloured applicants who may be in the immediate vicinity of the officer and so overhear the telephone conversation and this was the case on this occasion.' He added that 'the same service is given to applicants of all races at this office'. In a subsequent letter to the Council he stated: 'You will no doubt realize that we may have to put the question "Will you accept a Coloured Worker?" a hundred times or more a week, and even if only for a change an officer may vary the form of words used to the inquirer. . . . The question when put to an employer gives them a lead to state that they do not accept other races, Cypriots, Gibraltans, Maltese, Irish, Scots or Welsh, if in fact they have an objection or prejudice to having one of these people in their employ.' (National Council for Civil Liberties, June 1961)

[20] The Manager of an Employment Exchange was reported to have said: 'At the moment there is a shortage of jobs for unskilled men. Many immigrants fall into the unskilled category. A lot of employers' stipulations (not to send them Coloured or Irish labour) may be the result of trade union agreements. Often employers will not mix certain races. *Our job is to provide exactly what is wanted. . . .*' (*Leamington Spa Courier*, 18 and 25 August 1961)

(ii) Private employment agencies[1]

[21] One agency, which we considered typical, said, 'We dare not send coloured people along for interview with this or that company as they have made it quite clear that they will not consider employing coloured people. We know that if we persist in putting them forward we shall not be invited to supply personnel to meet their future needs.' (Christopher Brocklebank-Fowler *et al.*, *Commonwealth Immigration*, Bow Group, 1965, p. 29)

(c) *Employee opposition to employment of members of minority groups*[2]

[22] Miners at a colliery near Barnsley asked the management not to sign on any worker who was not *British by birth*. There were five foreigners (Poles and Hungarians) out of 2,140 miners at the pit. An industrial relations officer of the National Coal Board said the Board would not recruit 'foreign' labour. (N.C.B. Press Summary, 5 June 1962) At another colliery, near Wolverhampton, miners were reported as expressing concern at the employment of 'coloured' workers, while English workers were made redundant elsewhere (*Express & Star*, 14 May 1962)

[23] A chapel of a trade union branch voted by thirty-eight votes to twenty-four to oppose the employment of coloured workers. After the meeting, the father of the chapel and his deputy resigned in protest and the branch secretary dissociated the union from the vote, stating that the union had a number of coloured members. (*Daily Herald*, 11 April 1961)

[24] A branch of a national union submitted a resolution to a Trades Council, calling for a limitation of coloured unskilled immigrant labour. (*Leicester Mercury*, 17 May 1961)

[25] English stewardesses working for B.O.A.C. opposed the introduction of Asian girls as stewardesses on the San-Francisco – New York run, on the alleged ground that Asians would be allowed to wear ear-rings, nail varnish and stiletto heels, unlike English girls. (*The Times*, 4 August 1961; *Guardian*, 12 August 1961)

[26] Forty night-shift workers at a North London factory refused to work with three new coloured workers. The management refused to make any concession and the trade union shop stewards supported the management in this. The men returned to work. (*Guardian*, 7, 8 and 11 January 1965)

[27] At [a soft drinks firm] the manager [stated]: 'There's no discrimination in race, religion or anything else here. Most workers are local cockneys but we've had almost every nationality here except Germans. I'm Jewish myself and I won't have them.' He had employed coloured men and women for some years and found them no slower than local labour at picking up the job. The women, however, were not very popular with fellow-workers on the following grounds: body odour ('you can't get away from it'); a tendency to refuse their turns at cleaning jobs which all normally did in rotation; excessive exuberance and aggressiveness in groups. My informant told me that he had tried an experiment

1. Another example is case 4 above
2. Further examples in this category are cases 9, 10, 11, 12, 45

in the early days of coloured labour by putting a rather intelligent West Indian woman in with a particular group where the shop-stewardess had 'her knife into coloured girls'. He had hoped that personal contact might break down this feeling, but unfortunately this did not happen. The group sent the coloured woman to Coventry and 'ganged up on her' during the toilet breaks until she could stand it no longer and left. (Sheila Patterson, *Dark Strangers*, Penguin ed. 1963, p. 102)

[28] A West Indian was employed by a haulage firm after showing his union card. His qualifications and union membership satisfied the shop steward who first noted his employment. Within a week, however, a new shop steward took over and a meeting was called by the stewards at the firm. At this meeting a majority agreed to strike unless the coloured worker was dismissed. A number of coloureds had previously been employed among this department, but none of them had been quite so dark-skinned as the West Indian in question. The firm suspended the West Indian during talks with union officials, who put pressure on the stewards and rank and file to call off their strike. The management believed that the union had the responsibility to settle the problem. (National Council for Civil Liberties, February 1964)

[29] Over 100 lorry drivers came out on an unofficial strike in East London because they objected to the taking on of a coloured man on the grounds that he might be 'exploited' by the firm and not paid normal overtime. The firm refused to dismiss him and more workers came out on strike. He was a union member and the management said it intended to keep him. (*Guardian*, 14, 18 and 28 February 1964)

[30] Workers at a cartage company refused to work with a British-born coloured fitter and threatened to strike. The chief engineer decided, in view of this, to dismiss the man, whose qualifications were described as 'ideal'. A majority of the workers later revoked their decision, but the coloured fitter was reported to be unenthusiastic about working alongside them. (*Guardian*, 21 September 1962)

[31] Workers at a factory at Banbury voted for a 'colour bar' after a Pakistani had been engaged by the management. The Banbury branch of the National Union of General and Municipal Workers and the Banbury Trades Council opposed the workers' decision, but the management paid off the Pakistani worker after only one day. (*Topic*, 23 June 1962; *The Times*, 14 and 15 June, 1962)

(d) *Offences of corruption resulting from alleged discrimination in employment*

[32] A furnace chargehand was indicted at Birmingham Assizes on a charge of taking money from Indian workers in return for favours. It was alleged that he had threatened them that unless they paid him money, they would lose their jobs or overtime would be stopped for them. Summing up, Mr Justice Phillimore said the broad question was whether the allegations were true or were a frame-up. He said: 'Whatever their views on immigration may be an English jury can always be trusted to hold the scales fairly quite regardless of colour.' The accused was found not guilty. (*Sheffield Morning Telegraph*, 1 December 1965)

[33] It was alleged that Pakistanis had paid fees of £25 to £30 for jobs at a rubber factory at which eighty of the 350 workers were Pakistanis. The firm investigated and one chargehand was dismissed and a departmental head suspended. No evidence, however, was uncovered of more than packets of cigarettes and a few shillings changing hands. (*Guardian*, 25 June 1962)

[34] A mill manager and a Pakistani boilerman were accused of selling jobs to Pakistanis at the mill. The mill employed thirty-two Pakistanis in a total staff of sixty to seventy. The sums which changed hands were said to be between £5 and £25. (*Yorkshire Post*, 12 and 14 March 1964)

II. VOCATIONAL TRAINING

[35] A boy aged sixteen, born in Britain of West Indian parents, began work at a London Electricity Board depot as an apprentice and was being trained under a scheme approved by the National Council for the electricity industry. Some workers objected to the boy on grounds of colour, but the management informed them that it did not intend to operate a colour bar. (*The Sun*, 1 November 1965)

[36] An 'unofficial' strike was threatened in the London docks following a rumour that coloured men were being trained as dockers. Officials of the Transport and General Workers' Union said the rumours were untrue. They said jobs in the docks normally stay in East End and Bermondsey families, dockers having first chance to nominate relatives for vacancies. This made it virtually impossible for outsiders to get in but 'this does not mean that there is a colour bar. . . .' (*Sun*, 10 April 1965; *Evening Standard*, 20 April 1965)

[37] Fifty white employees in the bolt-making section of a firm went on strike because a West Indian was being trained there. Spokesmen for the strikers said: 'This is not a colour bar. But we feel we may lose our our own jobs if there is a flood of coloured labour into the department.' The Amalgamated Engineering Union condemned the strike and supported the management. After six days on strike the men returned to work. One of the shop stewards said white men ought to have been given preference. (*Daily Telegraph*, 3 February 1965; *Yorkshire Post* 1 February 1965)

III. PROMOTION

(a) *Work Assignment*

[38] London Transport have until recently declined to distinguish white from coloured workers on the ground that this would merely encourage differentiation. A careful 'head-counting' investigation by reporters at London bus garages tended, however, to confirm the claim that coloureds do not get promotion.

At one garage for instance, 20 per cent of the 500 workers are coloured, yet while 30 per cent of the conductors are coloured only 10 per cent of the drivers are coloured. A West Indian bus driver said:

'You've got to drive twice as well as a white man to get the job.' Statistics released by London Transport revealed that 15·6 per cent of the 27,250 London bus workers are coloured. There are 13,235 drivers of whom 985 or 7·4 per cent are coloured. Of the 9,815 male conductors 29 per cent are coloured.

Officials of London Transport categorically denied all allegations of discrimination. An assistant operating manager said there were no coloured inspectors because 'no coloured man has shown himself good enough'. (*Sunday Times*, 6 June 1965)

[39] A Pakistani was upgraded from crane driver to the charge of a machine in a steelworks. Eighty workers threatened to strike and the Pakistani was forced back to his old job. (*Sunday Times*, 23 February 1964)

[40] Forty dustcart drivers, led by a trade union branch secretary, threatened to withdraw their labour on public holidays and for snow clearing if a coloured man was promoted to dustcart driver, which would have meant a considerable wage rise and authority over dustmen on his route. It was reported that the dispute ended after 'higher level union talks'. (*Daily Herald*, 10 and 20 October 1963)

[41] A letter in the journal of a chain store group of companies, written by an anonymous employee, alleged that nearly all coloured workers with the group were relegated to portering jobs. The chairman of the group denied this and said 'more coloured people than ever have been given responsible jobs in the last two or three years in selling, stock-keeping, clerical or secretarial work'. He added that language was, however, a difficulty. (*The Sun*, 11 May 1965)

[42] An area training officer of a large Midlands firm alleged that people with B.Sc. degrees from India had to sweep floors in some places because of agreements between firms and unions. (*Birmingham Evening Dispatch*, 18 June 1962)

[43] The Vice-President of the Pakistani Welfare Association alleged that factory managers and foremen in some areas were using the Commonwealth Immigrants Bill as an excuse for refusing promotion to Pakistanis. (*Guardian*, 18 December 1961)

[44] An Indian was appointed acting inspector by a bus company after six years' service. Most crews were said to have accepted the appointment, but a trade union delegation told the company that they were concerned lest the whole complement of inspectors should ultimately become coloured. (*Leamington Morning News*, 7 December 1962)

(b) *Foremen and Supervisors*

[45] Eight night-shift workers were dismissed at a Lancashire firm for refusing to take orders from a Pakistani who was standing in as foreman. The production director who dismissed them said: 'They have confessed to me that if a white man had given instructions they would have obeyed.' One of the workers told a reporter: 'We have no objection to working alongside them [Pakistanis]. But we do object to taking orders from them.' Seven of the eight were later taken back after a promise that the Pakistani man would only transmit orders in future from the production manager or shift manager, and he would

remain in his position as a mechanic. (*Guardian*, 26, 28 and 29 June 1965; *Lancashire Evening Telegraph*, 25, 26 and 29 June 1965; *Daily Mail*, 26 June 1965)

IV. TERMS AND CONDITIONS OF EMPLOYMENT

(a) *Wages and Hours of Work*

[46] Forty-one coloured workers in a plastics factory in Luton went on strike against wage reductions claiming this was racial discrimination and did not affect white men in the same factory. They claimed, too, that white men were being brought in as blacklegs. They later returned to work at the reduced rates. The management claimed that the rate had been cut due to poor business in the moulding shop where it just happened that most of the men are coloured. (*Guardian*, 15 and 16 August 1962)

[47] Fleckers in the London fur trade alleged that coloured workers were being used to break a closed shop and to undercut their wages. (*Daily Mail*, 26 and 27 April 1962)

[48] It was alleged that four coloured workers in a Midland firm worked seventy hours each a week without overtime pay, for a wage of £11 to £13 a week. A number of these allegations were investigated by the Transport and General Workers' Union. The Union's District Organizer said these rumours concerning 'back-street' factories were mostly anonymous and therefore difficult to check or remedy. (*Birmingham Post*, 13 September 1961)

(b) *Separate toilet facilities for workers of different groups*

[49] Workers threatened to strike if they had to continue sharing toilet facilities with Asian workers at a factory in Smethwick. The National Chairman of their union expressed total opposition to any form of discrimination of this kind and there were protests from the Indian High Commission and the Indian Workers' Association. The management abandoned its plan for segregated toilets but stated that a few Asian-style lavatories might be put up for those who wanted them. (*Birmingham Post*, 1 and 9 June 1965)

[50] A Leeds Textile firm introduced a separate toilet for thirty Pakistani employees to 'ease a difficult situation'. This led to sharp protests from the Pakistani and Muslim Association. (*Yorkshire Post*, 19 and 23 October 1963)

[51] Coloured workers at a Smethwick factory protested against a plan to have a separate entrance to the works and separate washing facilities for coloured workers. The Amalgamated Union of Foundry Workers declared its opposition to this plan and 'any form of racial discrimination'. (*Manchester Evening News*, 2 June 1965)

(c) *Objections by workers to sharing living quarters or canteens with members of other groups*

[52] At Fleetwood, Lancashire, three deckhands on a trawler which carried eight deckhands and a coloured apprentice refused to sail if they had

to share quarters with the coloured man. The trawler was thereupon obliged to put back to port after some hours, causing the owners a loss of £1,000. The three deckhands were charged [presumably under s. 376 of the Merchant Shipping Act, 1894] with the offence of an unlawful combination to disobey lawful commands while engaged to serve on a sea-fishing vessel. One of them was sentenced to two months' imprisonment, and the others were fined £20 and £10 respectively. The chairman of the magistrates said the court took a very serious view of the case: 'The sooner you three realize that a man, whatever his colour, has the same rights and privileges in this country as you have, the better'. (*Lloyd's List*, 3 May 1965; *The Times*, 3 May 1965)

(d) *'Ethnic' work groups*

[53] See above, Chapter 5, pp. 77–9.

(e) *Special rules regarding clothing, appearance etc.*

[54] A local Transport Department prohibits its employees from wearing beards which do not conform with the requirement of regulations, that is of 'cleanliness and tidiness'. The Chairman of the Transport Committee refuse to lay down a standard for beards. In December 1962 a Pakistani was dismissed for non-compliance with this rule. (*The Times*, 18 December 1962.) The Indian Workers' Association alleged in 1965 that Sikhs wearing beards and turbans were refused employment by the Transport Division of the Corporation, on these grounds. They alleged that Sikhs employed by the Transport Division were clean shaven, although they might prefer to observe these customs, if it were not that they felt they might lose their jobs. This allegation was put to the General Manager of the Transport Division by the National Council for Civil Liberties. The General Manager did not reply specifically to this point but stated that the employees themselves 'do not seek to lay emphasis on their customs and religious beliefs'. (National Council for Civil Liberties, August 1965)

[55] A local Transport Committee reversed a decision that Sikhs in its employ as drivers and conductors must wear peaked caps and not turbans. It later settled that the colour of such turbans was to be blue. (*Guardian*, 10 and 18 October, 21 November 1962: *Birmingham Mail*, 27 March 1963)

[56] A Pakistani who was dismissed as a trainee bus conductor because he would not shave off his beard successfully sued the Bradford Corporation for wrongful dismissal. The trainee, who said he wore his beard for religious reasons, was awarded £21 1s. 10d. damages and costs in the county court.

He was accepted for training as a conductor in December 1962 and nothing was said about his beard. But on the second day of his training his instructor said he must remove it. The instructor referred to a rule requiring employees to report for duty properly dressed and clean in appearance. The trainee was dismissed on his third day of training and the Corporation claimed that he had failed satisfactorily to respond to his tuition by shaving off his beard.

Judge Stansfield held that the beard was not scruffy or unsightly but 'of a neat and rather distinguished variety of which many Englishmen would be delighted to be the proud possessor'. He held 'I do not think they had any valid reason at all for terminating his employment in the manner in which they did. I think it was an unwarrantable interference with the freedom of the individual.'

He said the damages represented the pay the trainee would have received while in training and a week's wages after completing his training. (*The Times*, 26 November 1963)

V. DISMISSAL PRACTICES

[57] An assistant matron at an old folks' home alleged that she had been asked to resign because of her colour. (*Daily Mail*, 6 May 1961)

[58] On the question of redundancy policy [the spokesman of a construction firm] said: 'In a slump the coloured workers will go first, and quite rightly. There should be job priority for local people.' (Sheila Patterson, *Dark Strangers*, Penguin ed., p. 120)

[59] [At a light engineering factory] coloured labour [was] regarded as an undesirable necessity, temporary and expendable in the event of a recession. I was told that the management would change to white labour any day if it became available. . . .

By the time I revisited [this factory] two years later, there had in fact been some redundancy and the firm had put off several hundred full- and part-time workers, mainly women. As my informant had prophesied, coloured workers had borne the brunt of the redundancy, and now constituted 9 per cent of the male labour force and 13 per cent of the female full-time workers. [At the earlier time the proportions were 11 per cent and 20–30 per cent respectively.] (Sheila Patterson, *Dark Strangers*, Penguin ed., pp. 106–7)

VI. NATIONALIZED INDUSTRIES, PUBLIC SERVICES AND LOCAL AUTHORITIES

(a) *Transport*

(i) British Rail

[60] Over forty railway passenger guards protested to British Railways against the promotion of two coloured men to be relief passenger guards. They alleged that coloured men are treated more leniently than white railwaymen 'because the Railways management is frightened of being accused of colour prejudice'. A British Railways spokesman denied this and said both men had been employed for five years and were being promoted in the normal way on eligibility and merit. The National Union of Railwaymen sharply rebuked the passenger guards who had taken part in the protest and reaffirmed its 'no colour bar' policy while calling for a measure of control over immigration to avoid flooding the labour market. (*Birmingham Post*, 27 March and 15 April 1961)

[61] It was alleged that none of the large number of coloured workers

employed by British Railways were among the 1,000-strong staff at the main line station of Paddington, because of the attitude of the management.

A Western Region public relations official called it 'not a colour bar – just a question of colour preference'. A spokesman at the station was reported to have said, 'There are enough European applicants for the jobs. All things being equal we prefer taking on coloured people. They are more satisfactory'. In October 1961 it was reported that coloured porters were still not employed at Paddington. (*Railway Review*, 23 and 30 June 1961; *Daily Herald*, 17 and 19 June 1961; *Evening Standard*, 7 October 1961)

(ii) Municipal Road Passenger Transport[1]

[62] An omnibus company which is jointly owned by the Corporation and the Transport Holding Company (the latter being a public corporation which has the controlling interest) had, in 1963, 1,300 vehicles. In 1962 it carried 255 million passengers. For the ten years before 1963 the company maintained a policy of not recruiting coloured workers for its buses although some were employed on maintenance work at its garages. A 'test' case was arranged in March 1963. A nineteen-year-old coloured boy was granted an interview but this was cancelled when the company learned he was coloured. A West Indian community leader thereupon called for a boycott of the company's buses and there were widespread protests. The general manager of the company refused to alter the company's policy giving as reasons the absence of a labour shortage, a 'white' waiting list, the expectation that coloured recruitment would lead to an exodus of white staff and that coloured busmen in London were 'rude and arrogant'. He said the decision was that of the company and not the unions. Subsequently the chairman of the Transport Holding Company said: 'In future there will be no colour bar on [the] buses at all. . . . It just could not be tolerated.' Following a directive from London, the general manager of the company opened negotiations with the union. The local Trades Council adopted a statement deploring the incidence of racial discrimination. (I.R.R. *News Letter*, June 1963, pp. 4–7, ibid., July 1963, p. 13)

[63] At a conference of delegates from London Transport's eighty bus depots a resolution was passed 'opposing the influx of immigrants into this country and their employment in London Transport'. The Transport and General Workers' Union subsequently declared this resolution invalid, and at a later conference the representatives of London busmen passed a resolution by sixty-five votes to fourteen, with two abstentions, opposing racial discrimination. (*Sunday Times*, 14 May 1961; *Daily Mail*, 15 May 1961; *Commercial Motor*, 7 July 1961)

[64] Bus crews in Sheffield threatened to strike because two conductresses had been suspended for refusing to work with coloured drivers. Sheffield Corporation's Transport Department emphasized that the Corporation's policy was one of non-discrimination. (*Sheffield Telegraph* 7 October 1961)

---

1. Further examples are cases 38 and 54 above

(b) *Electricity Supply*[1]

[65] A skilled Jamaican electrician was refused an interview by a local office of the Electricity Board despite an admitted shortage of electricians on the grounds that consumers might be 'shocked and scared' if visited by a coloured workman in their homes. After consideration by the East Midlands Board and the Electrical Trades Union, he was invited to attend for interview. By then he had found alternative employment and declined to attend. His new employer said: 'He's a skilled man and a most satisfactory worker. . . .' (*The Times*, 11 July 1961; *Leamington Spa Courier*, 7 and 14 July 1961)

(c) *Bank of England*

[66] The Financial Secretary to the Treasury (Mr N. MacDermott) in reply to a question in the House of Commons by Mr R. Freeson, M.P., stated that employees at the Bank of England were required to be British by birth and parentage. He would not direct the Bank to remove this condition of employment. (*The Times*, 5 June 1965)

(d) *Post Office*

[67] A delegate at the Post Office Engineering Union Conference on 17 June 1964 alleged that whenever coloured men joined the cable depots of the Post Office they 'were immediately made labourers, whatever skills they might have, while white men are put straight into a technical grade'. Spokesmen for the Union's executive deplored this suggestion and said it was the first case of alleged racial discrimination of which the executive had heard and it would be extensively investigated. A G.P.O. spokesman said later: 'We have no colour bar at the Post Office at all.' All the cable depots' labourers were white men and 'the filling of vacancies depends on the qualifications of those who apply'. (*Yorkshire Post*, 18 June 1964)

(e) *National Health Service*

[68] In 1961 only 3 per cent of the student nurses in teaching hospitals in the Oxford area were non-European, whereas the comparative figure for non-teaching hospitals was 21 per cent. (J. M. Maclyuire Report to the Oxford Area Nurse Committee, 1961, quoted by R. B. Davison, *Commonwealth Immigrants*, p. 45)

(f) *Education Authorities*

[69] In reply to an inquiry by the National Council for Civil Liberties, the Director of Education of a Midlands city stated: 'The number of coloured teachers in the . . . city education services has varied between six and twelve. There is no question of any percentage being applied but I am bound to say that our policy is dictated to some extent by the fact that we have a quota imposed by the Department of Education. We have no difficulty in appointing the maximum within the quota and we are therefore able to choose. In choosing as between white and coloured or British-born or immigrant of any colour, we consider only

---

1. Another example is case 35 above

the suitability for the post in question. . . . We have employed coloured teachers for many years and have never had difficulties with their teaching white classes. . . . We receive many applications which cannot be considered because our quota is already full.' Another education authority informed the Council that as much as 75 per cent of the 'immigrant' applicants could not be given teaching appointments because their English was inadequate. (National Council for Civil Liberties, July–August 1965)

(g)   *Local Authorities and general facilities*

[70] A woman complained to the Brighton public library committee that she found it 'offensive to be served by a Native'. This complaint was firmly rejected by the committee. (*Daily Express*, 4 January 1961)

[71] A rural council endorsed a recommendation by its town development committee not to accept 'at this stage' applications from firms interested in moving from London into their area, which employed large numbers of coloured workers. The decision of the council apparently arose out of the interest in moving to the area under an 'overspill' scheme, shown by a firm employing eighty workers, twenty-five of whom were coloured. (*The Times*, 24 and 25 February 1965; *Cambridge News*, 24 February 1965)

VII.   SELF-EMPLOYED AND PROFESSIONAL PERSONS

(a)   *Discrimination in regard to insurance affecting self-employment*

[72] A West Indian businessman who used his van for business purposes was fined for driving without insurance. He alleged that he had approached at least fifteen companies for insurance on his van and had had his money returned as soon as it was learned that he was coloured.

A spokesman for the British Insurance Association later denied that there was any discrimination but one broker reported that at least 180 companies operated a ban, either by refusing to insure a coloured man until he had lived in Britain for up to three years, or by increasing premiums by 25 per cent on the grounds that West Indians are temperamentally worse risks than other drivers. (*Daily Mail*, 1 July 1961; *Daily Herald*, 1 July 1961)

(b)   *Licences to carry on business*

[73] Taxi-drivers in Warwick unsuccessfully opposed an Indian bus driver's application for a licence on the grounds that taxi-driving was 'an intimate business' and 'the general public would prefer to be driven by a white man'. (*Daily Mail*, 21 September 1963; *Birmingham Post* 24 September 1963)

VIII.   TRADE UNION PRACTICES[1]

(a)   *Membership*

[74] A delegation of coloured dockworkers complained to their union that

1. For examples of trade union reactions where discrimination is alleged see cases 22, 23, 24, 26, 28, 31, 36, 37, 39, 40, 44, 47, 48, 49, 51, 53, 63, 65, 67

they were only allowed to hold a 'miscellaneous' union card, a 'regular' card being obtainable by white workers only, while they all paid the same union subscription. A district secretary of the union said the allegations were nonsense and there had been a misunderstanding. There were a lot of coloured men in each of the four grades of workers; registered men, branch men, miscellaneous branch men and non-union men. After a meeting the coloured workers accepted assurances that there was no racial discrimination within the union. (*South Wales Echo*, 2, 10 and 17 June 1964; *Western Mail*, 3 and 6 June 1964)

(b) *Unofficial action*

[75] Forty Indian and Pakistani workers went on strike over technical grievances and the refusal of management to accept one of their leaders, an M.A. of Punjab University, as their spokesman. The men later returned to work, but came out again and were dismissed. The union district secretary said he could not support them in their second walk-out having advised against it. (*Guardian-Journal*, 25 February 1964)

Appendix II. Collective Agreements and Union Rules in Regard to Non-British Workers: Summary of information Supplied by Trade Unions:(a)

Union	Description of Workers	1. Date 2. Duration 3. Parties	Recruitment Provisions	Terms and Conditions of Employment	Union Membership	Redundancy
1. Amalgamated Moulders Union (b)	Italian	1. 26 August 1946 2. Not operated 3. Engineering Employers' and Light Castings Ironfounders'	Mutual consent of employer and workrooms at each foundry directly concerned	T.U.*	Temporary membership condition of employment	To be returned to homes as and when position can be met by employment of British labour
2. Amalgamated Society of Textile Workers and Kindred Trades	a) European Volunteer Workers b) Members of Polish Resettlement Corps or their dependents if alien	1. a) 14 October 1947 b) 6 March 1947 2. Not specified 3 J.I.C. Silk Industry	No suitable British labour available	T.U.*	To be encouraged	To be discharged before any British workers. (Redundancy agreement 14 July 1964 applicable to all employees)
3. Amalgamated Union of Building Trade Workers	Foreign Nationals	1. Since end of war 2. Reviewed from time to time 3. Not specified	Consultation before employment in Terrazo industry	—	—	—
4. Amalgamated Union of	Italian	Same as 1 above				

218

	Foreign (until acquiring British nationality)			Condition of Employment	First to be dismissed after part-time British workers
5. Amalgamated Weavers' Association		1. 1 December 1953 2. 2 months' notice to terminate 3. U.K. Manufacturers Association	15 per cent quota of total operatives in specified groups (subject to variation)	As for British	—
6. Association of Cinematograph Television and Allied Technicians	Aliens etc. not qualifying for membership or temporary membership of union	1. 24 February 1958 2. 3 months' notice to terminate 3. British Film Producers Association. (Similar agreements with other employers)	(a) Preference to be given to available members of union (see 'Union Membership'). (In practice this means employment of technicians from abroad is opposed unless members not available or suitable. (b) Foreign directors and producers permitted on 10 per cent of productions	MUST BE: (a) British subject by birth or naturalization; or (b) citizen of Republic of Ireland or (c) British protected person; or (d) have resided required number of years in U.K. which are necessary for recognition of him by Home Office. (Persons not qualifying may be admitted as temporary members with same privileges as members.) (Rules as amended 1965)	

Union	Description of Workers	1. Date 2. Duration 3. Parties	Recruitment Provisions	Terms and Conditions of Employment	Union Membership	Redundancy
7. British Airline Pilots' Association	Non-British subjects	—	—	—	Members must be British subjects	—
8. Civil Service Clerical Association	Non-British Subjects by Birth	Civil Service Nationality and Security Rules Recognized. (See page 178)	Restricted	—	—	—
9. Heating and Domestic Engineers (d)	a) Immigrant b) Foreign c) Coloured	1. Since 1947 2. Continuing 3. a) and b) with Courtaulds c) with 'most industries catered for'	Accepted if have necessary craft qualifications. Otherwise accepted as auxiliary section members	Not less favourable than for British	—	—
10. Inland Revenue Staff Federation	Non-British subjects		Same as 8 above			
11. Leeds and District Ward Pressers, Twisters and ...	Foreign		Same as 5 above			

			short visits with approval of union		U.K. for 12 months	
13. National Association of Card Blowing and Ring Room Operatives	Foreign	1. 12 November 1947 2. 3 months' notice to terminate 3. Federation of Master Cotton Spinners' Associations Ltd.	If British Workers NOT available, 10 per cent quota	As for British	Condition of employment	First to be dismissed
14. National Union of Dyers Bleachers and Textile Workers (see also 23 below)	a) Spanish Females b) Italian Females	1. Recent 2. Not specified 3. Not specified 1. Early post-war years 2. Open-ended 3. Wool (and Allied) Textiles Employers' Council Bradford	Limited	Housed in hostels provided by employers. As for British	As for British	—
15. National Union of Hosiery Workers	Foreign Nationals (employed continuously in this industry for less than 5 years)	1. Not specified 2. Continuing 3. Not specified	Only where suitable British labour not available. 10 per cent quota	On completion of 5 years' service. As for British	To be encouraged	First to go (unless suitable British workers not available)

Union	Description of Workers	1. Date 2. Duration 3. Parties	Recruitment Provisions	Terms and Conditions of Employment	Union Membership	Redundancy
16. National Society of Pottery Workers	Foreign	1. 1946 2. Continuing 3. British Pottery Manufacturers' Federation	Consent of union required (i.e. right of veto)	—	Condition of employment	—
17. National Union of Railwaymen	Foreign Nationals	1. 20 May 1959 2. Continuing 3. British Rail	If suitable British Labour not available	a) *Temporary Basis Only* (if recruited for starting as above) until naturalized b) Not eligible for permanent Posts (starting grade as above) before naturalization c) If placed in vacancy in Step 2 or higher (this involves training) permitted to remain therein for 2 years, after which (if	—	a) Not to be displaced from starting grade positions because British labour available after recruitment b) Displaced from Step 1 positions before British nationals. Temporary foreign before temporary British irrespective of date of entry

18. National Union of Seamen (e)	Non-European Seamen	1. 1 March 1965 2. Continuing 3. Shipping Federation Ltd.	a) No existing ship presently wholly or partly manned by European seamen shall change to non-European seamen other than those domiciled in U.K. and members of N.U.S. without approval of N.M.B. b) Where an owner desires to man a new ship or newly acquired ship by other than Europeans case shall be submitted to N.M.B. (Criteria by which N.M.B. to be guided specified)	service counts for seniority or future promotion if transferred to permanent staff on becoming British subject (from July 1960)	—	See under 'recruitment'	—

Union	Description of Workers	1. Date / 2. Duration / 3. Parties	Recruitment Provisions	Terms and Conditions of Employment	Union Membership	Redundancy
19. Power Loom Carpet Weavers and Textile Workers Association	Foreign	1. 1951 / 2. (not operated) / 3. Kidderminster Manufacturers	—	—	—	First to be dismissed
20. Professional Footballers' Association	Non British-Born Subjects	—	—	—	Not eligible to take part in any competition under jurisdiction of Association without 2 years' residential qualification within U.K.	—
21. Saddleworh and District Weavers and W.T.W. Association (affiliated to National Association of Unions in Tex-	Foreign Male Labour	1. Not specified / 2. ,, ,, / 3. ,, ,,	Totally excluded	—	—	—

Cloth Pattern Weavers Association	Females

ABBREVIATIONS

* T.U. = 'In accordance with recognized or agreed trade union rates of wages and under full trade union conditions.'

As for British = 'In accordance with existing agreements applying to British workers.'

NOTES

(a) A questionnaire was addressed, early in 1966, to 162 unions affiliated to the Trades Union Congress (representing $8\frac{3}{4}$ million of Britain's 10 million organized workers). Of the 103 unions which replied, 81 had no relevant provisions

(b) The engagements of this union have since been transferred to the Amalgamated Union of Foundry Workers (see footnote (c))

(c) This union has since become amalgamated with the Amalgamated Engineering Union

(d) This union has since become amalgamated with the National Union of Sheet Metal Workers & Coppersmiths

(e) In addition to this Agreement, there is an Established Service Scheme (operative since 31 March 1947) which expressly excludes from its scope 'Asian and African crews'. For this union's agreement regarding rates of pay of deck and engine-room ratings, see above, p. 76

Appendix III

*MEMORANDUM OF AGREEMENT BETWEEN
ENGINEERING EMPLOYERS' FEDERATION AND
CONFEDERATION OF SHIPBUILDING AND
ENGINEERING UNIONS*
RACIAL DISCRIMINATION IN EMPLOYMENT

1. The parties to this Agreement wholeheartedly endorse the opposition expressed by the Confederation of British Industry and the Trades Union Congress to racial discrimination in employment. They also subscribe to the view that allegations of discriminatory practices, either by employer or employed, can more suitably be considered and dealt with through voluntarily-established machinery than through statutory measures.

2. In the event of a question arising between an employer and his workpeople involving allegations of discrimination in employment, the matter should be dealt with in accordance with the terms of the Provisions for Avoiding Disputes.

3. The parties accept that there may be instances where this procedure is not applicable, e.g. where there is no dispute between an employer and his workpeople but a person considers that because of discrimination either by one party or the other, he is being denied the opportunity of employment or advancement.

4. In order to deal with such questions it is agreed that the following special arrangements shall apply:

(a) There shall be set up in the area covered by each federated Association a small committee or, if necessary, committees comprising an equal number of representatives of the Association and of local union officials appointed by the appropriate district committee of the Confederation.

(b) A secretary or joint secretaries to each committee shall be appointed.

(c) Any person who feels that he is the subject of discrimination in the field of employment in the works of a federated employer and whose case is not appropriate for discussion in terms of the Provisions for Avoiding Disputes shall be entitled to report details of the case to the secretary or secretaries of the committee covering the area in which the federated establishment is located.

(d) If, after investigation, the secretary or secretaries of the committee cannot dispose of the question, the complainant shall be entitled to have his case considered by the committee.

(e) If, after hearing the complainant and representatives of the company or workpeople complained against, the committee finds that discrimination has been established, all practicable steps shall be taken by the committee to ensure that the discriminatory practice ceases forthwith.

(f) The secretary or joint secretaries shall be required to submit annually to the Federation and Confederation details of each case considered in terms of the provisions of this Clause. Such details shall include a report of the outcome of action taken in any case where a complaint of discrimination was found to be established.

5. The terms of this Agreement will be brought to the attention of the Ministry of Labour with the request that Employment Exchanges be advised of its contents. Any complaints regarding discrimination in federated establishments can then be forwarded to the secretary or joint secretaries of the appropriate committee for action.

6. The special procedure contained in Clause 4 of this Agreement will, if required, be available for dealing with cases of alleged discrimination in non-federated engineering establishments.

Signed on behalf of:

Engineering Employers' Federation

Confederation of Shipbuilding and Engineering Unions

Dated: 26 July 1967

TABLE 1

Occupational Distribution (per cent): Commonwealth and Irish Citizens Resident in England and Wales, Born in Specific Countries (1961)

| | ALL PERSONS RESIDENT IN ENGLAND AND WALES | | IRELAND[1] | | INDIA | | PAKISTAN | | CARIBBEAN[2] | |
	Males per cent	Females per cent	Males per cent	Females per cent	Males per cent	Females per cent	Males per cent	Females per cent	Males per cent	Females per cent
(a) Total economically active	100 (14,649,080)	100 (7,045,390)	100 (297,180)	100 (152,660)	100 (57,490)	100 (23,630)	100 (13,430)	100 (1,270)	100 (58,070)	100 (31,540)
(b) Occupations										
1. Farmers, foresters and fishermen	5·1	1·1	1·8	0·2	1·6	0·6	0·4	0·8	0·3	0·1
2. Miners and quarrymen	3·1	0	1·2	0	0·4	0	0·1	0	0·5	0
3. Gas, coke and chemical workers	0·8	0·2	0·9	0·2	0·9	0·2	0·7	0	1·3	0·1
4. Glass and ceramics workers	0·4	0·5	0·3	0·2	0·2	0·3	1·0	0	0·6	0
5. Furnace, forge, foundry, rolling mill workers	1·4	0·1	1·6	0·1	1·3	0	1·3	0·8	2·8	0·4
6. Electrical and electronics workers	3·0	0·8	1·9	1·3	2·8	0·9	1·1	0	2·4	1·5
7. Engineering and allied trades workers n.e.c.	14·7	3·6	13·7	5·4	12·8	2·0	8·4	0	15·0	7·8
8. Woodworkers	2·7	0·1	2·9	0·1	0·9	0·1	0·5	0	6·3	0·3
9. Leatherworkers	0·6	0·9	0·3	0·6	0·2	0·4	0·2	0	0·5	1·2
10. Textile workers	1·0	3·6	0·4	1·7	1·5	0·5	8·2	0	1·0	1·8
11. Clothing workers	0·6	5·1	0·4	2·5	0·3	2·7	0·9	0	0·7	11·8

Occupation										
14. Makers of other products	1·2	1·7	1·6	1·7	1·3	1·4	2·6	0	3·3	3·2
15. Construction workers	3·5	0	6·3	0	0·7	0	0·1	0	1·1	0
16. Painters and decorators	2·0	0·2	2·8	0·1	0·4	0	0·6	0	2·1	0·3
17. Drivers of stationary engines, cranes, etc.	1·9	0	3·4	0	1·0	0	0·9	0	2·5	0
18. Labourers n.e.c.	7·5	1·3	20·0	1·8	6·7	0·9	27·7	0	24·2	4·3
19. Transport and communications workers	8·4	1·9	7·3	1·9	8·2	2·0	7·5	0·8	11·4	1·7
20. Warehousemen, storekeepers, packers, bottlers	3·3	3·9	3·8	4·1	2·8	2·6	2·7	2·5	3·4	5·5
21. Clerical workers	7·1	25·5	5·2	15·9	12·7	39·3	5·3	36·3	3·0	6·6
22. Sales workers	8·0	12·7	3·5	7·8	6·6	6·1	4·3	8·0	0·7	1·0
23. Service, sport and recreation workers	5·2	21·6	5·7	29·8	4·6	13·3	7·5	9·5	6·0	20·7
24. Administrators and managers	3·8	0·5	1·9	0·3	4·7	1·1	2·2	0·9	0·3	0·1
25. Professional technical workers, artists, etc.	8·0	10·0	6·2	20·1	18·6	22·3	8·6	36·3	3·1	22·6
26. Armed forces	2·0	0·2	2·8	0·2	4·5	0	2·5	0	1·1	0·3
27. Inadequately described occupations	1·6	1·9	2·0	1·9	2·5	1·8	3·6	2·5	4·1	5·2

Source: General Register Office *Census 1961 England and Wales: Occupation Tables* (ten per cent sample) (London: H.M.S.O. 1966) Tables 26 and 30.

[1] Includes Northern Ireland and Irish Republic

[2] British Guiana (Guyana) Jamaica, Trinidad and Tobago, and other Caribbean territories

TABLE 2

Industrial Status (per cent): By Birthplace in Six Commonwealth Countries¹ and Resident in Six Conurbations² (1961)

	ALL PERSONS (England and Wales)		PERSONS BORN IN 6 COMMONWEALTH COUNTRIES[1] RESIDENT IN 6 CONURBATION:[2]	
	Males per cent	Females per cent	Males per cent	Females per cent
(a) Total Economically Active	100 (14,649,080)	100 (7,045,390)	100 (116,060)	100 (51,690)
(b) In Employment				
1. *Self-employed without employees*	4·9	3·0	3·2	1·7
2. *Employers and managers*				
(i) *Large establishments*[3]	3·6	1·1	1·4[5]	0·4
(ii) *Small Establishments*[4]	7·0	3·0	3·3	1·3
3. *Foremen and supervisors*	4·4	1·9	1·2	0·8
4. *Other employees*	77·3	88·6	85·3	90·6
(c) Out of Employment	2·8	2·4	5·6	5·2

Source: General Register Office *Census 1961: Commonwealth Immigrants in the Conurbations* (London: H.M.S.O. 1965) Table A.7. *Census 1961: Occupation Tables* (1966) Table I.

[1] Jamaica, rest of British Caribbean, India, Pakistan, Africa (other than South Africa), Cyprus and Malta
[2] Tyneside, West Yorkshire, S.E. Lancashire, Merseyside, West Midlands, Greater London
[3] Twenty-five or more employees
[4] Under twenty-five employees
[5] None of these were employers

TABLE 3

Socio-Economic Groups (per cent): By Birthplace in Six[1] Commonwealth Countries and Resident in Six Conurbations[2] (1961)

	ALL PERSONS (England and Wales)		PERSONS BORN IN 6 COMMONWEALTH COUNTRIES[1] RESIDENT IN 6 CONURBATIONS[2]	
	Males per cent	Females per cent	Males per cent	Females per cent
(a) Total working population	100 (16,330,780)	100 (7,646,930)	100 (109,560)	100 (49,020)
(b) Socio-Economic Group				
1. *Employers and managers – large establishments*	3·6	1·2	1·6	0·4
2. *Employers and managers – small establishments*	5·9	2·9	3·4	1·8
3. *Professional workers – self-employed*	0·8	0·1	0·8	0·2
4. *Professional workers – employees*	2·8	0·7	3·5	1·0
5. *Intermediate non-manual workers*	3·8	9·3	3·1	17·7
6. *Junior non-manual workers*	12·5	34·9	11·3	23·1
7. *Personal service workers*	0·9	11·8	3·6	8.4
8. *Foremen and supervisors – manual*	3·4	0·5	0.5	0·1
9. *Skilled manual workers*	30·4	8·4	27·9	8·5
10. *Semi-skilled manual workers*	14·7	15·6	19·8	28·9
11. *Unskilled manual workers*	8·5	6·7	18·3	5·8
12. *Own account workers (other than professional)*	3·6	2·6	2·5	1·2
13. *Farmers – employers and managers*	1·0	0·2	0	0
14. *Farmers – own account*	1·0	0·2	0	0
15. *Agricultural workers*	2·3	0·7	0	0
16. *Members of armed forces*	2·0	0·2	0·5	0·1
17. *Indefinite*	2·8	4·0	3·2	3·2

Sources: Derived from General Register Office *Census 1961 England and Wales: Commonwealth Immigrants in the Conurbations* (London: H.M.S.O., 1965) Table A.5.; and *Census 1961: Occupation Tables* (1966) Table 19.

[1] Jamaica, rest of British Caribbean, India, Pakistan, Africa (other than South Africa), Cyprus and Malta

[2] Tyneside, West Yorkshire, S.E. Lancashire, Merseyside, West Midlands, Greater London

TABLE 4

Unemployment (per cent): By Birthplace in Six Commonwealth Countries and Resident in Six Conurbations (1961)

	ALL PERSONS (ENGLAND AND WALES)		PERSONS BORN IN 6 COMMONWEALTH COUNTRIES[1] RESIDENT IN 6 CONURBATIONS[2]	
	Males per cent	Females per cent	Males per cent	Females per cent
(a) Total economically active	100	100	100	100
(b) Total unemployed (including unemployment due to sickness)	2·8	2·4	5·6	5·2

Source: General Register Office, *Census 1961: Commonwealth Immigrants in the Conurbations* (1965) Tables A.3 and A.8. *Census 1961: Occupation Tables* (1966) Tables 1 and 13.

[1] See note (1) Table 3
[2] See note (2) Table 3

Immigrant Population of Britain by Birthplace (1966)

	Total Population	Outside British Isles	Ireland[1]	Africa[2]	Caribbean[3]	India	Pakistan	Rest of Commonwealth[4]	Europe	Other Foreign Countries
ENGLAND & WALES	47,135,510	1,780,600	878,530	88,510	267,850	232,210	73,130	280,610	559,850	278,440
Northern Region	3,264,410	38,830	17,230	2,180	930	5,030	1,570	7,470	15,300	6,350
Yorkshire & Humberside Region	4,669,200	111,260	47,430	3,830	12,510	14,890	15,010	12,000	36,940	16,080
North Western Region	6,615,240	132,260	121,660	6,490	14,560	16,150	8,550	17,230	46,490	22,790
East Midland Region	3,262,290	89,250	43,090	3,000	12,670	14,290	2,590	9,580	34,530	12,590
West Midland Region	4,909,350	173,510	119,440	5,860	41,880	38,730	17,290	15,570	39,840	14,340
East Anglia	1,539,960	58,660	12,770	1,950	2,920	3,310	760	7,290	16,910	25,520
South East Region	16,651,690	1,039,630	442,630	57,930	173,620	125,890	25,180	182,700	316,680	157,630
South Western Region	3,559,930	99,770	43,010	5,750	6,970	11,460	1,490	22,420	34,680	17,000
Wales	2,663,440	37,430	21,270	1,520	1,790	2,460	690	6,350	18,480	6,140
SCOTLAND	5,168,210	83,860	69,790	4,750	1,340	8,090	2,030	19,200	27,940	20,510

Source: General Register Office, 10 per cent SAMPLE CENSUS 1966 (H.M.S.O. 1967)

1. Includes Northern Ireland and Irish Republic
2. Commonwealth countries, colonies and protectorates only
3. Includes Barbados, Guyana, Jamaica, Trinidad and Tobago and other Caribbean countries
4. Principally Canada, Australia, New Zealand, Cyprus, Malta

Select Bibliography

This bibliography includes some but not all the references in the footnotes and adds a number of other writings from which information on race relations in industry and the legal aspects of race relations may be garnered. To avoid making the list unwieldy there has been marked discrimination against foreign sources.

Abbreviations used in the references:

I.R.R.   Institute of Race Relations
L.Q.R.   Law Quarterly Review
M.L.R.   Modern Law Review
I.C.L.Q.   International and Comparative Law Quarterly

In regard to the case citations in the legal parts, readers will find an explanation in Glanville Williams, *Learning the Law*, 7th ed. (London: Stevens, 1963).

I. RACE RELATIONS IN INDUSTRY

(1) *General Works*

Allport, G. W. *The Nature of Prejudice* (Cambridge, Mass.: Addison & Wesley, 1954)

Bacon, E. F. 'Race Relations in an Industrial Society' *Race*, IV, 2 (1963), p. 37

Banton, M. *Race Relations* (London: Tavistock, 1967)

Benedict, R. *Race and Racism* (London: Routledge & Kegan Paul, 1942)

Borrie, W. D. *The Cultural Integration of Immigrants* (Paris: UNESCO, Population Studies Supplement, 1950)

Eisenstadt, S. N. *The Absorption of Immigrants*, International Library of Sociology and Social Reconstruction (London: Routledge & Kegan Paul, 1954)

Hunter, G. (ed.) *Industrialisation and Race Relations* (London and New York: Oxford University Press for I.R.R., 1965)

Montagu, M. F. Ashley, *Man's Most Dangerous Myth: the fallacy of Race* (New York: Harper & Row, 3rd rev. ed., 1952)

United Nations Educational, Scientific and Cultural Organization, *The Positive Contribution by Immigrants* (Paris: UNESCO, 1955) [Chapter on United Kingdom]

——, *The Race Question in Modern Science* (London: Sidgwick & Jackson, 1956)

——, *Research on Racial Relations* (Paris: UNESCO, 1966) [Articles reprinted from *International Social Science Journal*, including one on Britain]

United Nations Sub-Commission on the Prevention of Discrimination and

Protection of Minorities, *The Main Types and Causes of Discrimination.* Memorandum Submitted by the Secretary-General. UN Doc. E/CN 4 Sub. 2/40/Rev. 1, 1949

(2) *Britain*

(i) Books, Articles, etc.

Alavi, H. 'Pakistanis in London', Supplement to I.R.R. *News Letter*, July 1963

Banton, M. *The Coloured Quarter* (London: Cape, 1955)

——, *White and Coloured: the behaviour of British people towards coloured immigrants* (London: Cape, 1959)

Bayliss, F. J. and Coates, J. B. 'West Indians at Work in Nottingham', *Race*, VII, 2 (1965), p. 157

Bell, R. 'Smethwick (Staffordshire)', Supplement to I.R.R. *News Letter*, September 1966

Brocklebank-Fowler, C. *et al. Commonwealth Immigration* (London: Bow Group, 1965) [Pamphlet]

Butterworth, E. 'Immigrants in Bradford', Supplement to I.R.R. *News Letter*, December 1963

——, 'Leeds', Supplement to I.R.R. *News Letter*, March 1964

Chadwick-Jones, J. K. 'Italian Workers in a British Factory: a study of informal training and selection', *Race*, VI, 3 (1965), p. 191

Chitty, C. W. 'Aliens in England in the Sixteenth Century', *Race*, VIII, 2 (1966), p. 129

Collins, S. *Coloured Minorities in Britain* (London: Lutterworth Press, 1957)

Constantine, L. *Colour Bar* (London: Stanley Paul, 1954)

Davison, R. B. *Black British: Immigrants to England* (London, New York, Toronto: Oxford University Press for I.R.R., 1966)

——, *Commonwealth Immigrants* (London, Melbourne, Bombay: Oxford University Press for I.R.R., 1964)

—— *West Indian Migrants: social and economic facts of migration from the West Indies* (London, New York, Toronto: Oxford University Press for I.R.R., 1962)

Deakin, N. D. (ed.) *Colour and the British Electorate, 1964: six case studies* (London: Pall Mall for I.R.R., 1965)

Desai, R. *Indian Immigrants in Britain* (London: Oxford University Press for I.R.R., 1963)

Economist Intelligence Unit, *Studies on Immigration from the Commonwealth.* Part 4, The Employment of Immigrants (London: E.I.U., 1962–3) [Pamphlet]

——, *Commonwealth Immigrants and the future population of the United Kingdom* (London: E.I.U., 1965) [Pamphlet]

Eggington, J. *They Seek a Living: West Indian Migration to Britain* (London: Hutchinson, 1957)

Foot, P. *Immigration and Race in British Politics* (Harmondsworth: Penguin, 1965)

——, 'The Strike at Courtaulds, Preston', Supplement to I.R.R. *News Letter*, July 1965

Freedman, M. (ed.) *A Minority in Britain* (London: Vallentine, Mitchell, 1955)

Gartner, L. P. *The Jewish Immigrant in England, 1870–1914* (London: Allen & Unwin, 1960)

Glass, R. *Newcomers: The West Indians in London* (London: Allen & Unwin, 1960)

——, 'The New Minorities', *The Times*, 30 June and 1 July 1965

Goodall, J. 'Huddersfield', Supplement to I.R.R. *News Letter*, October 1966

Gould, J. and Esh, S. (eds.) *Jewish Life in Modern Britain* (London: Routledge & Kegan Paul, 1964) [esp. E. Krausz, 'The Economic and Social Structure of Anglo-Jewry', p. 27]

Griffith, J. A. G. *et al. Coloured Immigrants in Britain* (London: Oxford University Press for I.R.R., 1960)

Gwynn, J. B. 'Some Economic Aspects of Immigration', I.R.R. *News Letter*, March 1965, p. 13

Hartley, B. 'Halifax (West Riding of Yorkshire)', Supplement to I.R.R. *News Letter*, February 1965

Hepple, B. A. *The Position of Coloured Workers in British Industry*. Report for the Conference on Racial Equality in Employment (London: N.C.C.I., 1967) [mimeographed]

Hill, C. S. *How Colour Prejudiced is Britain?* (London: Gollancz, 1965)

Hooper, R. (ed.) *Colour in Britain* (London: B.B.C., 1965) [esp. S. Patterson, 'Work', p. 75]

Israel, W. H. 'Slough (Bucks)' Supplement to I.R.R. *News Letter*, September 1964

——, *Colour and Community: a study of coloured immigrants and race relations in an industrial town* (Slough Council of Social Service, 1964)

Jackson, J. A. *The Irish in Britain* (London: Routledge and Kegan Paul, 1963)

Jenner, P. 'Some Speculations on the Economics of Immigration', in Wolstenholme, G. E. W., and O'Connor, M. (eds.) *Immigration: medical and social aspects* (London: J. & A. Churchill, 1966)

Jones, C. *The Economic Status of Coloured Families in the Port of Liverpool* (Liverpool University Press, 1940)

Lawrence, D. 'Nottingham', Supplement to I.R.R. *News Letter*, June 1966

Leech, K. 'Stepney', Supplement to I.R.R. *News Letter*, November 1964

——, 'Migration and British Population 1955–62', *Race*, VII, 4 (1966), p. 401

Lester, A. and Deakin, N. (eds.) *Policies for Racial Equality*. Fabian Research Series 262 (London: Fabian Society, 1967)

Little, K. L. *Negroes in Britain: a study of racial relations in English society* (London: Routledge & Kegan Paul, 1947)

Maddox, H. 'The assimilation of Negroes in a dockland area in Britain', *Sociological Review* New Series: 8, 1 (1960), p. 5

Marsh, P. *Anatomy of a Strike. Unions, Employers and Punjabi Workers in a Southall Factory* (London: I.R.R. Special Series, 1967)

Mishan, E. J. and Needleman, L. 'Immigration: Excess, Aggregate Demand and the Balance of Payments', *Economica* 46 (1966), p. 129

——, 'Immigration: Some Economic Effects', *Lloyds Bank Review* 81 (1966), p. 33

National Council for Social Service, *People and Work: co-operation for social welfare in industrial communities* (London: N.C.S.S., 1960) [Chapter on employment and social life of coloured workers]

Needleman, L. 'The Economic Effects of Immigration', I.R.R. *News Letter* (New Series) I, 2 (1967), p. 16

Patterson, S. *Dark Strangers: a study of West Indians in London* (London: Tavistock, 1963; Harmondsworth: Penguin, 1965)

——, *Immigrants in Industry* (London: Oxford University Press for I.R.R., 1968) [expected date]

——, (ed.) *Immigrants in London*. Report of a study group set up by the London Council of Social Service, 1963 [Pamphlet]

Peach, C. 'West Indian Migration to Britain: the economic factor', *Race* VII, I (1965), p. 31

——, 'Under-enumeration of West Indians in the 1961 Census', *Sociological Review* (New Series) 14 (1966,) p. 73

Political and Economic Planning, *Report on Racial Discrimination* (London: P. E. P., 1967)

Radin, B. 'Coloured Workers and British Trade Unions', *Race*, VIII, 2 (1966), p. 157

Reid, J. 'Employment of Negroes in Manchester', *Sociological Review* (New Series), 4, 2 (1956), p. 199

Rex, J. and Moore, R. *Race, Community and Conflict: a study of Sparkbrook* (London: Oxford University Press for I.R.R., 1967)

Richmond, A. H. 'Applied Social Science and Public Policy concerning Racial Relations in Britain', *Race*, I, 2 (1960,) p. 14

——, *Colour Prejudice in Britain: a study of West Indian Workers in Liverpool, 1942–51* (London: Routledge & Kegan Paul, 1954)

——, *The Colour Problem* (Harmondsworth: Penguin, 1961)

Robb, J. H. *Working-class Anti-Semite: a psychological study in a London borough* (London: Tavistock, 1954)

Roth, C. *A History of the Jews in England*, Second ed. (Oxford: Clarendon Press, 1949)

Senior, C. and Manley, D. *A Report on Jamaican Migration to Great Britain* (Kingston: Government of Jamaica, 1955)

Sivanandan, A. *Coloured Immigrants in Britain: a select bibliography* (London: I.R.R., 1968)

Slade, R. 'Sheffield (West Riding of Yorkshire)', Supplement to I.R.R. *News Letter*, July 1965

Social Surveys (Gallup Poll) Ltd. March 1955 (No. 427); June 1958 (No. CQ77); September 1958 (No. 2577); May 1961 (No. 4024)

Stephens, L. *Employment of Coloured Workers in the Birmingham Area* (London: Institute of Personnel Management) Occasional Paper No. 10, 1956

Tannahill, J. A. *European Volunteer Workers in Britain* (Manchester University Press, 1958)

Wickenden, J. *Colour in Britain* (London: Oxford University Press for I.R.R., 1958)

Wright, P. *The Coloured Worker in British Industry with special reference to the Midlands and North of England* [Ph.D. thesis, University of Edinburgh, 1966]

Young Fabian Group, *Strangers Within* (London: Fabian Society, 1965) [Pamphlet]

Zubrzycki, J. *Polish Immigrants in Britain* (The Hague: Martinus Nijhoff, 1956)

(ii) Official Reports, etc.

Alien Immigration, Report of the Royal Commission. Cd. 1741, 1903

Board of Trade, Report of the Committee appointed to inquire into certain questions affecting the mercantile marine. Cd. 1606–9, 1903

——, Report on the supply of British seamen, the number of foreigners serving on board British merchant ships and the reasons given for their employment etc. 1886. [by Thomas Gray, Asst. Secretary]

Commonwealth Immigrants Advisory Council, Third Report, Cmnd 2458, 1964 [Employment of immigrant school-leavers]

General Register Office, Census 1961 England and Wales: Commonwealth Immigrants in the Conurbations (London: H.M.S.O., 1965)

——, Census 1961 England and Wales: Occupation Tables (London: H.M.S.O., 1966)

Home Office, Immigration from the Commonwealth. Cmnd. 2739, 1965

——, Instuctions to Immigration Officers. Cmnd. 1716, 1962 and Cmnd. 3064, 1966

——, Statistics on the control of immigrants under the Commonwealth Immigrants Act, 1962. 1962–3: Cmnd. 2379, 1964. 1964: Cmnd. 2658, 1965. 1965: Cmnd. 2979, 1966

House of Commons, Report of Select Committee on Emigration and Immigration (Foreigners). 1888

——, Report of Committee on Lascars and other Asiatic Seamen. 1814–15.

——, Reports of Committee on Navigation Laws. 1847–8

National Committee for Commonwealth Immigrants, The First Six Months (London: N.C.C.I., 1966)

——, Report for 1966 (London: N.C.C.I., 1967)

Race Relations Board, Report for 1966–7, 1967

Youth Service Development Council, Immigrants and the Youth Service. (London: Dept. of Education and Science, 1967)

(3) *United States of America*

Bullock, H. A. 'Racial attitude and the employment of Negroes', *American Journal of Sociology*, 56 (1951), p. 448

Doriot, G. F. (ed.) *The Management of Racial Integration in Business* (New York and London: McGraw-Hill, 1964)

Greer, S. 'Situational pressures and functional role of the ethnic labour leader', *Social Forces* 32 (1953), p. 41

Ginzberg, E. *The Negro Potential* (New York: Columbia University Press, 1956)

——, *The Negro Challenge to the Business Community* (New York: McGraw-Hill, 1964)

Hope, J. 'Industrial integration of Negroes: the upgrading process', *Human Organisation* 2 (1952), p. 5 [Describes how International Harvester Co. put Negroes in positions over whites with union cooperation]

Hughes, E. C. 'The knitting of racial groups in industry', *American Sociological Review*, 11 (1946), p. 512

Marshall, R. *The Negro and Organised Labor* (New York and London: Wiley, 1965)

Myrdal, G. *An American Dilemma: The Negro Problem and Modern Democracy* (New York: Harper and Row, 1944)

Silberman, C. E. *Crisis in Black and White* (New York and London: Cape, 1965)

Weaver, R. C. 'Negro labor since 1929' in A. M. Rose (ed.) *Race Prejudice and Discrimination* (New York: Knopff), p. 117

United States Commission on Civil Rights, 1963 Report (Washington, D.C.: Government Printing Office, 1963)

(4) *Other Foreign Countries*

Da Silva, M. Paranhos 'Equality of Opportunity in a multiracial society: Brazil' *International Labour Review* 93 (1966), p. 477

Descloitres, R. 'Foreign Workers in Europe', I.R.R. *News Letter* (New Series) I, 2 (1967), p. 37 [reprinted from O.E.C.D. *Observer*, December 1966]

Doxey, G. V. *The Industrial Colour Bar in South Africa* (Cape Town and London: Oxford University Press, 1961)

Gavin, R. 'Correcting Racial Imbalance in Employment in Kenya', *International Labour Review* 95 (1967), p. 61

Kraak, J. H. *et al. De Repatriëring uit Indonesië* (Amsterdam: Instituut voor Sociaal Onderzoek van het Nederlandse Volk *et al.*) [no date] [Investigation concerning the integration of Indonesian repatriates in the Netherlands, esp. Chapter 28 about work adaptation]

Lewin, K. 'The Free Movement of Workers' (1964–5) 2 *Common Market Law Review*, p. 300

Menon, P. M. 'Towards Equality of Opportunity in India', *International Labour Review* 94 (1966), p. 350

2. RACE RELATIONS AND THE LAW

(1) *Britain*

Brocklebank-Fowler, C. *Race Relations – Legislation and Conciliation* (London: Bow Group, 1967)

Fiddes, E. 'Lord Mansfield and the *Somersett* case' (1934) 50 L.Q.R. 499

Griffith, J. A. G. 'Legal Aspects of Immigration', Part IV in *Coloured Immigrants in Britain* (London: Oxford University Press for I.R.R., 1960)

Hall, J. S. 'Racial Discrimination' (1965) 115 *L. J.*, p. 706

Henriques, H. S. Q. *The Jews and the English Law* (London: Oxford University Press, 1908)

Hepple, B. A. 'The Race Relations Act 1965' (1965) 29 M.L.R. 306

Hindell, K. 'The Genesis of the Race Relations Bill' (1965) 36 *Political Quarterly*, p. 390

Kahn-Freund, O. 'Attacking the Colour Bar – A Lawful Purpose' (1959) 22 M.L.R. 69 [comment on *Scala Ballroom (Wolverhampton) Ltd.* v. *Ratcliffe*]

Jowell, J. 'The Administrative Enforcement of Laws Against Discrimination' [1965] *Public Law*, p. 119

Lester, A. 'Racial Discrimination and the Law', Supplement to I.R.R. *News Letter*, May–June 1965 [Broadcast on B.B.C. Third Programme, 29 April 1965]

Nadelhaft, J. 'The *Somersett* case and Slavery: Myth, Reality, and Repercussions', *Journal of Negro History* 51 (1966), p. 193

O'Higgins, P. 'English Law and the Irish Question' (1966) 1 *Irish Jurist* (New Series), p. 59

Rowson, S. W. D. 'Some Private International Law Problems arising out of European Racial Legislation 1933–45' (1947) 10 M.L.R. 345

Sharp, G. *A representation of the injustice and dangerous tendency of tolerating slavery in England* (London, 1769 and *Appendix* 1772)

Street, H. *Freedom, the Individual and the Law* (Harmondsworth: Penguin, 1967) [Chapter 11 on Racial Discrimination]

——, [with Howe, G. and Bindman, G.] *Anti-Discrimination Legislation* (London: P.E.P., 1967)

Thornberry, C. 'Law, Opinion and the Immigrant', (1962) 25 M.L.R. 654

——, 'Commitment or Withdrawal?' *Race*, VII, 1 (1965), p. 73

——, 'Law and Race Relations in Britain', I.R.R. *News Letter*, February 1965, p. 10

——, *The Stranger at the Gate*. A study of the law on aliens and Commonwealth citizens. (London: Fabian Society, 1964) [Pamphlet]

Williams, D. G. T. 'Racial Incitement and Public Order' [1966] *Crim. L.R.* 230

——, Note on *Jordan* v. *Burgoyne* (1963) 26 M.L.R. 25

World Jewish Congress, *Legal Curbs on Racial Incitement: a survey of international measures and domestic legislation* (London: W. J. C., 1965)

(2) *United States of America*

Berg, R. K. 'Equal Employment Opportunity under the Civil Rights Act 1964' (1964) 31 *Brooklyn L.R.*, p. 62

Birnbaum, O. 'Equal Employment Opportunity under Executive Order 10925' (1962) 11 *Kansas L. R.*, p. 17

Berger, M., *Equality by Statute: legal controls over group discrimination* (New York: Columbia University Press, 1952)

Bonfield, A. E. 'The Role of Legislation in Eliminating Racial Discrimination', *Race*, VII, 2 (1965), p. 107

Dyson, R. B. and E. D. 'Commission Enforcement of State Laws Against Discrimination: a comparative analysis of the Kansas Act' (1965) 14 *Kansas L.R.* p. 29

Giaccone, F. X. 'Techniques of the New York State Commission for Human Rights' (1963) 29 *Brooklyn L.R.* p. 185

Ginsburg, G. J. 'Non-discrimination in employment: executive order 10925' (1961) *Mil. L.R.* p. 141

Greenberg, J. *Race Relations and American Law* (New York: Columbia University Press, 1959)

Kansas Anti-Discrimination Commission, Annual Report, 1961

Kansas Commission on Civil Rights, Annual Reports, 1962–

Leskes, T. 'State Laws Against Discrimination', in M.R. Konvitz, *A Century of Civil Rights* (New York: Columbia University Press, 1961)

Means, J. E. 'Fair Employment practices, legislation and enforcement in the United States', *International Labour Review* 93 (1966), p. 211

New York State Commission Against Discrimination, Annual Reports, 1951–61

New York State Commission for Human Rights, Annual Reports, 1962–

Norgren, P. H. 'Government contracts and fair employment practices' (1964) 29 *Law and Contemporary Problems*, p. 225

Norgren, P. H. and Hill, S. E. *Toward Fair Employment* (New York: Columbia University Press, 1964)

Powers, N. T. 'Federal procurement and equal employment opportunity' (1964) 29 *Law and Contemporary Problems*, p. 468

Price, W. S. 'The Affirmative Action Concept of Equal Employment Opportunity' (1965) 16 *Labor L. J.*, p. 603

Ruchames, L. *Race, Jobs and Politics* (New York: Columbia University Press, 1953)

Sovern, M. I. *Legal Restraints on Racial Discrimination in Employment* (New York: Twentieth Century Fund, 1966)

Wortman, M. S. Jr. and Luthans, F. 'The Incidence of Anti-discrimination clauses in union contracts' (1965) 16 *Labor L. J.* 523

Note, 'An American Legal Dilemma – Proof of Discrimination' (1949) 17 *U. Chicago L.R.*, p. 107

Note, 'Anti-Discrimination Law as a Vehicle for a Private Civil Action' (1964) 17 *Vanderbilt L. R.*, p. 1506

Note, 'Enforcement of fair employment under the Civil Rights Act of 1964' (1965) 32 *U.Chicago L.R.*, p. 430

Note, 'Right to Equal Treatment: administrative enforcement of anti-discrimination legislation' (1961) 74 *Harvard L.R.*, p. 526

(3) *Canada*

Eberlee, T. M. and Hill, D. G. 'Ontario Human Rights Code' (1964) 15 *U. Toronto L. J.*, p. 448

Hughes, G. 'Prohibiting Incitement to Racial Discrimination' (1966) 16 *U. Toronto L. J.*, p. 361

Laskin, B. 'Canada's Bill of Rights: a dilemma for the courts?' (1962) 11 I.C.L.Q., p. 519

McWhinney, E. 'The New Canadian Bill of Rights' (1961) 10 *American Journal of Comp. Law*, p. 87

Schmeiser, D. A. *Civil Liberties in Canada* (Toronto and London: Oxford University Press, 1964) [Chapter VI on Racial Discrimination]

Note, 'Race Relations and Canadian Law' (1960) 18 *Faculty L.R.* (Toronto), p. 115

(4) *International Law*

Ferguson, C. C. jr. 'U.N. Convention on Racial Discrimination: civil rights by treaty' (1964) 1 *Law in Transition Quarterly*, p. 61

International Labour Organization, Report of the Committee of Experts on the Application of Conventions and Recommendations. Report III. (Geneva: I.L.O., 1963)

Netter, F. 'Social Security for Migrant Workers', *International Labour Review* 87 (1963), p. 31

Schwelb, E. 'The International Convention on the Elimination of All Forms of Racial Discrimination' (1966) 15 I.C.L.Q., p. 996

Addendum

RACE RELATIONS BILL 1968

On 9 April 1968, after the final proofs of this book had been corrected, the Government published its Race Relations Bill. The issues raised by the proposed legislation are discussed at length in the book. For the benefit of the reader, the major relevant provisions of the Bill are summarized below, with cross-reference (in brackets) to the appropriate parts of the book. It will be observed that in several significant respects the Bill falls short of the proposals made in this book. The Bill is liable to be amended by Parliament and, in any event, will apply only to acts of unlawful discrimination committed after it comes into operation.

1. *Unlawful discrimination.* The Bill makes discrimination unlawful, whether as a course of conduct or on a single occasion only (p. 137), if it is on the ground of colour, race, or ethnic or national origins (pp. 24–6). It covers discrimination in respect of engagement, terms of employment, conditions of work, opportunities for training and promotion and dismissal (pp. 30, 62–82, 109–24), discrimination by employers' and workers' organizations and other business and professional bodies in respect of the admission and expulsion of members and the benefits afforded to them (pp. 30, 82–6, 125–8, 218–25), and the publication or display of discriminatory advertisements and notices (pp. 30, 69). The main exceptions are for (*a*) an employer with not more than ten employees (during the first two years of the Act's operation, decreasing in the third year to five persons) – (pp. 30–1); (*b*) an employer who discriminates in good faith for the purpose of securing or preserving a 'balance of persons of different racial groups employed in the undertaking or in a particular part of the undertaking which is reasonable in all the circumstances' (pp. 21, 27–31, 50, 64–5, 71–2, 77–9, 86, 87, 155, 171, 203); (*c*) domestic employment (p. 30); (*d*) employment wholly or mainly outside Great Britain; (*e*) employment on a ship or aircraft if the employee was engaged or applied for it outside Great Britain (pp. 42–6, 65–6, 99, 223); (*f*) ships where crew members of different races would otherwise be obliged to share sleeping accommodation (pp. 66, 77, 210); (*g*) acts certified by a Minister to have been done for the purpose of safeguarding national security (pp. 26, 180). Statutory provisions relating to employment are unaffected (pp. 33, 44). The Bill makes it unlawful to incite or to aid and abet another person to discriminate unlawfully, and employers are made responsible for acts of discrimination done by employees in the course of their employment, and principals for acts done by agents within the scope of their authority.

2. *Conciliation and enforcement.* The present structure of the Race Relations

Board (with increased membership) and the conciliation committees is retained (pp. 136–43) but assessors may be appointed to assist these bodies. Complaints relating to employment, trade unions and employers' organizations must go first to the Minister of Labour (i.e. the Department of Employment and Productivity). If he is satisfied that there is a suitable voluntary body to consider the complaint he must give that body four weeks to do so (exceptionally this period may be extended); if it fails he must refer the matter to the Board. The voluntary body must give the parties written notice of what has been done about the complaint; a person aggrieved then has one week (or exceptionally a longer period) to complain to the Board, which may either dismiss the complaint, refer it back to the voluntary body or investigate the matter itself. If there is no suitable voluntary body, the Minister must refer the complaint to the Board for investigation by them or a conciliation committee (pp. 144–7, 155–71). The Board also has self-initiating powers, but in employment cases these must first be referred to the Minister of Labour and then follow more or less the same procedure as for specific complaints (pp. 143–4).

Conciliation has to be attempted once the Board, conciliation committee or voluntary body (as the case may be) has determined that there has been an unlawful act (p. 147). If conciliation fails, or an assurance against discrimination is not being complied with, the Board must decide whether or not to bring civil proceedings in a specially designated county court, or in Scotland a sheriff court. Two assessors, with special knowledge and experience of problems connected with race and community relations, must be appointed in each case (pp. 147–50). The court will have power to grant injunctions, and the corresponding orders in Scotland, restraining the defendant from engaging in discriminatory conduct, if satisfied that there has been a course of conduct which is likely to be repeated. Damages for expenses reasonably incurred and also for loss of opportunity may be awarded (pp. 106–7). A declaration may be made that an act is unlawful (p. 150) but no provision is made for an order of reinstatement (pp. 107–8). The court is not freed from the formal rules of evidence (pp. 102, 149) although in deciding whether or not a person has engaged in a course of conduct, it may consider any relevant act of discrimination. The rule that evidence of communications, other than an assurance against future discrimination, is inadmissible in court proceedings has been retained (pp. 140, 147). Existing common law remedies are not affected (pp. 141, 151–2).

3. *The Crown*, public bodies and police authorities are bound by the Bill (p. 134). An exception is made in respect of rules restricting employment by the Crown or prescribed public authorities 'to persons of particular birth, citizenship, nationality, descent or residence' (pp. 178–80). The conciliation and enforcement machinery cannot be used against the Crown, prescribed public bodies and police authorities, but the Secretary of State must ensure that complaints against them are investigated.

Table of Cases

Index

Abel-Smith, B. and Townsend, P. (cited), 19
Absorption: theories of, 20
Advertisements and pre-employment inquiries, 69, 201-2
Air Force, 33, 180n.
Aliens Act 1905, 47-8
Aliens: collective agreements relating to, 33-4, 199, 218-25; discrimination against, 31-7; occupations barred by statute, 33; promotion of industrial unrest by, 33; reform proposals, 199; Royal Commission on immigration of (1903), 47; Select Committee on immigration of (1888), 46-7; union rules relating to, 34; work permits required by, 32-3
Aliens Employment Act 1955, 33, 178n.
Aliens Order 1920, 45n.
Aliens Order 1953, 33
Aliens Restriction (Amendment) Act 1919, 33, 44, 199
Amalgamated Engineering Union, 81-2, 83, 208
Amalgamated Moulders' Union, 218
Amalgamated Society of Textile Workers and Kindred Trades, 218
Amalgamated Union of Building Trade Workers, 218
Amalgamated Union of Foundry Workers, 81, 218
Amalgamated Weavers' Association, 219
Anti-colour-bar activities: legal aspects of, 114-15, 118-19, 121, 122, 123

Apprenticeships, 73 (*see* Industrial training of immigrants)
Army, 33, 180
Army Act 1955, 33
Association of Cinematograph and Television and Allied Technicians, 34, 219
Association of Engineering and Shipbuilding Draughtsmen, 169
Attorney-General (*see* Race Relations Act)
Au pair girls: foreign, 193-4

Baird, J., 129
Bank of England, 183, 214
Banton, M. (cited), 17-18, 70-1
Bayliss, F. J. and Coates, J. B. (cited), 56, 59
Bell, R., 130n.
Berger, Morroe (cited), 167
Bindman, Geoffrey, 6
Birkett, Mr Justice, 102, 106
Birmingham: immigrants in, 15, 16
Bonham-Carter, Mark, 136
Bradford: Corporation, 80; immigrants in, 15; police liaison officers in, 181
British Airline Pilots' Association, 34, 220
British Columbia: anti-discrimination law in, 35
British Nationality Act 1948, 32
British Rail, 75, 114-15, 182, 212-13
British Shipping (Assistance) Act 1935, 45
Brockway, Lord, 3, 129-31
Brooke, Henry, 130
Brownlie, I. (cited), 35n.

Index

European Economic—*cont.*
nationality discrimination in, 35–7; sex discrimination in, 26
European Social Charter, 192
European Volunteer Workers, 49–50, 218
Europe: Council of, 192, 194
Evans, Herbert (cited), 47

Factories Act 1961: Jewish sabbath and, 80; segregated facilities and, 115–16
Factory and Workshop Act 1901, 48
Fair Wages clauses (*see* Government, contractors)
Fiddes, E. (cited), 40n.
Flanders, Allan (cited), 157–9
Foot, Paul (cited), 46, 78
Foreign workers (*see* Aliens)
Fox, Alan (cited), 161
France: bilateral treaties with emigration countries, 194

Gartner, L. P. (cited), 48
General Post Office, 214
George, M. D. (cited), 41
Glass, Ruth (cited), 13, 53, 69, 74
Goodall, John (cited), 50n.
Government: contractors, 183–7, 199; financial support for legislation, 152; model employers, 178–83; nationalized industries and, 182–3, 213–14; White Paper on Immigration (1965), 6, 14, 21 (*see* Civil Service Nationality Rule; Crown; Labour, Ministry of)
Grunfeld, Cyril (cited), 121
Gunter, R. J., 66, 71
Gurden, H. (cited), 4n.
Gypsies: occupations of, 25; unlawful discrimination against, 24–5

Hackney: Citizens Liaison Council, 172; local authority contracts, 187
Hahn, Oscar, 146
Halifax: Pakistanis in, 56
Hardwicke, Earl of, 47
Hastings, Sir Patrick, 102, 106
Heating and Domestic Engineers' Union, 76, 220

Henriques, H. S. Q. (cited), 39n.
Highways Act 1959, 25
Hill, Clifford (cited), 75
Home Office, and E.V.W.s, 49
Houghton, D., 131
Housing: effect on job discrimination, 15, 145
Howe, Geoffrey, 6
Huddersfield: coloured unemployed in, 58
Hungarians, 2
Hunt Committee Report (1967), 16, 21, 28, 68–9
Hunt, J. A. (cited), 93n.
Hutchins, B. L. and Harrison, A. (cited), 160

Immigration: automation and, 59–60, 62; balance of payments and, 60n.; cheap labour and, 58–60; Government policy and, 6, 57, 63, 195–6; Jewish, 46–7; judicial policy and, 111; numbers and distribution of immigrants, 233; seasonal employment and, 194–5; trends in, 13–15 (*see* Aliens; Commonwealth Immigrants Act 1962)
Ince, Sir Godfrey (cited), 70
India, scheduled castes in, 29 (*see* Coloured persons)
Indian Workers' Association: of Great Britain, 21, 175; of Southall, 79
Industrial Courts Act 1919, 147; industrial court under, 114, 147, 184–5
Industrial Training Act 1964, 73, 118n.; industrial training boards under, 148
Industrial training of immigrants, 64, 72–5, 87, 200, 208 (*see* Apprenticeships)
Industrial tribunals: appeals in respect of dismissals, 117–18; proposed human rights jurisdiction, 148–50, 152, 199
Inland Revenue Staff Association, 220
Inns of Court, 126

250